*For Makenzie, Randy, and Stephanie,
once again, with love*

Safe Passage

Recovery for Adult Children of Alcoholics

Stephanie Brown, Ph.D.

JOHN WILEY & SONS, INC.

New York • Chichester • Brisbane • Toronto • Singapore

Library of Congress Cataloging-in-Publication Data

Brown, Stephanie, 1944–
    Safe passage : recovery for adult children of alcoholics / Stephanie Brown.
       P.   cm.
    Includes bibliographical references.
    ISBN 0-471-54888-X (cloth). — ISBN 0-471-53221-5 (paper)
    1. Adult children of alcoholics—Psychology. I. Title.
HV5132.B75   1992
362.29′23—dc20   91-4692

Printed in the United States of America

10 9 8 7 6 5 4 3 2 1

Preface

Like many of you picking up this book, I was born and raised in "an alcoholic family." I lived and breathed parental alcoholism and I survived it. My life with alcoholism is not something that has been "solved," or finished, or erased. It's in my bones, in my roots, and in my history. And now, it is also in its place. I am a child of an alcoholic and I have come to terms with parental alcoholism.

My book is about recovery—about breaking free, starting over, coming home. It's about the pain and sorrow, the joy and discovery of growing up all over again. But this time around, there's hope.

What's it like to be a child of an alcoholic? What happens to kids whose lives are shaped—sometimes, literally, inside and out—by the realities of a parent's alcoholism? Horrendous trauma, confused and distorted reasoning, unhealthy family dynamics, poor nurturance, and poor modeling are only some of these realities. For many children, they form a legacy of massive defense, despair, and destructiveness.

Families have lived with parental alcoholism for as long as there have been alcoholic beverages. The problem is nothing new. What is new is to be naming it, talking about it, and literally rewriting life histories to include it.

As adult children of alcoholics, we are in the midst of a revolution in how we think about ourselves and how we live. We are suddenly aware of deception all around us and within us, deception so insidious and so pervasive that we can't see it or move around it. But now, at least, we know it's there.

Parental alcoholism is still blatantly denied as a common occurrence in our culture and a widespread fact in "normal" family experience. Countless millions of children are growing up within family systems, and a broader cultural milieu, that not only tolerate, but support and incorporate all the pathology necessary to allow people the privilege of drinking all they want to whenever they want to while denying the consequences.

As a culture, we are only beginning to take off our blinders and to challenge the premises of that privilege. We are questioning the deep but faulty beliefs that make it easy for us to live with the reality of parental alcoholism, to deny its existence, and to explain it in a way that maintains it.

Our revolt against this deception is what we are passing on to our children, who are now beginning to say, "No thank you, the old way's not for me." Whether they're making a wish or a declaration, they can't deal with parental alcoholism differently by simply willing it. Recovery takes much more.

What it takes is what this book is about. Recovery takes breaking the pacts of denial, naming parental alcoholism, and then rewriting family history to include all its facts. Recovery means saying what happened and meeting its impact head-on. Recovery comes from growing up again, this time with a new foundation of truth and a commitment to honesty. Challenge and loss are involved, as adult children of alcoholics break away from the unhealthy beliefs and behaviors that had bound them to disturbed and destructive first families. But recovery is mostly about development—the development of a new, healthy self.

From the popular social movement of adult children of alcoholics (ACAs, or ACOAs), started less than 15 years ago, have come an important introduction, a new foundation, and a loosely defined and still uncharted direction to recovery. The movement focuses on "making real the past" and on learning new ways to think, feel, and behave in the present. Films and books sometimes portray this process as simple; it is not.

Knowing, really *knowing*, what happened and what it was like is not enough and will not automatically lead to change. Deep change requires a reconstruction of inner-core beliefs and a challenge to all the defenses that have been set up to protect children caught in the unhealthy alcoholic family system.

The popular movement's introductions and guidelines for recovery were a vital first step. This book is the next step for an ACA who has been introduced to recovery and needs to examine the deeper process of change—what it is and how it occurs.

Many ACAs want professional therapy, or are at least curious about what it might offer, but they don't understand how or why it could be helpful. Perhaps this book will remove their uncertainty. The words of ACAs in treatment are quoted throughout, and many examples are drawn from ACAs who are in formal psychotherapy as part of their recovery.

Why so much emphasis on people in treatment? In another life, this book was a textbook for professional therapists;* this popular version is equally grounded in clinical research. ACAs in treatment are the only ACAs we know about, and their treatment has reciprocal benefits. Even as they receive the professional help they are seeking, they give back to the professionals treating them an expanded knowledge and enriched understanding that may someday allow us to make statements about *all* ACAs. For now, this book can talk about only people who have sought professional help.

The therapeutic process needs to be demystified. I have intentionally retained detailed examples of ACAs in long-term treatment, to illustrate the complexities involved and to demonstrate how change can result from "rewriting" history, challenging defenses, developing new insights, and taking action. Serious change has no magic and no quick cures. Instead, it requires a long view, a developmental view, to understand both what happens to children growing up in an alcoholic family and what happens over the long term during recovery.

Common themes and tasks are found in the in-depth process of recovery described here, but there is much individual variation as well. Readers, whether ACAs or not, will, I hope, be stimulated to learn more about the recovery process, and ACAs will be reassured about seeking help.

This is not a how-to book, nor does it cop out with "answers that only you can provide." There is no promise here to make the

---

* Stephanie Brown, *Treating Adult Children of Alcoholics: A Developmental Perspective* (New York: Wiley, 1988).

life of an ACA better. If anything, the book spells out why change is so hard. Recovery is tough stuff, and ACAs need all the best resources that can be mustered—the powerful social movement, the enormously supportive and effective self-help network (particularly Alcoholics Anonymous and Al-Anon), and good professional treatment.

Is there such a thing as recovery without any help? Many of us would like to think so. With the number of ACAs so massive, a belief that everyone who grew up with an alcoholic parent requires help to deal with the realities and consequences of this childhood experience seems too depressing to contemplate.

Our culture's preference for pick-yourself-up-by-the-bootstraps, tough-it-out self-improvement tends to encourage belief that recovery can be accomplished without any help. Ironically, self-reliance is a value that ACAs develop well, in order to cope with an unhealthy family. This same value later stands in the way of change and growth.

The idea that "self-recovery" is the best course, or even an adequate course, reinforces both a cultural belief in the power of the human will and a sense that seeking help or relying on support is a failure. The critically important benefit in seeking help is that it frees the ACA from *having* to recover alone. ACAs often had to grow up alone. Is their recovery really to be more of the same?

I do not expect that formal, in-depth psychotherapy could be provided to all ACAs, nor would they all necessarily need long-term treatment. A full understanding of who needs what is still not possible, but therapists—and their patients—know that many ACAs can gain tremendous benefit from formal treatment, both short-term and long-term. Increasing the opportunities for affordable and accessible treatment from well-trained therapists remains a formidable, but absolutely essential task.

The self-help movement, sparked by the granddaddy organization of Alcoholics Anonymous, offers the most viable, accessible, affordable help that is currently available. Self-help groups and the kinds of problems they address have grown phenomenally, and some of the negative stereotypes of support groups have begun to phase themselves out. More people are checking into these groups for more kinds of problems and are finding enormous gain through these communities of shared experience. The label "self-help" couldn't be farther from reality.

What's ahead in the book? Briefly, the chapter groupings:

- describe the ACA phenomenon and sketch out the background of current understanding;
- go into "what it was like," looking especially at the environment and the concessions that maintain the unhealthy foundation and destructive patterns of the alcoholic family;
- examine the impact of parental alcoholism on childhood development—how kids learn who they are and why growing up is bound to be problematic when parental alcoholism is involved;
- look directly at the consequences of living with parental alcoholism and at how kids cope;
- detail the stages and tasks of the in-depth, difficult process of recovery—what happens to people in treatment and what's involved in their process of change.

The final chapter asks: What is progress? What is the redevelopment process that I call "growing up, growing out, and coming home?" What does it feel like and how will an ACA know that anything has changed?

A few additional lines about how to read this book—and what not to read into it—are in order here. The book is rooted in individual development—loosely, the idea that what comes first influences what follows. Growth occurs in predictable stages and each stage has predictable tasks. Healthy development—physical, psychological, and spiritual—is a building process, the successful completion of one stage after another. Problems along the way will influence everything else that follows.

Parental alcoholism is a big problem along the way for many, many children. By tracing several different levels of development, or "tracks," none of which is simple or isolated from the others, crossfertilization and cross-contamination are revealed. There is also much repetition. Some of the most crucial factors, such as emphasis on denial and defense, appear over and over. The mosaic of childhood and adult experience contains patterns, and many of these patterns overlap; critical factors reappear in different guise, with different meaning or emphasis.

I mentioned earlier that many examples are from group therapy. Just what kind of group am I talking about? Much of my

professional work with ACAs over the past 15 years has been centered on long-term interactional group therapy (developed and articulated by Irvin Yalom), which operates on four major premises:

1. Sharing experience in the present—who's who and what's
   going on in people's lives;
2. Sharing experiences from the past—remembering and
   feeling what really happened;
3. Examining what goes on among members of the group—
   what is called the "here-and-now";
4. Relating the present—the way ACAs see, feel, think, and
   behave with each other in the "here-and-now"—to the
   past.

Operating as a small social microcosm, the group creates an
environment in which members can look closely at themselves to
see and learn what couldn't be recognized or known before, and
to challenge old ways of seeing things and old ideas that no longer
hold true.

This particular kind of therapy is very hard work. Although
ACAs look at their first families in this process, the major focus is
themselves. Group members agree to be reflective, to be open to
learning about themselves, and to return over and over again, *especially* when the going gets rough and they want to flee from the
group and not return.

Ultimately, the formal work is done. ACAs aren't remade, nor
have they shed the past. But, they have come through it again, this
time for real, with their eyes open and with a new "story" to tell.

Throughout the process of recovery, which never really ends,
most ACAs long to "go home," to find a healthy family to reclaim, to
find parents now able to hear and to give, to find that everyone now
has a new, recovering family story to share because truth has become a family affair. Sometimes this happens. But more often, the
ACA finds that home lies up ahead, not in the past. Home lies in
finding a personal truth.

Toward finding that home, and the new beginning that awaits
there, I hope this book offers a safe passage.

STEPHANIE BROWN

September 1991

Acknowledgments

I have had the great good fortune to work professionally in the field of alcoholism for nearly 20 years. To work with people affected by alcoholism, and to think, write, and teach about this baffling and damaging disease, has been an incredible, richly rewarding, challenging, and humbling experience.

Many, many people have helped in countless ways, and I thank them all. A few deserve special mention.

Thomas and Katherine Pike have been dedicated to helping people recover from alcoholism for over 40 years. Their wisdom, generosity, and example have been extended to all those who sought their help.

Deep thanks and appreciation to the staff of the Mental Research Institute for their support of the Family Recovery Research and Curriculum Development Project. In its early stages, this study has gathered support from all corners—members of AA and Al-Anon, treatment centers, professional clinicians and researchers. Special thanks to Yale and Eugenia Jones, Ben Hammett and Rudy Driscoll for their support of this research, and to my colleagues Dr. Virginia Lewis, co-director, and Margo Chapin, Project Coordinator.

I extend my deep appreciation and gratitude to the many members of A.A. and Al-Anon who have volunteered to share their experience, strength, and hope over the years, to help others who had not yet "come home." None of my work would have been possible without their generous gifts of time and self.

The same tribute is owed to my clients, or "patients." So much of what I know now, I learned right along with them. Sometimes, I was no more than a week ahead of them; at other times, for sure, I've been more than a week behind. We take our journey together.

My profound respect and my thanks go to my friends in the ACA social movement, the wonderful gang who started NACOA, the National Association for Children of Alcoholics.

Warm thanks also to my long-time editor, Herb Reich, for his support, and to Maryan Malone, at Publications Development Company, for her remarkable skill and talent.

Finally, thanks and love to my husband Bob Harris and our daughter Makenzie, for all and everything.

I'm one of the lucky ones in the world; my work is deeply rewarding, touching, enriching, and fun. I'm one of those who survived, and I now have the privilege and the honor to "carry a message," as members of A.A. might put it. I offer that message here, with the deepest gratitude for all that has come before and all that has been given to me.

S.B.

Contents

I

Overview

1

Introduction

My name is Sheila and I am the child of an alcoholic.
My mother always drank. I could see it, smell it; and I had
to deal with it constantly, but I couldn't really know it
until now.

Sheila is one of the estimated 28 million adults and young people who grew up in a family with one or two alcoholic parents. She is an adult child of an alcoholic (ACA, or ACOA). Her mother always drank, but not until Sheila read about parental alcoholism and heard the term ACA could she finally allow herself to know the painful reality that she'd lived with all her life.

Children of alcoholics (COAs) and adult children of alcoholics have always been among us, and formal research reports date back to 1945. Yet, only within the past 10 years has this enormous group been openly named, described in painful detail, and identified as a distinct population requiring intervention and treatment.

The popular media picked up on the group's rapid, phenomenal recognition and ran with it, fueling a powerful national social movement and jolting a denying nation to attention. By gaining coverage in national newsweeklies, leading newspapers and syndications, and TV news reports and specials, the ACA popular movement has had a tremendous impact on many thousands of individuals and families who have lived with parental alcoholism, and on public awareness. Professional interest is just beginning to catch up.

This book spends time with Sheila and people like her, to find out what it means to be an ACA—what it's like growing up, how the alcoholic family works, what happens to kids in such a family, how they cope, and what happens in recovery.

Growing up with an alcoholic parent is both a *common* experience, with similarities to other ACAs' experiences, and a *unique*, individualized part of each ACA's history. One of the most important aims of this book is to cover both: to review the similarities that are popular knowledge, and to individualize the elements of this common experience.

WHAT IS ALCOHOLISM?

Alcoholism has been known and recognized for centuries as an individual behavioral problem. For a long time, it was thought to be a disturbance of will or character. In the past 40 years, alcoholism has been accepted as a disease. The afflicted individual drinks too much and cannot stop.

The alcoholic always has received a great deal of attention. The pain, the sorrow, and even the comedy of being alcoholic have been portrayed in literature and drama for centuries, though alcoholism was rarely named or dealt with directly. Yet, who could miss the centrality of alcoholism in works like Eugene O'Neill's *Long Day's Journey Into Night?* The characters themselves could miss it, that's who! And so could the audience, and people like Sheila.

During centuries of medical treatment, alcohol was believed to be a cure for various ills and was prescribed by physicians as a primary treatment. Today, alcoholism is designated as a primary illness that must be treated directly. The emotional illness, marital difficulties, or physical ailments that usually accompany alcoholism are now recognized to be consequences of the drinking rather than causes. This is a major change in thinking, although there is by no means general agreement today about any aspect of alcoholism. No cause or cure is known, and controversy dominates both research and popular knowledge.

DENIAL

Despite the controversy, one fact is rarely disputed: the alcoholic individual doesn't know about the alcoholism. Or rather, the alcoholic denies knowing about it. Denial is surely the most significant stumbling block preventing individuals from seeking help. They do not know, or they deny, that they need it.

Denial has a sidekick: the self-excuse. Alcoholic individuals develop a thinking disorder, in addition to their behavioral problem of out-of-control drinking. The thinking disorder allows them to deny point-blank that they have any problem with alcohol *and* to explain the reality of the drinking behavior in a way that allows it to be maintained. This is quite an accomplishment. In essence, an alcoholic says: "I am not drinking too much and I need to drink this much because . . . ." This amazing distortion of perception and logic is a central part of alcoholism. By simply saying, "It isn't so," the alcoholic overrides the evidence, the concern expressed by family members, or the diagnosis of a professional.

Denial is not unique to the drinker. If it were, alcoholics would more quickly become isolated, anxious, and disturbed, because their behavior and their explanations for it would be unacceptable to those who count in their lives. But this rejection of their behavior rarely happens early; often, it never happens at all. Those close to the drinker come to think the same way! Doctors, employers, friends, and spouses all deny to some degree that the alcoholic drinks too much, and they echo the drinker's explanations. For them, alcoholism is a reality only when it's once or twice removed from their experience. It may be a central, dominating factor that is influencing an entire family, but this truth cannot be known by that family. Consequently, the family stays out of the spotlight and out of treatment. No one recognizes that the children in the family suffer from growing up in this environment, and that they give a pseudonym to their parents' alcoholism.

Later chapters will look more closely at denial and at the dynamics of this kind of family system—how it works and how it affects the individual members. To grow up in such a home environment and not be considerably or even dramatically affected by it is very difficult, if not impossible. In many families, denial is like a polluting haze that settles over all family members,

enveloping and limiting them, and distorting and coloring everything they see.

The popular movement exposed denial, named reality, and,
through the label ACA, provided a new emphasis on parental alcoholism as a major factor in a child's development. By pointing to the
source, the movement gave new direction to study of the child developing in an alcoholic family. Suddenly, everything looked different—
sharper and clearer—and everything made sense. Naming reality
meant that it *can* happen to me. Alcoholism can now exist on my
block, in my family, and even for me. As Sheila said after seeking help:

> By learning that I am the child of an alcoholic, I can open up the
> secrets. My life makes sense when I can know the truth.

Why is it often nearly impossible for the drinker and those
close to the drinker to know the truth? Because, from the view of
those locked into alcoholism, the truth will destroy the family, its
values, the bonds among its members, and the beliefs that bind
them together. In the alcoholic family, alcoholism is the tie that
binds. This book looks at how alcoholism develops, how the family
adapts and accommodates to the behavior and thinking of the
drinker, and how everyone in the family is quite literally shaped,
inside and out, by this central organizing principle.

Over and over, attachment—the need for human contact, involvement, and connection—is seen to be based on shared denial
and on distorted perceptions and explanations about alcoholism.
The need for attachment and close relationships overrides concerns about truth or reality; kids mustn't grow up with a view of
reality markedly different from the family's version. Maintaining
the family's version is seen as essential for survival. Thus, all members of the family tacitly agree on their "story," the beliefs and
patterns of behavior they know are required to keep their own
system intact. For a child, these beliefs and behaviors become the
base for individual development. The child will see them as truth,
reality, and normality, and they will provide the detail map for the
child's view of self and world. In a family skewed and distorted
by alcoholism, the models of adulthood will be equally skewed and
distorted. In the closed system of this kind of family, locked up in
its own logic and shared perceptions, no one can see what can't be
seen or know what can't be known.

FOCUS ON THE CHILDREN

Expanding the focus of alcoholism to include the drinker, the family, and the children has profound consequences. Alcoholism has an entirely new look, when seen through the eyes of children or adult children. There may be many more children, or sibling units, of alcoholics than there are acknowledged alcoholic parents to match. Parental alcoholism may be revealed as far more prevalent than was ever believed. The alcoholic family may actually constitute one kind of "normal" childhood experience, in the sense that so many children live with it. Breaking the denial pacts and telling the truth may challenge the cultural belief that alcoholism is deviant and always extreme in its manifestations.

The name of the "children of alcoholics" movement says something important about the family as a unit. The movement focuses on understanding and exploring the child's experience within the context of the childhood environment, and names parental alcoholism as the overriding factor in that environment. The family focus is incredibly powerful. It assigns primacy to the alcoholism and therefore suggests that a child's development can be understood in relation to it.

The children of alcoholics movement provides an exit to a different version of reality and ultimately to a new family story. The movement offers children of alcoholics a safe harbor and a new "family," represented by books, pamphlets, news items, a national association, self-help groups, and professional treatment. In these, they find the support and the backing to tell a different story.

Thousands of children and adult children are now doing just that: telling a different story, from a different point of view. Their new label provides permission to know what really happened, to articulate it, and to incorporate the realities of childhood family life into a new family portrait or story, which is the heart of recovery.

THE ALCOHOLIC FAMILY

My name is Matt. I was born and raised in the family of alcohol and that's what my life has been about. But I can't tell you much more: my *whole* life has been about alcohol and I am only beginning to sort it through to know what that *really* means. I am just starting to look at the childhood family album and wonder: what's wrong with this picture?

How would you feel if you could walk into your childhood home again, if it were not changed in any way? Would it actually be the way it looks in the family album?

As ACAs begin to reconstruct the reality of their childhood environments, they find that their album photos and the reality don't match. Matt remembered only too well:

> As I think about it, I feel a knot in my stomach. You know, I often feel like they looked. When I put myself mentally back at home, I can feel the tension, hostility, and fear, and an intense feeling of disgust.

The alcoholic family has been described broadly as one of chaos, inconsistency, unpredictability, unclear roles, arbitrariness, changing limits, arguments, repetitious and illogical thinking, and perhaps violence and incest. The family is dominated by the presence and the denial of alcoholism. The alcoholism becomes a major family secret, most often denied inside the family and certainly denied to outsiders. This secret becomes a governing principle around which the family organizes its adaptations, its coping strategies, and its shared beliefs, to maintain its structure and hold the family together.

In this global portrait, the secret and the resulting disorder and disruption are at the center of the frame. The need for a family, or family-systems, point of view only becomes more apparent, and the need to understand the environment, more urgent. What actually happened in the home and what was the family atmosphere like?

Howard Blane, a prominent, long-standing researcher in the field of alcoholism, characterized the family situation this way:

> [There are] family tensions, strife and bitterness; threats of corporal punishment are the lot of children in a family with an alcoholic member. Chances for these youngsters to become emotionally or socially deviant are high.

The constants in most descriptions seem to be chaos, isolation, and inconsistency. With alternating emptiness and emotional turmoil, the family life of children of alcoholics could be described as unhealthy. Chapter 2 is entirely directed to describing the alcoholic family, and expands on the issues raised in this overview.

Before proceeding, acknowledgment of the work of early researchers provides background on the cultural beliefs on alcoholism that existed in past decades. Against this background, the success of efforts in the past ten years becomes remarkable.

BEGINNINGS

Much of the early writing on the children of alcoholics focused on a description of the alcoholic as a father (the alcoholic was still thought to be solely the male) and the family climate in which the child was raised. Although they are descriptive, these studies formed the background for the suggestion of problems. Family researcher Joan Jackson suggested that, as a whole:

> Family members are influenced by the cultural definition of alcoholism as evidence of weakness, inadequacy, or sinfulness; by the lack of cultural prescription for the roles of family members, and by cultural values of family solidarity, sanctity and self-sufficiency.

She suggested that, in adapting to these roles, the family goes through stages that include denial of the problem, social isolation, and behaviors geared to relieve tension rather than control drinking. Jackson characterized the family as feeling guilty, ashamed, inadequate, and, above all, isolated from social support.

Other researchers also accented themes of family disruption, related to inconsistencies between drinking episodes and periods of sobriety. These writers suggested that each drunken episode is shattering and disillusioning to a developing child who is repeatedly subjected to extremes of hope and bitter disappointment.

The child in such an inconsistent situation has been compared to a "hungry, laboratory animal tempted with goodies and frustrated by barriers." What these early researchers didn't describe was how the child felt, or the impact on its development. Janice, an ACA who now remembers, fills in the blanks:

> I remember feeling "icky" and embarrassed. My vulnerability was dangled in front of me and used against me manipulatively. I'm

beginning to realize how frightened I am of letting myself care, and especially to feel that I care.

Well-known alcoholism researcher Dr. Ruth Fox observed that inconsistency makes it difficult for the child to develop consistent standards of behavior, and that the emotional warmth and support needed for the development of a sense of self-worth are seriously lacking. Fox noted that, if the child can step outside of the family, he or she is likely to become delinquent. But a child who is frightened of the outside world "feels hopelessly trapped in the hostile, growth-inhibiting isolation of a battling family." The child comes to believe that the drinking bouts or fights between the parents are his or her fault. The youngster may develop feelings of frustration and guilt that often result in emotional disturbance.

Seldon Bacon, one of the earliest researchers to explore the impact of alcoholism, suggested that alcoholism is incompatible with marriage. Stressing family disruption, he noted:

> Alcoholism makes close interpersonal relationships more difficult, increases suspicions, provides a safe retreat from reality and allows immaturity, cynicism, aggressiveness, egoism and self-pity fuller play.

Because of early beliefs that nearly all alcoholics were men, Bacon focused on males. Becoming a father, he suggested, is upsetting and fearful to the alcoholic because he is used to playing the emotional role of little boy. Perceiving dimly that he does not want his own child, he may be anxious about its safety and comfort.

Jackson anticipated the importance of understanding roles, which was also highlighted in the early popular literature. She suggested that roles are often distorted in an alcoholic family because the father (again assumed to be the alcoholic) acquires the stance of a naughty child. As a result, both boys and girls may have problems in identification.

Fox noted that girls may identify other males with their fathers and thus develop fear, distrust, and hatred for members of the opposite sex. She saw that battles over discipline of the children are almost always present in the alcoholic family, and the children suffer confusion about expectations. Children may be used as pawns, played back and forth by the mother or father, or they may receive the misdirected anger or overindulgence of a frustrated parent.

William and Joan McCord, researchers at Stanford University, suggested that if a child's needs are erratically satisfied and frustrated, they will increase in intensity until they become the most powerful motivating force in the child's life. They summed up alcoholics as fathers:

> They are unstable members of their families as well as their communities. They perform roles as fathers in a passive or dictatorial manner; they are prone to express frustration through conflict with wives, rejection of sons, and the imposition of a radically punitive discipline on their children.

All of these early researchers foresaw some of the developing problems for families, brought on by alcoholism. They could not have anticipated the breakthroughs that have come in recent years, or the alcoholic-population explosion that resulted from not restricting the label of alcoholic to men only. They certainly could not have anticipated the term that is now in common usage—adult children of alcoholics. This freely used term is not simple to define, but, for any difficult term, there has to be a definition before there can be a discussion that makes the same sense to every reader. Let's take a look at who exactly adult children of alcoholics are.

WHAT DOES "ADULT CHILD" MEAN?

In response, skeptics picture full-grown adults in bloomers, or Lily Tomlin as the endearing Edith Ann—a grown-up snuggled into her gigantic oversized rocker, delighted with herself as a child.

Before the widespread use of this new term, we had adults and we had children, but we didn't have both in the same person at the same time. Adults might behave like children or vice versa, but generally we could tell them apart. Now we're worried that maybe we can't.

The label "adult child" acknowledges a reality: as adults, we are also the children of our past. We can remember our childhood as it was, not the way we wished it could have been or the way we were told it was. And we can think about ourselves as adults, affected in a multitude of ways by our childhood experience.

This concept is not new to psychologists or developmental experts. What is new is a meaning of "adult child" that establishes a dual identity and looks at individuals as adults chronologically and functionally, and, at the same time, as "adult children" with a past that influences the present.

The term actually represents a very positive breakthrough. It allows people to think about themselves and their own personal histories with much less guilt and, ultimately, with less blame. Initially, though, it can be frightening.

It also raises all kinds of thorny problems for the justice system and for other institutions that have never had to deal with "adult children." Assuming that (A) it's correct to understand an individual's adjustment and behavior as an adult in terms of that person's childhood experience, then (B) does it follow that an adult who commits a murder is not responsible because he or she had a brutal alcoholic parent? Many would agree that B does not follow from A, but the logic and the arguments are by no means clear yet.

The problem is especially complicated in mental health. What should the focus of treatment be for an ACA? Who needs treatment? Is this an individual or a family problem? Who is the patient? If adult mental health problems are now to be understood as a direct consequence of childhood environment and experiences, what diagnosis is valid? Should an alcoholic adult be viewed or treated differently if the individual is a child of an alcoholic parent?

These dilemmas create all kinds of problems for the current diagnosis and treatment system because there has never been any such thing as an adult child—as a patient or a diagnosis. Yet, calling oneself an ACA provides a spark of instant recognition and identification, and a tremendous opportunity for personal change. How this new, raw knowledge will become institutionalized remains to be seen. One thing is sure: it's not likely to go away.

Let's look more closely now at what it means to be an ACA.

II

Family Development

2

The Alcoholic Family Environment

What's it like in the alcoholic family? Chapter 1 gave a global view and a list of negative adjectives. The bottom line on the alcoholic family reads: Unhealthy. Popular media have described and depicted what an alcoholic household feels like, what sort of atmosphere, mood, and tone it has. But the articles are short, and the TV specials are sprinkled with interruptions and comfortably timed to end before the late news.

This chapter takes a long, close look at the environment of the alcoholic family, which is the context for the child's experience of family life. Let's look first at an ideal family. The comparison will give a better understanding of the deviations that exist in the alcoholic home.

THE IDEAL FAMILY

Human society has always had families. There have been different kinds with different customs, but we've always had them. Families have been one of the most significant factors, if not the key factor, in individual development, according to theorists in psychology, sociology, anthropology, and other fields. Jerome Kagan, an eminent psychologist, states that the family is the unit to which

loyalty is given and from which identity is derived. The concept of
self, Kagan says, is dependent on the resources, status, and socially
perceived qualities of the family group, and the fate of each person
rests with the vitality, reputation, and success of that same kinship
group. That description makes it hard to overestimate the importance of the family to every aspect of a child's development.

The child enters the family totally dependent on it for care.
The caregiver member, usually a parent or both parents, takes the
child from its total dependence through stages of its development
that eventually socialize it, or make it a member of the family's and
the outside world's society. Kagan notes that this process of attachment to the caregiver creates a special receptivity in the child to
being socialized by that particular person. The child will accept
from that person whatever standards are modeled and will establish harmonious relationships under that person's guidance. An
insecure, faulty, or pathological attachment puts the child at risk
and may result in serious disturbances.

In simple terms, children learn from their parents. Standards
of behavior, values, attitudes, and deep beliefs about themselves as
individuals and about their families and their world come through
their most trusted, and often their only, channel of information—
their parents. Children learn by watching, by imitating, and by
identifying with parental models. In Kagan's words: "Parents
are the role models with whom the child identifies; parents should
display behavior the child classifies as good, for a five year old
who perceives parents as nurturant, just and virtuous and identifies with them, will come to regard him- or herself as possessing
those desirable qualities." A fundamental of child-raising is easy
to find here: children must believe they are valued if they are to
grow up valuing themselves. In an "ideal" or "perfect" family
(which doesn't exist), or even in a "good enough" family (which
does exist), this will happen.

Theodore Lidz, a psychiatrist specializing in schizophrenia,
also describes the importance of the family in human adaptation.
He suggests that the family fosters and directs the child's development by carrying out a number of functions. The parents must
provide basic nurturance, fulfilling not only the child's physical
needs but also his or her emotional needs for love, affection, and a
sense of security. The quality and the nature of this care, and the

bond that exists between parent and child, will influence the child's emotional development—its vulnerability to frustration, anger, aggressivity, and anxiety, and the feelings of hopelessness or helplessness the child experiences under various conditions.

THE FAMILY'S EFFECT ON CHILDREN

The family also teaches the child about roles, within the family and in the broader social system outside it, and about language and culture, which are necessary for social adaptation and for cooperative interactions with others. The whole collection of the child's normal processes of emotional, intellectual, social, and physical development will take place under the direct and indirect guidance and influence of the key person or persons to whom the child is attached. Kagan reminds us that children learn unconsciously, by watching and listening, and by reflecting on what they see and hear. These developmental processes are probed in more detail later. For now, it is enough to say that parental alcoholism can't be hidden (except superficially), and children can't escape its influence. Parents' ability to provide care and emotional availability to their children is a frequent casualty. Their influence on the organization of the family, and on what their kids learn about close relationships and the meaning of a family, is not diminished. It just becomes negative.

Parental alcoholism has a direct impact on what children learn about their culture. They will see it as their parents see it and they will negotiate relationships and social interaction outside the family in the same ways their parents do.

Later in the chapter, we'll see that these social and cultural functions are extremely important. Children learn a system of logic and meaning that matches the culture of their family, but doesn't carry over to the outside world.

The ideal family, if there were such a thing, would accomplish these tasks in a healthy, adaptive manner. No individual or family meets the ideal, but children with an alcoholic parent often fall far short of receiving the necessary positive foundation at every level. Our comparison with the alcoholic family environment will show how.

THE ALCOHOLIC FAMILY

In Chapter 1's global portrait, the alcoholic family environment was chaotic, unpredictable, and inconsistent; it had arbitrary, repetitious, and illogical thinking; not infrequently, it was guilty of violence and incest. These are characteristics of a family that is out of control, with no means to regain it.

The alcoholic is number one in the family, setting the shifting rules and tone to which everyone else must adjust and respond. The child's needs, feelings, and behavior are always secondary to those of the alcoholic and are often regulated by the needs of the drinker. Here are some details about this family environment.

Chaos When Matt was looking through his family album, he was not likely to see chaos or open disorganization. Few alcoholic families *look* upset, disheveled, or out of control. Defensive adaptations and efforts at coping often successfully mask the underlying chaotic realities. These realities are the overriding dominance the alcoholic exercises over the family, and an ever present sense of impending doom: things are or soon will be out of control. Family members must always be ready to react.

Many ACAs recall a particular symbol that represented the illusion of stability, such as bookshelves filled with never opened texts. Others remember the importance of maintaining "appearances." Sally remembers the ironing board, always up in her living room. If her mother could do the ironing, things must be under control.

The potential for instability is a constant; daily routines may be upset at any time. Families often adjust to the sense of chaos and it even gains an ironic predictability. Sheila explains:

> The chaos was the only thing I knew for sure. I always could rely on the unexpected and the knowledge that I'd have to quickly adjust— turn my attention to the crisis at hand and get into gear. I always grew up "on guard." It was the only way to survive.

Adjusting to this kind of chaotic environment takes an enormous amount of energy and attention. Many children adjust to the demand for reaction and even come to count on a behavior or sequence of events that requires particular reactions from them. Many ACAs have a sense of boredom when reality is too calm.

They've adjusted to the high threshold of action or energy necessary to maintain an unhealthy system's balance. Unfortunately,
they pay a tremendous price for the hypervigilance and outwardly directed attention that result from this "ready" stance.
Many ACAs seek treatment because they are chronically tense,
anxious, and "on guard." They may have sleep problems, or they
can't concentrate on anything but signs of danger. They certainly
can't relax enough to turn their attention to building or experiencing a close, safe relationship. Hank illustrates some of these
difficulties:

> I always expect a hostile environment. People are just like fierce
> animals. My general attitude is to approach everyone with suspicion
> and an expectation that I'll be betrayed.

> I enter new situations on guard. Then I make a quick assessment of
> the environment: will I be trapped by someone so I'll make a mis-
> take, break a rule, or humiliate myself? You've got to stay one step
> ahead or you won't survive.

Inconsistency and Unpredictability   Inconsistency in parental
behavior and logic chronically interferes with establishing predictability. Children cannot feel secure, when the family's rules
and roles are constantly changing; they are not free to turn their
attention to their own internal development. Children will find it
especially difficult to establish standards of behavior and logical
thought, if their parents model arbitrary and inconsistent behaviors, and unstable values and thinking.

Inconsistency is often evident in the standards of authority
and the limits that are set. A behavior considered funny today
will be harshly punished tomorrow. A permission granted today
will be rescinded or forgotten tomorrow. As Matt flips the pages
in the family album and sees the smiling faces, his recollection is
bitter:

> I'll never forget the anger and humiliation I felt as a teenager. On
> Tuesday, I asked my Dad for permission to use the car for a date on
> Saturday. He said, "Sure." Saturday came and I was ready to go. He'd
> been drinking all day and lashed out at me: Who did I think I was,
> expecting to get the car? I was ungrateful and unhelpful and I wasn't
> going anywhere.

Not surprisingly, after a few experiences like this one, Matt was more cautious about counting on anything from his father. He vividly recalls the event and feels anger as he talks about it. Mike, accustomed to disappointment, says he reacted differently:

> My mother's unpredictability was so distressing. I was always on guard and shielded from her violence and rage. I insulated myself emotionally and physically by just checking out. I don't know where I went mentally, but I sure left. Now I don't feel anything and I can't even remember much of what happened.

Inconsistency is also evident in changing explanations for behavior and events. Today's explanation is contradicted, edited, or forgotten tomorrow. Distortions or contradictions in logic are necessary to support denial and rationalization, and the effects of alcohol interfere with clear thinking and with memory. Many children and adults report their frustration at hearing the same story repeatedly from a drinking parent who had no idea the story had been told before—many times. They refer to a "haze" or confusion that often characterizes the family atmosphere.

> There was a tendency toward being "numb" about feeling—what goes on, what people say and what they see. Tony used to operate in a "haze." Mike was always numb and still is. Bonnie is sure her sense of confusion and "haziness" about her family and her interactions with others are due to the chronic haze of their drinking.

Inconsistency and confusion in logic also have an impact on perception. Children come to believe that they do not see things accurately. As adults, they recall being told by a parent that what they were seeing—the drunken parent—was not what they were seeing. Sometimes, this correction is so simple, so seemingly minor, that the child finds it hard to appreciate the complete undermining of perception that occurs. Sandra remembers:

> I used to be so upset listening to my parents argue and fight late into the night, screaming and even hitting each other. I tried to tell my mother how much this scared me and she laughed, saying, they weren't fighting, but having "discussions."

Inconsistency affects children in their dealings with other people as well. They cannot learn to predict the consequences of their behavior because of the changing rules and logic. As a result, they suffer constant fear, uncertainty, and deep distrust of others.

Many of the effects of inconsistency get condensed by ACAs who share a life-style of being "on guard." They describe themselves as constantly watchful, hypervigilant, and defensively mistrusting toward others. When they think about the reality of the alcoholic environment, and not the album pictures, they see now that it was usually impossible to guess what was coming next; when it was easy for them to predict what was coming next, they were helpless to "manage," ward off, or control anything or anybody.

> Joyce describes her father's cruelty and love for her: she could never predict how he would be or what behavior from her would elicit an angry, cruel response. Pleasing men is important. But she is always certain she will fail and it will be her fault. It must have been her fault that she got beaten up on certain occasions and not on others.

Other ACAs share memories of chaos, lack of control, and violence.

> Jack describes having no control over his parents as a child—his mother beat him, often in an uncontrolled manner. She would be violent and abusive, then guilty and ingratiating as she needed to hear from him that he loved her.

Tension   Mike has no strong reactions or feelings, just a watchful stance, which he calls the "children of alcoholics shuffle." Tension rarely leaves the atmosphere in an alcoholic home. It resides there permanently, regardless of outward signs of disturbance. Some ACAs talk about a mood, or a general air, that hangs over the family like a cloud; others call it a vacuum that sucks everyone in. Many ACAs can feel tension, hostility, and fear when they return mentally to their childhood home.

As the dissonance increases between the realities of alcoholism and the denial of its presence, and as the pressures of inconsistency build, the family's defensive posture tightens. Because family members "know" they are sharing a secret, the fear of discovery looms large within and outside the family. One way to cope with the fear of discovery and to deny it at the same time is to have an enemy who is "out to get us." All the feelings of fear, anger, and desperation that belong to the reality within the family, but can't be known or recognized, can then be directed at the common enemy. Children are told that the family must stick together and that the world outside is a hostile threat and is not to be trusted.

Within the family, frequent or periodic outbursts of anger, rage, or violence may be the norm. Many ACAs remember that their fear of parental arguing and violence outweighed their concern about the drinking. In a later chapter, we'll trace this atmosphere of tension into ACAs' adulthood. Many ACAs are tuned outwardly to be watchful and vigilant toward their environment; internally, they live with a constant sense of unease or outright anxiety.

Shame   In characterizing their families' atmosphere, many adults recall intense feelings of humiliation and shame. Often, they were painfully and publicly embarrassed or ridiculed by a drunk or hostile parent. Jack's sense of humiliation in public places was constant:

> I hoped people would know I wasn't like those two.

Adults often wanted to fade into the woodwork as children, to minimize humiliation or abuse. Being visible was dangerous; not only did they run the risk of being held responsible for causing the parent to drink, but they were the likely target for hostility. Safety rested in not being seen, or even in "not existing." John recalls:

> My father was frequently angry and cruel, suddenly critical and attacking toward me. I remember feeling awful as a child. I tried to disappear, standing right there in the middle of everything. I'd go numb and check out. Now, as an adult, I spend a great deal of time and effort testing out with others just how bad I really am.

Adults may experience deep and constant feelings of shame and will organize their access to feelings and their relationships with others to avoid awakening them. These ACAs equate emotional awareness and emotional involvement with others with having to feel shame. How and why they have this belief may be unknown to them. The fear of feeling shame and the conviction that shame is what relationships bring are linked to the inability to control others and a fear of being taken by surprise.

Shame is a reaction of being exposed, or having something that was hidden revealed, without conscious control. The fear of being visible, exposed, or revealed, without one's awareness, is terrifying. The feeling of being out of control may be equated by the ACA with being drunk, like the alcoholic, or out of control in some other horrible way. Maintaining vigilance over oneself and over others is seen as the only way to avoid this experience.

But all the vigilance in the world won't wipe out shame. For many ACAs, shame is the one feeling that maintains a sense of connection to parents; it is the painful one that says, "I do exist." Nancy finally recognized that her chronic sense of shame really wasn't hers, but belonged instead to her parents. As a child, she experienced the shame and humiliation they should have been feeling but did not, because of their denial and their drunken state. When she thought about what it would be like not to feel their shame, Nancy couldn't imagine it. All she could think of was "loss": loss of her bond with them. She learned much more about this awful feeling in group therapy.

> Nancy experienced fear and emotional constriction before each meeting. During the week, she thought a lot about what occurred in group, but as she drove to the meeting, she grew "foggy" and confused. Finally, she realized that she expected the therapist to do or say something ridiculous, illogical, or hostile. She would then be embarrassed on the therapist's behalf and ashamed for the therapist's loss of control. But if she didn't feel that way, it would be worse. She wouldn't exist!

Nancy's experience triggered memories for others who recalled painful feelings of humiliation and shame in the past and present.

> Lena identified with the humiliation her parents should have been feeling but were not because they were so clouded with alcohol. She filled in enormous gaps in feeling that her parents weren't experiencing. As a result, she was also thought of as overemotional and "hysterical" a good deal of the time.

When a therapy group becomes an ACA's new "family," the ACA can work toward awakening and reexperiencing memories, feelings, and beliefs from childhood. Sometimes, just remembering is what counts, because it's finally safe enough to know. At other times, there's more. ACAs in treatment work toward reexperiencing the past *in the present*, in order to challenge its validity or appropriateness to the present. ACAs are troubled, in large part, because the defenses they developed for coping and surviving in the childhood family don't match reality outside the family and don't work in any kind of healthy way in establishing adult relationships. The ACA usually doesn't know what's wrong and has no idea how to change what isn't working. A long time and a lot of hard and painful work are needed, to interrupt and challenge the unhealthy connections to the past.

In the group therapy setting, Brent showed how past issues of shame interfere in the present. He became visibly agitated and upset when several members began discussing their feelings and sexual attraction toward one another. In a burst of anger, Brent left the room. Returning the next week, he reported intense feelings of shame and explored the relationship between what had occurred in the group and his childhood experience:

> I had to continually watch my mother and father behave erratically and unpredictably. I felt I had to control them or be forced to watch them embarrass me. It's very difficult for me to spend time each week in group, listening to people reveal themselves to a degree I can't control and in a way that makes me feel disoriented when I leave. But I also think I have no choice. I have to come back. I have to be here. You guys have the power to embarrass me and you will, for sure; and I can't leave because then I'll be alone.

Brent continued to experience tremendous anxiety and shame. He began to realize that these feelings were awakened by experiences with others, but actually belonged to him. A few months later, as he realized just how much these feelings were a part of him, there and waiting, ready to be aroused by virtually anyone, he mused:

> Are all of us ACAs a little weird? I always felt such shame and embarrassment at the stigma of being the child of an alcoholic. It's in my bones, in my skin. No matter what, it's always there. Anybody who misbehaves brings up my bad feelings about me.

Two predominant aspects of the alcoholic family system (the subject of the next chapter) cross over to characterize and dramatically shape the environment: emphasis on control, and changing parental roles. Control is a central theme, a core part, of the family's faulty belief system. Like denial, it is ever present. Changing parental roles contribute to the inconsistency, unpredictability, and tension of the environment.

Emphasis on control serves as a major defense and is a part of the false self that develops in reaction to the trauma of parental alcoholism. For now, we'll look at the emphasis on control as a response to the chaotic, frequently out-of-control, environmental context.

Control The alcoholic family is dominated by the centrality of alcoholism and by its denial, which is supported by a strong belief in control. The drinking individual maintains two core beliefs:

1. I am not alcoholic.
2. I can control my drinking.

These beliefs form the heart of the alcoholic's identity and the view of self and others in the environment; perceptions and beliefs about the world *must* fit these two beliefs. Incoming data that challenge them must be altered to fit, ignored, or denied.

These beliefs are also central to the identity of the alcoholic family, that is, the family's "story" when denial is intact. The story reads: There is no alcoholism and we have no lack of control. The chaos, inconsistency, and unpredictability are denied; they become incorporated into the family's sense of normality or are attributed to some other problem.

In the face of strong and continuing denial, the struggle to control a situation that cannot be controlled is the overriding reality. As Sheila put it:

We were constantly coping with it.

Children take on their parents' unsuccessful struggle for control over alcohol. The children believe that they can cope with conflict and chaos by controlling themselves and others.

Because they often assume major responsibilities in the family, children learn early how to cope with rapidly changing situations.

They are adept at shifting roles from child to parent and often engage in attempts to "manage" the actions of others. Some children achieve a sense of control by paying attention to timing. Sally had a special strategy:

> I knew I could get what I wanted with the proper timing. Mom was most remorseful and receptive in the late morning, before she started sipping sherry through the afternoon. She said yes to almost anything at 11:00, while the same request would get an angry no at 3:00.

Sally reports feeling guilty now because she "manages" and manipulates other people so well. She actually believes that she has the power to control others and cannot see the flaw in this reasoning: her "management" or control of others was always a *response* to someone else's control, or lack of it. Underneath her belief in control were painful feelings of desperation, helplessness, and deep need, never alleviated and therefore covered and ultimately denied in the interest of survival. The costs of this denial are again illustrated by Sally.

> She describes deep, painful feelings in a rational, matter-of-fact way. Sally realizes that her need to "look good"—to be in control and to "manage" the reactions of others—is a guiding principle. She can't imagine "really" feeling.

Many children of alcoholics believe that they can gain a measure of control, and therefore safety, in their interpersonal relationships by "managing" the ways in which others see them. This is another false belief. No one has the power to control others' interpretations and responses. ACAs often become anxious, or close to panic, when they recognize that their belief in control of the perceptions of others is false. They may feel suddenly vulnerable and unsafe. As we'll see later, it takes a very long time for ACAs to be able to challenge their belief in their own control, because it is such an important defense. When it is finally challenged, their initial feelings of being helpless, desperate, and needy may be much more frightening than a false, even magical, belief in control.

Roles   Role assignment is critically important and essential to any system. Knowing who belongs and who does what ensures stability in the system, regardless of whether the roles are healthy or appropriate. Kagan and other developmental theorists suggest that the clear assignment of roles is extremely important to a family's sense of itself and its own development. A revolution in culturally approved role assignments within the nuclear family is occurring in the present generation of adults, as women move into the previously male-dominated work world and challenge the tradition of female responsibility for the home.

In the alcoholic family, the pattern of the drinking behavior—whether stable or erratic—affects role assignment and stability. The nonalcoholic parent, if there is one, may regularly assume the roles and responsibilities of both father and mother, with the alcoholic incapacitated and excluded from the family's routine. The alcoholic may become another child, taken care of, cleaned up after, and not consulted in decision making. Inconsistency may be minimal in such a home, although the inactive, childlike parent creates confusion for children. In later years, they have difficulties in how they see themselves, because they have not had an appropriate model.

Parents may change roles, depending on the drinking behavior of the alcoholic. Some alcoholics drink "periodically" or in a "binge" pattern that is alternated with periods of sobriety and stability. Their families adjust to the alternating patterns; all members are ready to switch roles when the alcoholic begins to drink. Dan describes these changes:

> When my Dad began to drink, my Mom suddenly became wary and vigilant, as if she would need to take control to make it safe for us. The tension rose dramatically and it felt like a war zone as she took command. Sometimes, she actually protected us, but we lost her too as she turned her emotional attention to the crisis at hand and couldn't respond to our needs till my Dad stopped drinking again.

Parents may take turns: one assumes responsibility while the other one drinks, and vice versa. Both parents present confusing and erratic models for their children and deprive them of predictable emotional availability. The consequences of the lack of any consistent, stable parental figure are severe.

Frequently, a child substitutes for one or both parents, assuming major responsibility for managing the home and for caring for younger children or an incapacitated parent. The child's substitution may create a cross-generational coalition or a triangle with a nonalcoholic parent. Shirley changed roles on any given day:

> I remember helping my mother feel better by being a good girl. I was always "on duty," cheerful and available to take charge of my younger brother and sister. In many ways, I stepped into the mother role whenever she signaled that she was dropping out. I even became a companion for my father when my mother wasn't available.

Most adults in treatment eventually share a conscious sense of having missed childhood. Some yearn for a fantasied sense of closeness, achieved through a secure relationship with a parent. They speak of an imagined and longed-for inner freedom or spontaneity, the kind of freedom a child ought to experience in a safe and stable family; Kagan described it as part of the ideal or "normal" family. In an atmosphere of tension, unpredictability, and inconsistency, where one's safety is a constant concern, such freedom, if it's possible at all, gets short-circuited by the need to take responsibility for others too early. Sheila experiences a sense of longing and missed opportunity:

> I never have expectations for others. But sometimes I imagine what it would be like to feel the freedom of a child blossoming with a delighted parent cheering me on. Can you just imagine what this would be like?

Many adults become aware of their longing to be cared for when they consciously try to provide for their own children what they did not receive themselves. As they see their children "blossom," the pain of what they missed is awakened. One ACA made a personal vow:

> As a child, I swore I'd "be there" for my kids so they'd never have to experience the loneliness and the fear I lived with constantly. I often look at them and feel intense envy for what they've gotten from me that I missed getting from my parents.

The longing for what was missed is constant, whether expressed directly, as in the above examples, or indirectly. Christmas frequently evokes painful memories. Brad recalls:

I never had a father or family for Christmas because they were always drunk. It was pretty hard to be a kid.

Christmas added more chaos. Brad's father was always saying he might not be with them next Christmas, which was terribly distressing. Kate still has a hard time at Christmas:

I remember feeling needy all the time, like a dull ache. As Christmas rolls around, I feel a deeper sadness about not having a parent who would take care of me so I could have feelings myself.

The winter holidays are hard because they intensify the regular worries. If the parents are sober, will they take a drink at New Year's? Will the holidays disrupt a tenuous stability of sobriety or intensify the drinking? Carl gives us an example that accents the disruption and the impact on roles:

I never enjoyed Christmas. My father was sober on and off and there was often a disaster around his drinking. I tried to withdraw and blend into the wall, but it was hard because I usually had to fix something major and take charge. December was a sure signal that it was time for Dad to drink. Embarrassing and painful situations would follow.

Taken as a whole, the chaotic, unpredictable, inconsistent, tense environment of the alcoholic home, characterized by feelings of shame and an emphasis on control and shifting roles, is an environment of trauma. What does that mean for the children who live there?

The Trauma of the Alcoholic Home   The alcoholic home, whether it's perceived to be "normal" or "abnormal," is now widely accepted to be traumatic. Does that mean that it's painful and difficult? Yes, and more. Psychiatrist Henry Krystal defines trauma as the "overwhelming of the self's normal preservative functions in the face of inevitable danger."

What many kids experience as "everyday" routine and normal "life context," what *is* their life, is also by definition traumatic. In addition, episodes of "acute" trauma may punctuate the "normal" atmosphere. Acute trauma might include a single experience, or many experiences, of violence, incest, or terrible fear when they come home to an empty house. A child might also experience trauma through having watched violence or the abuse of others. We are beginning to appreciate that the experience of being a "witness" is extremely traumatic, with severe consequences. Many ACAs must struggle with survivor guilt and anguish because they escaped direct brutality when another family member did not.

The child's normal, natural ways of adapting and defending itself become stretched to the limit. Sometimes, the trauma is so severe that the normal defenses won't work at all, and the child must resort to more primitive adaptive strategies. We'll be discussing these defenses in the next chapter. Later in the book, when we look closely at the consequences of living with parental alcoholism, we'll see more about the effects of living in a traumatic environment. It takes a serious toll.

Let's now move to an examination of the alcoholic family as a system.

3

The Alcoholic
Family System

In this chapter, we'll look at the alcoholic family as a system. That means we'll focus on the way the family works, the way the household functions. We've seen how opposite from an ideal family, and how different from a good enough family, the alcoholic family is, with chaos, inconsistency, tension, and shame in permanent residence.

Experts who study family systems explain how family members relate to each other and how they behave so that they can maintain a family's sense of balance, or equilibrium—what is called, technically, homeostasis. A very important concept about homeostasis is that it is a point of balance, not a judgment of health or well-being. All groups, organizations, or families strive naturally toward achieving and maintaining a sense of internal stability, a point of balance.

The alcoholic family, contrary to popular belief, often functions quite well. But, with alcoholism at the center of their life, family members have developed their own techniques of reacting, adjusting, and enduring so that the household stays a household and the family members can still function as a family. Their system is rigid and unhealthy. But it works; it is in balance. Let's see how that happens.

31

HOW THE SYSTEM WORKS

Alcohol: The Central Organizing Principle

> You'd see a family with alcohol at the head of the table, so to speak. My father's alcoholism organized everything about our family, but everyone would tell you it wasn't so. My father was drunk every night, but no one could talk about it. We knew that drinking provided relief from the stresses of Dad's difficult job, but we couldn't know or talk about the fact that the drinking itself was a problem.

The family this ACA was describing became dominated by the presence of alcoholism and the denial of that presence. Other ACAs, remembering their childhood, give similar descriptions; the alcoholic home challenges all our hallowed ideals about what a family *should* be like. Maintaining their secret—the reality of alcoholism—while denying it at the same time, becomes the central focus around which the alcoholic family is organized. Theorists say that family life has a "central organizing principle." For the alcoholic, and then for the family as a whole, the central organizing principle is alcohol. How does such a central focus come about?

The Alcoholic's Turn Toward Alcohol   As alcoholism develops, changes in drinking behavior and changes in thinking occur. The person experiences an increasing need for alcohol and a corresponding increase in the denial of that need. The two core beliefs mentioned earlier—

> I am not an alcoholic
> I can control my drinking

—dominate the person's thinking. To maintain these beliefs, the alcoholic begins to exclude from awareness any information that might prove that the beliefs are wrong.

The preoccupation with not being alcoholic and the focus on alcohol grow and eventually encompass the individual's life. Having alcohol available and having the opportunity to drink it become the only criteria for personal decision making. Relationships and activities not related to alcohol, such as church participation or association with nondrinking friends, are replaced by drinking activities and drinking friends.

The individual's whole life then becomes dominated by alcohol. Sometimes this shift is gradual and subtle, and sometimes it's sudden. Some alcoholics talk about slowly "crossing a line" into out-of-control drinking; others say that they never had control, that they were alcoholic from their very first drink.

Whatever the speed or the pattern of development, the change in the person's style of life may be described as a "turn toward alcohol." At this turn, the individual ceases to choose alcohol freely and begins to need it. The need for alcohol is most often unconscious, but it takes over the individual's behavior and thinking. The need to include more and more alcohol in one's daily life, without disturbing the central belief in self-control, becomes the dominant and incompatible focus of the alcoholic.

I loved the way drinking made me feel—warm, sexy, funny. I always felt out of it, frumpy and unattractive. With alcohol I could soar and be sexual. It was my freedom from my troubled adolescence. As soon as I discovered it, I looked for situations in which I could drink. I began to date older men and to run with a drinking crowd. My old friends seemed boring and stodgy to me.

As I look back, I realize that alcohol was playing an increasingly prominent role in my life, though I couldn't see any problems. My wife and I grew comfortable with our nightly cocktail, which became two and then three. We joined a wine-tasting social group and often built our weekend entertainment around tailgate parties or Sunday brunches. I became noted for my gin fizzes. Our lives slowly involved a lot of alcohol every day, but not in a way that seemed problematic to us or anyone else.

The Accounting System   To support the turn toward alcohol, the drinker develops what I call an "accounting system"—very individualized standards into which the drinking behavior must fit. The plus-side standard dictates what is "reasonable and appropriate" drinking, and says that kind of drinking is OK. The accounting system also has a minus-side standard for what is not OK—whatever constitutes alcoholism. For some people, having a drink before noon, four drinks before dinner instead of three, or hard liquor instead of beer or wine might be signs that they have crossed over to the minus side. Some individuals sustain a high level of alcoholic drinking for years and remain comfortable about it, because they have stayed inside the guidelines of their own accounting system. Dan demonstrates how OK can sometimes be defined:

> I always believed that alcoholics got committed to the nut house. I had loads of drunk driving arrests, a divorce caused by my drinking, and two lost jobs, but I always maintained I wasn't an alcoholic because I'd never been to the nut house.

When the need for alcohol exceeds the level or condition the individual has labeled reasonable and appropriate, reasons for being over on the minus side have to be found. Dan's were career explanations:

> I never used to drink before five. The work day was sacred and I had to be clearheaded. But as my promotions came along, I found the need to socialize with my colleagues and clients over lunch to be very important to my success. I'd always eaten in the company cafeteria, but now saw that as beneath me. Cocktails and wine are a necessary part of business lunches—so how could I refuse?

Dan used his own reasons and his denial to justify behavior that was previously unacceptable within his own accounting system. Eventually, he came to believe that, as an executive on the way up, he was still on the plus side when he drank at lunch. He thought about potential promotions nailed down over martinis and about the pride his family would feel as those promotions came to him. Instead, problems began to occur: he couldn't stay awake in the afternoon, much less be clearheaded. He denied each problem or came up with another explanation—never blaming the drinking. For example, his afternoon sleepiness was not due to his noontime cocktails but to his lack of sleep the previous night. He developed insomnia, which became a major problem and his excuse for his daytime fatigue. Drinking was now an inherent part of his daily life and altered his belief system about what constitutes success. Because he still saw himself on the plus side in his own accounting system, he could not pinpoint alcohol as a problem and certainly not as *the* problem.

The Family's Turn Toward Alcohol   Alcohol becomes the organizing principle for the family, as well as for the alcoholic—it "sits at the head of the table." Faced with the threat of the reality of alcoholism, family members must fit themselves into the denial pattern. Each person develops the same behavioral and thinking disorder as the alcoholic; each is controlled by the reality of alcoholism and, at the same time, must deny that reality. To preserve this inherent contradiction, all family members must adapt their thinking and behavior to fit the family's "story"; they must stand behind the explanations that have been constructed to allow the drinking behavior to be maintained and denied at the same time. The family's "story" becomes the family's point of view. The core beliefs that family members share give that point of view a sense of unity and cohesion, often against an outside world that is perceived as hostile or unsafe.

The strength of alcohol as an organizing principle is illustrated in family rules. Bonnie explains:

> There were two rules in our family: the first was "There is no alcoholism" and the second, "Don't talk about it."

Alcohol is special to the alcoholic, like a secret partner. It is an intruder to others in the family. In their perceptions and thinking, and in their personal relationships within and outside the family, they must make major, continuing adaptations. Often, they must develop the same distorted logic that the alcoholic finds necessary to maintain the denial of a problem. This is the family's turn toward alcohol.

Some images may help in understanding fully some of the terms we are using here. The centrality of alcohol means more than its having a place in the center of the family circle. It demands the family members' constant, watchful attention, their alertness to changes that will require their adaptive responses. In effect, all family members may as well be spending their lives seated around a table, staring intently at a large bottle of liquor standing at the center of the table.

The organizing function, or organizing principle, of alcohol is a way of describing how alcohol radiates its effects and demands to those gathered at the table. The large bottle affects their thinking, their view of themselves, and their life-style.

An image of the constant presence of alcohol makes it like a filter that colors all family relationships, perceptions, and feelings. Nothing is seen in natural, unfiltered light.

Alcohol's dominance in family life is akin to an uninvited in-law who moves in to stay, becoming the proverbial "elephant in the living room." The in-law's presence changes family interactions, roles, and even perceptions about events. Families may deny the presence of this permanent visitor, ignore it, or attempt to go around it. The visitor's impact is no less real and significant.

Each alcoholic family has a different way of including its secret in the family structure. An alcoholic mother describes her adaptation when she made the turn toward alcohol:

> I had four children and was very active in daytime school affairs. It was no problem. I had a standing policy; I'd volunteer in the morning and I'd "take" in the carpool. I could never "clean up" or "pick up"* because I couldn't predict what shape I'd be in when it came time to pick up.

Sometimes alcohol literally holds a relationship together or gives it meaning to begin with. One couple shares a secret partner in their marriage:

> My husband and I found each other through alcohol. We met in a singles bar, dated over Bloody Marys, champagne, white wine, and candlelight, and built our marriage around the cocktail hour. It's a special time for us. We both attribute "clear thinking" to alcohol. Everything looks better with a drink.

This kind of adaptation extends to other family members as alcohol becomes the dominating force around which rules are shaped and rituals are played out.

> The best time to ask my mother for extra money is at four o'clock in the afternoon. She is most relaxed then, and most likely to say yes. I never ask her for anything in the morning. She's too grouchy. But it has to be pretty close to four. If I wait till Dad comes home, she is often upset, or they're arguing.

> I should know better! You have to call home before 11:00 A.M. or my parents forget what we talked about. I really slipped up this time. I

forgot my parents' anniversary and had to call late that day. My parents were drunk and I got a letter a few days later chastising me for forgetting to call.

Whether the alcoholic's turn toward alcohol is subtle or sudden, family members must turn toward alcohol too, in order to preserve the family's belief in the alcoholic's ability to control his or her drinking. Or, they may persuade themselves that they have the ability to control the alcoholic's drinking. A child may say:

If I just figure out how to be a better kid, my Mom won't have to drink so much.

Members of A.A. refer to this skewed logic, in which cause and effect exchange places, as "alcoholic thinking." Start with some core beliefs, add an illusion of control, keep feeding in denial and excuses, and the family's logic will maintain that there is absolutely no problem at all, or, more commonly, that alcohol is a means to cope with something else that is identified as the major problem. This notion—that there is a problem, but it is something other than alcohol—is one of the core beliefs of the alcoholic and the family. A united front in not facing the problem holds the family unit together.

We learned early on that Dad needed his martinis at night, to unwind after a hard day at the hospital. His boss was the target of many an angry, bitter dinner hour as we all attacked this cause of our family's unhappiness.

Often, the major problem is identified as someone else within the family. Instead of banding together against an outside problem, the family may split internally as another member—usually the spouse—takes the blame.

My husband always told me if I were a better wife, more loving, sexually responsive, and less demanding, he wouldn't need to drink so much. I spent years trying to be that better wife, but his drinking didn't change.

Sometimes, the children learn that they are part of the excuse. Toni remembers:

Mom always reminded us, not too nicely, that we were the cause of the family's strife. If we didn't fight so much or if we got better grades, she wouldn't feel so upset all the time. I grew up knowing one thing for sure: I'd cause some problem today, though I couldn't determine how, why, or what.

The preservation of the drinking privilege and the denial of any difficulties with alcohol frequently require a scapegoat. To some degree, everyone in the family, including the alcoholic, feels responsible and guilty for not being able to solve the problem (or whatever has been labeled as the problem), or end the drinking (not identified as a problem), or change the situation. Each individual tries harder to figure out what he or she can do—be a better wife, do more weekend chores, get better grades. Nothing helps. Nothing changes. The seeds for severe problems are sown because of this perpetual double bind: what may be most visible and obvious, and is certainly most central, is also most vehemently denied *and* explained as something else.

Why would anyone go along with such a blatant denial or even with a subtle distortion? We know from experts in child development that all children need a very close human bond—what the experts call a primary attachment—in order to survive. Usually, the child's bond is with the parent, and preserving this bond, these experts say, is of utmost importance to the developing child. Any threat of disruption in the parent–child bond will cause tremendous fear and anxiety in the child.

One of the greatest threats to the family's attachment and solidarity (its balance) and to its sense of integrity, however false that sense may be, is any challenge to the family's denial about parental alcoholism. Children must join in the denial, or they risk betraying the family. All members readily accept the secret keeping, to maintain family ties. Everyone in the family fears that telling the truth about the drinking will result in loss of love, abandonment, and perhaps the breakup of the family.

Children learn not to trust their own beliefs about what is real and true, and not to say what they see. Parents interpret the family experience for them, giving the children an alcoholic perspective—the family "story." The children also learn not to test reality, because it will not match their parents' version. In this atmosphere, children's needs, feelings, and behavior are dictated by the state of the alcoholic at any predictable or unpredictable time in the drinking cycle. All members assume responsibility for maintaining stability in the alcoholic family system; they struggle to find ways of controlling a situation that cannot be controlled.

How is any stability possible? Largely through the use of what are called "defense mechanisms"—tricks of perception, attention, and thinking. What are these mental maneuvers and why are they needed?

DEFENSE MECHANISMS:
THE ART OF SELF-DECEPTION

The fields of psychology, psychiatry, human behavior, sociology, and anthropology all have an interest in how people think, behave, and adapt, in order to survive. Since Freud's discovery of the unconscious, a lot of attention has been given to how people think or don't think, how they feel, what they feel or don't feel, and what they see or don't see. There is now wide agreement that all human beings utilize mental maneuvers called defenses. Most people's defenses are the same, but few people are aware that they are using them. According to Daniel Goleman, a psychologist who writes for *The New York Times*, defenses are ways of knowing and judging—technically, cognitive devices—that all of us use to tamper with reality, in order to avoid pain. These attentional tricks that we use to deceive ourselves work directly as pain killers; they create blind spots in our perception and awareness. Any reality that is difficult, undesirable, threatening, or painful—the types of situation we are all faced with daily—can then be put in its place. Our defenses help us to sidestep it, minimize it, explain it as something else, or simply deny or reject its happening.

Defenses involve a variety of techniques for seeing things a certain way. These techniques were originally outlined in psychoanalysis. Goleman has summarized them in everyday terms. Some techniques are used more than others; all of them are found in the alcoholic family. If these are normal human defense mechanisms, what makes them problematic for the alcoholic and the alcoholic family? The degree to which they routinely operate and must be relied on to keep the family stable.

The alcoholic family becomes dominated by its need for defenses. It turns toward alcohol to avoid recognizing the reality and the pain of alcoholism. As that reality grows and dominates the family, the need for defenses also increases. In many alcoholic families, there are no free zones, no areas of seeing and recognizing that are not contaminated by the need for defenses. Understanding the kind, level, and degree of defenses necessary for a particular family is extremely important in understanding the role of alcohol as an organizer and its impact on the family's development. Let's look briefly at Goleman's descriptions, which are derived from Freud's terms, and apply them to the alcoholic family.

Repression   Goleman suggests that repression has come to mean "forgetting something and then forgetting that one has forgotten." What do people forget that they have forgotten? Anything that could give them pain: unacceptable sexual wishes, aggressive urges, shameful fantasies, awful feelings, and upsetting memories. The thought or the memory is simply erased. Because people have forgotten that they've forgotten, they don't know what to remember, or even that there is anything *to* remember.

Children and adults who have experienced trauma may use repression for sheer emotional survival. Many children of alcoholics use this defense to cope with their trauma. It is not unusual for adults to forget the parental drinking they witnessed as children, or, if they do remember it, to not recall the details. Some adults have no memories of childhood at all, or none before a certain critical age, or only sparse recall. Hank, seeking treatment as an ACA, was aware of big gaps:

> You know, I just can't remember too much about my childhood. It's sorta blank, except I know I moved a lot. It's funny, I can remember clearly the floor plans of the houses we lived in, but nothing that happened inside. It's hard, because I don't know where to start. I don't know what it is I don't know.

Denial   Denial is a very important defense mechanism for the alcoholic and the family. In its simplest form, denial says, "It isn't so." That statement is the slogan for maintaining the family secret and it is the first sentence in the family "story."

Denial is not a single entity. There are different kinds, levels, and degrees of denial, ranging from complete to partial to barely workable. Understanding the range and variation in denial is essential to comprehending differences between alcoholic families and—even more important—differences within the same family.

Goleman suggests that denial is the refusal to accept things as they are. How can ACAs hold a correct version of reality deep within themselves but not *really know* and verbalize that same truth? Because information has entered their unconscious memory, but it has bypassed or left their conscious awareness. An extremely important effect is that ACAs have a deep knowledge of reality, but do not consciously recognize that same reality. Let's look at some examples.

For some families, the presence or reality of alcoholism is "nonexistent." There may be hints of concern about a parent's drinking (perhaps Dad has begun to count Mom's drinks after dinner), but the possibility that alcohol itself may be a problem is unexplored. The belief that alcohol is a solution to another problem is tightly maintained.

> It's incredible to me now! My parents drank themselves to oblivion every night, yet at no time ever did anyone suggest that anything was wrong. No wonder I was frightened.

> I have just realized that my mother is an alcoholic. I am 35 years old. I have an older brother 38 and a sister 41. We lived with my mother's alcoholism for as long as I can remember and we never once talked about it. I told my brother and sister I was joining a group for ACAs and they were dumbfounded, then furious. It wasn't true! What was I saying about the family by joining such a group?

In some families, the presence of alcohol is acknowledged but the realities of alcoholism are not. The alcoholic and the family deny the centrality of alcohol and any problems or consequences. Any underlying concern is masked.

> My father always had a drink in his hand or within reach. Now that I think about it, it was kind of like his security blanket. We never thought much about it, although I remember being upset because his drinking came before a hello kiss from me.

Denial is mainly a perceptual trick. It says that what is happening isn't happening, even if everyone can see that it *is* happening. John, who remembers that alcohol was at the head of the table, says that it hadn't been invited for dinner:

I tried to get my Mom to do something about my father's drinking—
heck, even just to agree that he was doing it. She said, in essence,
"What you see is not what you see. It's not happening." Then she
added, "How could you say such a thing about your father after all
he's done for you?"

Some families add excuses, or what psychologists call rationalization, to their blatant rejection of reality. Denial says it isn't
so; rationalization says it *is* so but gives a reason that lets everyone
feel OK about it.

I didn't know mother was an alcoholic until she tried to commit
suicide and the hospital staff told us. We always knew she drank a
lot, but we referred to her drinking periods as "one of her moods."
Mother had a "look," slurred speech, and a funny walk that went
with these moods, but none of us ever openly related these traits to
alcohol. We explained her moods as the problem and accepted that
she needed alcohol to deal with them.

Mary's family offers another example of rationalization:

In our family, we knew my parents drank and it was OK to talk about
it. In fact, we talked about it all the time, because it was so important
to prove that they didn't drink too much! They were always reassuring each other that they didn't drink any more than Uncle Harvey or
Dad's boss, so they couldn't possibly have a problem. Sometimes they
wanted to drink before noon, which worried them, I think. So first,
they'd have this discussion about Uncle Harvey and what a souse he
was. Then they'd go ahead and drink, since they weren't as bad as
he was. Of course, we all felt sorry for Uncle Harvey and were glad
Mom and Dad were OK.

Goleman notes that rationalization involves excuses and alibis, the "slick lies we tell without flinching." Among the common
signals that a rationalization is coming are "It's for your own good"
and "This hurts me more than it hurts you."

Denial and rationalization can operate in subtler or more indirect ways as well. Some families recognize and acknowledge the
presence of alcohol and incorporate its centrality into the family's
beliefs.

> Everybody in my family drank. That's who we *were*! Alcohol was a
> part of our heritage, passed on from one generation to the next. As
> kids, we couldn't wait to join the grown-ups. Uncles, aunts, every-
> body had such a good time drinking.

Not surprisingly, this narrator is a recovering alcoholic who
has had to struggle with the sense that alcoholism was "normal" in
his family. It's what he knew, what insured his belonging. In his
own recovery from alcoholism, he's had to struggle with depression and the loss of a prized membership in a drinking clan that he
has abandoned by choosing abstinence.

Only rarely do all members of a family acknowledge alcoholism to be their central problem and the cause of other difficulties. I once told an airline seatmate that I had just come from a
conference on children of alcoholics. She raised her hand in the
I-am-one signal and easily reported the following:

> I was overwhelmed by it. My father's alcoholism was the scandal of
> the town and the center of our existence. His alcoholism organized
> all our lives. We didn't deny it. We were constantly dealing with it.
> When I left home and got some distance, I could see that there were
> lots of other problems in the family that none of us ever recognized,
> because everything was overshadowed by the focus on his drinking.

Out of the home for many years, with her parents now dead, she
explained that she had undergone years of psychotherapy to deal
with the consequences of her childhood family life. She wondered
whether many children of alcoholics have trouble with intimate relationships: Do they marry late, or with great fear? Do they necessarily
become alcoholic? She had obviously struggled with these questions
herself. I was amazed at her knowledge and asked whether she had
read a lot about children of alcoholics. Her reply was:

> No, I didn't know there was anything published.

As alcoholism progresses and encompasses more of the family's life, the need for denial increases. Children who don't join the
denial process very early find their own perceptions are continually
challenged. Belief in what they see is almost impossible for these
children to sustain.

> I can remember pleading with my father to do something about Mom's drinking. He became angry with *me*, saying there was nothing wrong and it was all my fault. After trying to get his help a few times with this result, I gave up trying.
>
> I was terrified of driving with my parents. Both of them drove around drunk all the time. Once I refused to get into the car, telling Dad he was drunk and I wasn't going anywhere with him. He hit me and shoved me in the car. My mother cried and told me never to criticize my father's drinking again. Look what I had done! I'd really upset him now. How could I spoil such a nice family outing?

The strength of the denial prevails, and the family becomes increasingly isolated and defensive. The reality of the alcoholism and the pressure to maintain the denial require the family to withdraw from friends and community activities. Frequent moves and job changes may intensify the sense of isolation.

> My father's alcoholism shaped our entire lives. He was so erratic and crazy, we were constantly coping. We tried to maintain an image of respectability, but he always blew it with some dumb or obnoxious drunken episode. Then he'd wake us up in the middle of the night, we'd grab a few things and move *again*. We were always "getting a fresh start."

The need for coping and for denial makes defensive strategies the family's first concern. Two threats never go away: discovery of the family's secret, and disaster resulting from the alcoholism.

Goleman outlines other psychological defenses that support denial and rationalization but are also very important in their own right, within the alcoholic family.

Projection   If we don't need to deny feelings or reality, Goleman suggests that we may project them instead. That is, we recognize the emotion, but believe and act as if it belongs to someone else. Our own feelings of anger become someone else's anger toward us. Projection lets us have feelings but not recognize them as our own.

Projection is a very common defense for the alcoholic; the spouse and children are often the recipients of all the disowned feelings.

> My father used to come home from work and be real moody. We'd wait for the explosion. It always came. He'd suddenly scream at my mother for being edgy or upset with him, and then he'd stomp out and head for the bar, muttering about what he had to put up with. We always got to be the bad guys, the excuse for my father to drink.

Isolation   Isolation blocks out the feeling that goes with an experience, but not the facts. Individuals may recall more than the floor plans in their homes; they may remember traumatic episodes and much detail about their daily life. But they have no feelings about any of these facts and they don't understand what all the hoopla is about, when others express shock or horror. A new member of an ACA therapy group is an example.

> Sally spoke about her childhood living with two alcoholic parents. She described being forgotten and left behind as the family went on vacation, missing dinner because no one called her, and other horrendous examples of neglect. She related these events matter-of-factly to a group whose faces registered dismay and horror at the reality described. Sally couldn't understand why they were upset; she was baffled by the pain so evident on their faces.

Sublimation   The final Freudian defense mechanism is sublimation, which shifts an unacceptable impulse to a socially approved end. A person's urges to scream might lead to a career as a political orator; another's feelings of emotional fragmentation and despair might find unified expression in some form of art. Goleman reminds us that Freud called sublimation the great civilizer. In this defense, more than in any other, the consequences of living with parental alcoholism are sometimes thought of as positive. One of the strongest urges for children of alcoholics is to tend to the ill and needy parent—to make the alcoholic well, or to spare the other parent (if there was one) more misery. Many health professionals now recognize that their choice of profession—as therapists, for example—was a natural outlet for a deep need to heal their families.

Selective Inattention   In addition to the defense mechanisms, Goleman mentions two other security operations. Selective inattention edits out the unpleasant parts of an experience. Simply failing to notice is the most common, everyday defense. The alcoholic family works overtime on this one; they fail to notice reality. Ironically, the failure works on another level. Because of the sense of danger, the very real inconsistency, and the unpredictability in the alcoholic environment, family members are often hypervigilant; they stay at crisis level, looking for signs and signals of impending disaster. Many children of alcoholics are so hyperalert to alcohol-related happenings, they cannot attend to anything else.

Automatism   The other security operation is automatism: we do what we do automatically, outside of awareness. According to Goleman, we fail to notice entire sequences of our own behavior. Alcoholic families develop very predictable patterns and behaviors and very rigid interactions, as part of their turn to alcohol. Yet no one in the families notices.

Later on, for alcoholics, ACAs, or families that break the denial pact and move into recovery, the patterns become obvious. They can even be quite humorous, especially to the recovering alcoholic. How can such realities and atrocities be funny? Because the logic is so ludicrous. A recovering alcoholic can poke holes in all the old defenses, because they're no longer necessary—and only then can they make sense in the most absurd way. A recovering alcoholic in Alcoholics Anonymous (A.A.) was greeted with the laughter of recognition and identification, when she recalled her pattern of denial and rationalization:

> I always told myself I didn't have a drinking problem. I could hold enormous quantities; but then I couldn't anymore. Suddenly, I was drunk on very little. I couldn't deny it so I had to explain it. I was quite pleased with myself when I decided that I'd developed an immunity to alcohol. It wasn't working like it used to, so I had to lay off for a while to enable it to work again.

If their family is not also in recovery, children of alcoholics find it hard to challenge the old distorted logic or to find humor in the memories. These children were victims of the distortions and, for them, each step of the unraveling process, each defense left behind, brings another loss of attachment. To uncover the deep and real truth that rests outside of awareness, the price list is loss, abandonment, and isolation.

Defenses and the family "story" serve to maintain the family's balance, to hold its members together as a system and as individuals, and to preserve the bond of child to parent and parent to child. Let's take a closer look at what holds the family together.

A FAMILY IDENTITY

Many groups and organizations develop a unified sense of who they are, of a common identity or purpose that shapes their interactions and the way they present themselves to others. Some corporations and businesses spend millions of advertising dollars to develop an identity that people will recognize and support; a solid identity can be worth that much and more.

The family also develops an identity. Psychiatrist and researcher David Reiss calls it a "family self," a shared outlook that guides the way the family approaches specific problems. This shared outlook is likely to be in the background, and may even be buried beneath the family's defenses. It consists of shared versions of experiences and of deep beliefs that make up the family's "story," identity, and explanations of itself as a whole. The shared versions of experiences guide, select, and censor information coming and going, in a way that repeatedly confirms and reinforces the family's view of itself. All information must protect the integrity and bonds of the family system. If necessary, family members must use the attentional defenses we have just looked at, to ignore or reinterpret any data that challenge the family's deep beliefs.

In the alcoholic family, the deepest beliefs often relate to alcohol. The alcoholic's false integrity rests on taking in information that confirms self-proclamations of not being an alcoholic and being able to control the drinking. The person then relies on an individual accounting system to verify that the proclamations continue to be valid.

The alcoholic family comes to rely on the same distorted accounting system; it perceives and selects information that confirms the family's deepest beliefs about itself as a whole. The alcoholic family identity—the sense of the family as a whole; "who we are"— is developed to protect these false beliefs.

The alcoholic family is organized to protect its alcoholic individual. Family members must sacrifice their individual points of view to the greater needs of the alcoholic and the alcoholic family system. The family may function quite well, and maintains its unhealthy integrity by supporting the alcoholic. While often the most dominant organizing force in the family, the alcoholic is also the most unhealthy and the weakest.

A family's shared beliefs are incredibly important and powerful because they provide the basis for attachment, for being a family and staying together. Reiss emphasizes that the need for unity is so strong that, even if beliefs don't fit objective reality, they will be adopted to satisfy the need for unity. The construction of reality is a family process. As the need for defenses increases, so do the skew and distortion of reality.

This is exactly what happens for the alcoholic and his or her family. The need to preserve two core beliefs—there is no alcoholism here, and nobody's out of control—organizes the family's behavior, perceptions, construction of reality, and relationships with each other and with the outside world. As Goleman notes, the need to preserve attachments in the family, coupled with an intense fear of abandonment, leads individuals to "blithely make alibis for the worst treatment and to skew their perceptions of blatant cruelty."

To maintain the secret of alcoholism, the family develops what Goleman calls a "collusive fog." Again, individuals sacrifice themselves to the needs of the family system, which is now dominated by strong collective defenses.

The alcoholic family often looks strong. It has deep beliefs and a unified view of itself. Its "story" to the world is tight. But the tighter the "story," the more fragile the "facts." As the alcoholism worsens, more joint defenses are needed. The system becomes top-heavy or entirely consumed by defending and preserving its shaky foundation. As one individual put it:

> You know those fumigating tents that cover houses completely? Alcoholism in my family was like that tent—it was everywhere; alcoholism was the air we breathed. Everything was touched and poisoned by it.

The alcoholic family may look just fine, but, using Goleman's political analogy, it is totalitarian at the core. Defense mechanisms are the psychological equivalents of censorship. The need for control is so strong that any dissenting opinion or alternative view of reality must be eliminated, choked off, filtered out, or explained away.

The alcoholic family is imprisoned by allegiance to a set of beliefs that keeps the dictator in power. The extraordinarily powerful human needs for attachment, belonging, and unity, and the fear of abandonment, loss, isolation, and loneliness if the dictator and the system were toppled, keep the allegiance from wavering.

The next chapter continues our exploration of the alcoholic family system. We'll take a fresh look at a whole collection of behaviors and sort them out to get a better understanding of the identity of all of the family members.

4

Unhealthy Codependence

In Chapter 1, I said that, for any difficult term, a definition has to come before a discussion. If there were a hall of fame for difficult terms, codependence would have one of the largest pedestals. "Codependence" is too complex, and has had too many definitions, to give it a quick two-liner. Even among experts and therapists, the atmosphere surrounding agreement on the concept of codependence is like a political party's nominating convention in a presidential year. We're all united in the same cause and in getting the same results, but oh how each of us wants our favorite nominee to get the nod.

WHAT IS CODEPENDENCE?

Codependence originally described a particular relationship pattern: one person's submissive reaction to the dominance or authority of another. When the term went public, "codependence" became less precise and lost much of its original usefulness. Codependence now sports, besides its noun form, the adjective "codependent," which doubles as a noun to identify a person, and a verb form to match any personal pronoun or subject that comes along. For virtually anything unappealing, unpleasant, or troubling in human interaction and behavior, codependent is a catchall accusation.

In the best of all possible worlds, we would be able to abandon the term codependence altogether, and start over. Unfortunately, the word is already part of our everyday jargon—and that is the heart of the problem. The term has been used too quickly, as a means of explaining too much.

Short of starting over, I propose we make some adjustments. First, let's confine the term codependence to discussion of adults who are operating within the framework of a system—the family, for example. Second, let's distinguish between healthy responding and unhealthy reacting. Why are these adjustments needed? Because use of "codependence" has covered the ground with crabgrass, and too many people are calling it a lawn.

WHAT HAS CODEPENDENCE COME TO MEAN?

Out walking with a colleague, I leaned down to pick up a piece of paper on the sidewalk. My friend looked sternly at me and said, "You're being codependent!"

A patient described how sad and guilty she felt because she refused to call her recovering alcoholic husband's office when he was quite ill. To do so would be codependent, in her new view. Yet she couldn't shake her equally strong feeling that, in proving herself free of codependence, she had also been unkind and ungiving.

An ACA was struggling to feel OK about his decision to temporarily put aside an opportunity for career advancement so that he could devote himself to caring for his terminally ill wife. "Friends are critical of my codependence, but it seems to me the only true and valid choice I have. Is there such a thing as healthy or positive codependence?"

The field of chemical dependence treatment has painted itself into a corner with new concepts and terminology that define strictly negative, all-or-none alternatives for behavior and belief. Using such definitions, everybody—regardless of whether they're actively addicted or in recovery—ends up in a pathological relationship to everybody else. No healthy alternatives are available.

Codependence started out as coalcoholism, a term for a partner's reactive, submissive response to the dominance of the drinking alcoholic. The term coalcoholic said a lot and said it well. The coalcoholic individual relinquishes initiative, accepts an unrealistic view of reality, and makes a turn toward alcohol, organizing his or her life around the central fact of the drinking just as the alcoholic partner does. This response ensures that one partner's developing alcoholism and the other's recognition and disapproval of it will not disrupt their relationship or throw their marital system off balance. The alcoholism and the alcoholic begin to dominate, and the coalcoholic complies and fits in. The alcoholic partnership becomes like a ballroom dance: the alcoholic leads and the coalcoholic follows in a way that keeps them dancing. The leader may stumble, drift away, step all over the follower, or even break up the dance by changing partners. The coalcoholic's response is to try to keep the dance going.

In similar ways, the members of any team, or organization, or family—technically, any system—will jockey their beliefs, roles, and behaviors, to find a balance point. Notions of balance and of patterns existing in relationships seem to be universal. It's not surprising, then, that others picked up on the idea of the alcohol studies field, borrowed the coalcoholism concept, and reissued it under a new name for a wider audience. Here, the trouble began.

The alcoholism/coalcoholism pairing could be correctly represented as two side-by-side but separate compartments with a wall, not a bridge or a tunnel, between them. There was no switching of sides and no one scaled the wall to start an exchange or interaction between the two situations. Even more important, both sides were considered to be in trouble—technically, they were both pathological.

The reissue kept the two-part framework intact but erased the old alcoholism and coalcoholism labels and substituted dependence and codependence. Figure 1 shows the reissue on the old framework.

When coalcoholism's spot was renamed codependence, *any* reactive, submissive response was included, and anyone who had one was confined to the codependence side of the wall. What was omitted in the reissue was this: being responsive and reactive is a very important part of mature, healthy behavior. Without these qualities, people cannot develop, or share, or sustain close

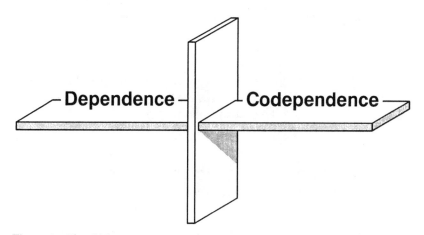

Figure 1. The old framework showing the replacement of alcoholism and coalcoholism by dependence and codependence.

relationships. It might just be healthy, kind, or generally OK to give priority to a terminal illness instead of a career, or make a phone call to a boss, or pick up some litter from a sidewalk.

This wretched outcome would be comical if it weren't such a common occurrence. Worse, this new concept of codependence has provided the excuse and justification for all kinds of manipulative, unkind behavior—the unbridled expression of anger, insensitivity to others, isolation, and an absorbed focus on the self—and has given no alternatives. A person is either the aggressor (the alcoholic or the otherwise dominant member of the duo) or the victim (the codependent or submissive member).

Dependence and codependence are *both* part of human behavior. They are not necessarily negative or unhealthy. We all need to respond to others and we need them to be responsive to us. This mutual need, known as interdependence, offers a middle ground in which healthy interactions are possible alternatives.

Codependence and dependence are both negative now; most people believe that either one is bad. I see two possibilities. One is to add the middle ground of interdependence, forming a bridge between the two compartments. The middle ground recognizes that individuals are both dependent and codependent and, given

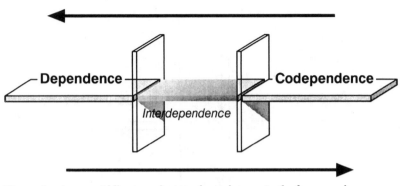

Figure 2. A new middle ground—interdependence—in the framework.

the opportunity, are capable of mixing the two. Figure 2 shows the middle ground in place.

The second possibility is to broaden the categories of dependence and codependence and make them neutral instead of negative. By adding the words "healthy" or "unhealthy" before dependence and codependence, as shown in Figure 3, we end up with four possibilities instead of two, which solves the problem. A particular attitude or behavior might very well be seen as an unhealthy dependent or codependent reaction in one situation and a very healthy dependent or codependent reaction in another.

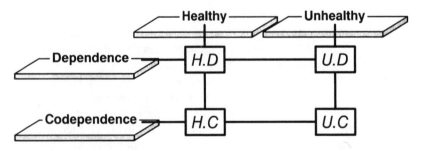

Figure 3. A broadened framework gives four possibilities instead of two.

WHAT IS UNHEALTHY CODEPENDENCE?

Unhealthy codependence is the logical result of the need to maintain attachment and of a sense of family unity that is held together by sharing false beliefs. Unhealthy codependence describes individuals who overorganize their lives around someone else or something else. In relation to alcohol, unhealthy codependence describes the adult who has become submissive to or controlled by the central place of alcohol in the family and/or by the dominance of the alcoholic.

Most often, unhealthy codependents are nonalcoholic partners, but alcoholics can also be unhealthy codependents to someone else's alcoholism. For example, if *both* parents are alcoholics, both may be unhealthy codependents as well. Or, an ACA may be an unhealthy codependent in relation to his or her alcoholic parent, and at the same time an alcoholic.

A person who is an alcoholic dependent or codependent is lacking, or has lost, the sense of "I am my own person." This sense of self-starting and independence—technically called the autonomous self—may have been submerged because of the family's turn to alcohol. Having lost that sense of self, the person cannot regulate closeness and distance toward others or develop strong relationships with them. Years may be spent reacting to the alcoholic rather than following or developing personal wishes or inner voices. Children raised in an alcoholic family may never acquire a sense of an independent self. Instead, they have a false sense of self that is so tied to the needs or dictates of the unhealthy parent that it is not recognized as being false and not easily given up.

The False Self   Four defensive maneuvers identify the false sense of self: an emphasis on denial (a major topic in Chapter 3), an inappropriate assumption of responsibility, all-or-none thinking, and a focus on control. This off-key quartet will get special attention in a later chapter; it gets top billing in descriptions of ACAs' defensive style. For now, let's look at some of its effects on how people see themselves.

Pam has a serious problem with taking on too much responsibility:

> I exist and I am important because I take care of my mother. If I didn't watch out for her every day, she would die.

The deep sense of responsibility Pam and others like her have acquired keeps them from recognizing that they have lost themselves in service to another and that the person they have sacrificed for is not and has not been emotionally available to them. They maintain a fantasy of attachment that may be quite different from reality.

Because of this insecure foundation, the partner or child often experiences deep fears of loss. If the dominating person is challenged, or if the sacrificer sees things differently or fails to respond, the person cared for will leave, or be hurt, or die. By assuming responsibility for the dependent and maintaining a reactive, peace-keeping stance, the reactive individual protects the sense of attachment, weak or unhealthy as it may be.

With its all-or-none perspective, the false self sees only all rights and all wrongs—black and white, with no possibility of shades of gray. Gray is hard; it asks ambiguous questions that can have more than one answer. A lot of anxiety can come from gray. When things are uncertain, they may need to be seen differently. Facts may have to be reordered and a few of them hidden away because they tell a conflicting story. An all-or-none view relieves anxiety but makes it difficult to form and maintain partnerships based on negotiation and compromise.

Within this framework, how is it possible to be involved with other people, without experiencing and acknowledging a painful loss of self? For most ACAs, the answer—all-or-none—is in line with their thinking:

> I can't have a relationship without controlling it or losing myself. Neither way is satisfying.

In the alcoholic family, "nothing is wrong" *and* someone must be held responsible for what is not wrong. The all-or-none thinking puts the ACA on the receiving end of blame, manipulated by someone else's dominance or control to accept responsibility for the problems that "don't exist."

In the polarized alcoholic family, no healthy parental role models are available. Someone is dominant and winning and someone is submissive and losing. Children often get caught between the two, unconsciously frightened at the potential and then the reality of growing up and having to identify with either parent.

Children and adults struggle unconsciously with the all-or-none choices in their family relationships. Pam describes herself:

> I am either alcoholic and powerful like my father or passive, weak, and depressed—a victim like my mother. There is nothing in between.

With the emphasis on two extremes, and with no healthy alternatives available, the focus on control is intense. The alcoholic family, as individuals and as a whole, seems to be chronically out of control. As one ACA puts it:

> I was always ready for the next crisis or disaster, the next drunken binge. Now, the only time I feel "off duty" is when I'm alone.

Within the alcoholic family system, usually the alcoholic is "in control." The ACA worries about being or becoming out of control, about who is in control now, and about being controlled by someone else.

Sam, always worried about being like his parents, notes his preoccupation with control:

> I feel the constant tension of holding myself together so I don't act it out. You know, lose control.

When these traits of the false self are enlisted in a situation of alcoholism, what is it like for the person, and what actually happens between people?

PARENTS AND UNHEALTHY CODEPENDENCE

With the onset of alcoholism and the need to deny it, the alcoholic's partner begins to adjust his or her life to the thinking and behavior of the alcoholic, in an attempt to gain a sense of control and stability. This turn toward alcohol is a behavioral and thinking disorder, just like alcoholism. The unhealthy codependent becomes obsessed with the behavior of the alcoholic and preoccupied about the alcoholic's welfare.

Let's move through the typical phases of this thinking disorder with one couple—Tom, the unhealthy dependent, and Marcy,

the unhealthy codependent. Marcy adjusts her view of herself and
the world to fit Tom's distorted logic. She and the family may hear
from Tom that her nagging and overcontrol are the real problems,
that he would not have to drink if it weren't for her. So she tries
harder to alter her behavior and her thinking, in an effort to
please Tom and solve the drinking problem. To no avail. Marcy's
self-esteem plummets. She denies for a long time that she feels
helpless, depressed, and victimized, because she believes it is her
own fault.

To counter her sense of self-blame, she bolsters her denial.
She tries an outward pose of superiority and pride that an-
nounces "nothing is wrong here." She begins to feel more shame
and increased isolation because her unconscious recognition of
the real problem is deepening. She becomes more obsessed with
the need to control Tom, to protect him and maintain the nothing-
wrong denial at the same time. Her futile struggle for control of
Tom results in chronic tension, anxiety, depression, underlying
resentment, and rage. She worries when Tom drinks and when he
does not. Will he come home, lose his job, get killed on the highway, or kill someone else with the car? She denies that she worries. For Marcy, now fully an unhealthy codependent, obsession
and preoccupation take over. Her time, direct attention, and un-
encumbered affection and emotion are less available for her children. The alcoholism is now a bigger worry for Marcy and a
central force in the family's life.

An obsession with alcohol may make both parents irresponsi-
ble, constantly or in spurts. They may alternate in the responsible
role, or one parent may take over completely. Whatever the pattern, only an extraordinary family can keep alcohol from interfering significantly, shaping parents' roles and behavior, and drawing
any healthy emotional investment away from the children. The
processes of denial and protection simply require too much emotional and physical energy to have enough left over to maintain a
good enough family.

For example, the issue of alcohol may be used as a hostile
weapon between the parents. The alcoholic parent drinks "at" the
other parent; the unhealthy codependent then responds through
the children, overprotecting them, out of a deep sense of guilt,
or perhaps expressing misplaced anger and hurt directly at the
children.

My mother would alternately lavish us with praise and attention and sudden outbursts of attack and rage.

The parents may become more and more preoccupied with their own relationship and its central focus on alcohol, leaving the children unseen and neglected.

At the first meeting of a new group, several members recalled the preoccupation and focus on the parents' problems as a major difficulty for them as children. "There was no room for me."

The alcoholic's initial emphasis on denial leads to underlying anger and constant fear. At first, the unhealthy codependent will attempt to control the situation through nagging, lectures, or extraction of promises from the alcoholic. Next, the unhealthy codependent will take action—hiding liquor, withholding money, or engaging in power struggles around the issue of drinking. By now, the family has an intense conflict over who is going to control whom. Any attempt at open or realistic communication is rejected. Instead, communication centers on attempts of family members to control one another.

Unhealthy codependence spirals into a vicious cycle that reinforces the protection of the alcoholic and the maintenance of the family denial. Coping with alcoholism, now the major concern, grabs and holds the attention of everyone in the family.

Terry had hoped to be a protector. She had just started to attend Al-Anon, and sought additional treatment because she could not get over her depression. She finally recognized that her husband was alcoholic, but she could not give up the idea that she could help him.

My friends in Al-Anon kept talking about "letting go," but I couldn't do this. I did not even know what they meant. I was immobilized, cried all the time, and could only think in terms of what I could do to make him change.

Now able to see more clearly, she traces the history of their life together; the central theme is alcohol.

As I look back, I now recognize that I stopped going to church when I married Mike because he thought religion was a crutch for people who couldn't face the tough realities of life. I altered my view to fit his and slowly cut my ties to my church and the friends I knew from there.

Mike already drank a lot, but because I loved him and wanted to be with him constantly, it was not a problem. I was Mrs. Michael Warden and I could follow his lead: so I drank with him, redefining my own values, goals, and what was important to me in life. Like Mike, I now wanted more time to relax and always looked for opportunities to have more fun times and a "quick one." I stopped making plans of my own, separate from him, in order to be able to respond to his needs. I now see that I never questioned any of these changes. I did everything possible to create an environment in which drinking was pleasant, acceptable, reasonable, and ever present. Our friends were drinkers and our lives revolved entirely around alcohol.

For a long time it was not a serious problem. I was anxious some of the time when Mike came home late or couldn't make it to work on time. But I covered up my worries. I called his boss to report that he had the flu, then nursed him back from his increasingly frequent debilitating hangovers. By afternoon we would share a drink and consider his "illness" a lucky holiday.

Mrs. Michael Warden never recognized that she was completely obsessed with the behavior and the welfare of her husband. She just wanted him to be happy, and he usually was while drinking. This pattern lasted for several years, until Terry was jolted by an unexpected effect:

I was virtually isolated from a nondrinking world that might have challenged my perceptions about my life and drinking. I began to have trouble keeping up with Mike, and I began to want more personal attention from him, which he could not give. I did not want him to be drunk so much of the time. Soon we were fighting over my need to control his drinking, and our close, "loving" relationship was fractured. The alcohol that brought us together was now driving us apart. It was now what we argued about constantly.

I began to drink less myself and to feel more and more depressed. For a long time, I kept protecting Mike and shouldering the blame for the unhappy atmosphere, so full of tension and arguments. If I could just control my anger and stop trying to control him, things would be better. I tried, but things didn't improve.

I felt a nagging sense of impending doom and bolstered my defenses. I denied my problem more vehemently, and mentally rejected all those I imagined were criticizing and condemning us. I believed more strongly that the world outside was judgmental and, like my husband, that people were always out to get whatever they could. You had to take care of yourself in a world like this. My days were full of worry about Mike's drinking. I drove by his favorite tavern several times a day and cut my activities completely so I could be ready to rescue him if necessary. But we still fought constantly.

I was always proud that our son Billy was such a little man and seemed so able to take care of himself. I never imagined his needs were unmet or that he was suffering as a result of his father's drinking and my preoccupation with it. I was dumbfounded when Billy's fourth grade teacher called for a parent conference. Billy was not quiet—he was withdrawn and depressed. The school recommended treatment for him. Billy's counselor insisted that both of us be involved. Mike refused; I agreed to see someone.

If a wife is alcoholic and her husband is not, events similar to Terry's may still occur. Either parent may assume the role of the other; the nonalcoholic parent may become both mother and father. Until recently, male alcoholics were slower to lose contact with the larger world than female alcoholics were. The men had more often held jobs outside the home and therefore maintained a continuing contact with a reality different from the home environment. For a partner who must maintain a continuing contact with two realities, the conflict may be intensely painful. Harry found that out first-hand:

I was an up-and-coming executive, good in my job, well-liked, good husband and father. Trudy was by my side, going up right along with me. I did OK for years while I altered my life to accommodate to her increasing drinking, unavailability, unpredictability, and shifting moods. I began to think of my wife as one of the children—I constantly called from work to see if she had remembered to do the shopping, arranged for Molly's skating lesson, and made our travel arrangements.

Eventually, I gave these duties to my secretary, who gladly took over. I worried about the kids constantly and often took them out to dinner when nothing was fixed at home. I kept trying to do more, to relieve Trudy of the stress and pressure she complained about.

I was jolted when I was offered a choice promotion. Suddenly, I was filled with shame and fear. I could not accept. The position demanded an executive wife, entertainment, and public visibility. Suddenly, I knew what had been true for years: Trudy was an alcoholic, and I had to keep her hidden. To accept the job would mean to reveal our family secret.

The spouse of the alcoholic, like the children, develops problems with interpersonal trust, intimacy, fear of being dependent, and an inability to trust perceptions.

CHILDREN AND UNHEALTHY CODEPENDENCE

The major focus of this book is on development and on understanding the complexities of what happens to children who grow up in a family with an alcoholic parent. Can we, or should we ever, consider using the term unhealthy codependence to describe children?

No, we should not. Children are automatically in a reactive, submissive position, in relation to their parents. All aspects of their development take place on the foundation of this dependent bond. Children have no choice but to follow the authority, direction, and dictates of their parents. In the alcoholic family, this direction is likely to lead to very restricted, defended self-development.

In our quest to understand the complexities of child development and the resulting ACA experience, we should omit the term codependence—whether healthy or unhealthy; it is too simplistic and overgeneralized. Most of all, the term implies choice, accountability, and responsibility. Children acquire these as distorted defenses of the false self, but they are not desirable acquisitions in this context.

Let's look at some of the consequences of the child's normal reactive position, when the parents are alcoholic and unhealthy.

Children in alcoholic families may not feel that their primary care is coming from their parents. They may concentrate on denial and peace-keeping, like the unhealthy codependent parent, or they may actually substitute for either parent, in dealings with the other parent or with siblings. They often get blamed for the family's problems. How many ACAs have heard the equivalent of:

If you kids wouldn't fight so much, your mother wouldn't have to drink.

Children learn not to care, not to have needs, or, when they do, to work them out on their own, regardless of age.

Both parents present confusing models of behavior and thinking, because of the distortions that are needed to sustain denial. Children can spot lies and alibis, and are befuddled at the disparity between what they see and what they are permitted to see and acknowledge as real.

They may not want to emulate either parent, but children will do so anyway, unconsciously. The nonalcoholic parent, if there is one, may be seen as a strong, dependable, joyless martyr, or as a weak victim, just like the children. The alcoholic also may be seen as weak, but full of needs, carefree, and loving. If the alcoholic is viewed as dominant, dictatorial, frightening, and mean, the child may want to avoid being like this parent at all costs, but may dread the other parent's victim position as well.

Separation from the alcoholic family is extremely difficult to achieve. Even after physical departure, or after parents have died, close emotional ties to the family remain. To leave is to give up hope; to abandon the family is to be abandoned. Staying emotionally attached is a way of holding on to an important role in the family and belonging to the fellowship of the family's denial.

For some ACAs, staying attached means becoming alcoholic. For others, it means being the perpetual rescuer, available in all emergencies—the grown-up version of the responsible child. Concern and involvement become preoccupations even for ACAs who no longer participate in the family. Failure to separate is a major barrier to forming healthy primary attachments to second families and causes great difficulty with intimate involvement in other significant relationships. The unfinished business in the first family precludes the perception of oneself as a separate, available partner.

Some ACAs relive their relationship with an alcoholic parent because they choose an alcoholic mate. Some avoid close relationships altogether, finding themselves more and more isolated and less and less able to trust. Those who marry and have children frequently feel that their main commitment is still to their parents. Frightened of needing to depend on another person, they often feel inadequate as parents.

Immediately after leaving home, students preoccupied with their alcoholic families may be unable to concentrate, and first-job trainees may be too distracted to commit to career goals. Focusing on themselves runs the risk that a calamity will occur in their family and they will not have done all that they could to avoid it. The young adults feel abandoned and are constantly frightened about the loss of one or both of their parents.

UNHEALTHY PATTERNS OUTSIDE THE FAMILY

Beyond the close day-to-day relationships and the core beliefs of the alcoholic family, other factors can have important and varying effects. Family size and structure, presence of extended family, number and spacing of siblings, marital status of parents, cultural pressures or expectations, and location of the home (inner city or "good" neighborhood; major metropolitan area or unattached city; suburbs or rural region)—all of these factors comprise the child's total experience of alcoholism. Because the factors vary, they affect the meaning each child attributes to alcoholism. That meaning is extremely important to the child's self-image in relation to the family and the broader culture. Technically, this is called the socialization of the child.

Socialization   In the family, the first and most important base of social involvement and social learning, we all learn the rules of culture, the do's and don'ts. Interacting and observing give us channels of information. Routine experiences that are permitted to be repeated and accepted inside and outside the home make up what any child comes to know as "normal." If the home has a pattern of parental alcoholism, how it's made a part of the family's daily life and how it's explained will have a critical impact on a child's developing self-image and his or her view of the family and the world. The realities that the alcoholic family permits to continue—a secret, denied inside and outside the home; a desperate struggle to appear normal; and a deep hostility to any intruder, especially the truth—become "normal" to the child.

The constant tension that results can create enemies outside the family; anger can then be discharged against those hostile antagonists who would threaten the family's tenuous sense of security. A retreat to its world of shared beliefs, and isolation from friends, community, church, and school, reinforce the family's denial. Tony remembers excursions into the outside world as sorties:

I hated to go out to dinner with my family. There was nothing wrong of course, but I had to endure the shame of watching my father get drunk, tip over drinks, argue with everyone, and often leave in a tirade. My father acted like he owned the world. Anybody who objected to his behavior or questioned him was the enemy.

At some point, the child in a family that says alcoholism is "normal" learns that it is not normal for other families or the world outside. Whether the realization comes suddenly or gradually, the child will not go much past entry into school before being aware that "something is wrong with my family." Memories of shame, humiliation, and embarrassment will accompany that awareness.

The need to appear normal is directly connected to adjustment and later developmental difficulties. Adults who have labeled themselves ACAs begin to challenge whether they were ever normal. Sheila tells us what can happen when the pact of denial is broken and nothing is there to take its place:

There was something wrong with my family and I knew it. I was damaged goods. Growing up was awful, but my troubles REALLY began when I left home. I had no foundation to make it in the world outside. I learned an abnormal form of reality at home and it didn't carry over. Suddenly I knew I was trying to look normal when I had no idea of what that meant. I was supposed to be an adult but I felt like a child, frightened and helpless. I was sure I'd missed something that others had gotten.

Jerry, born and raised in an alcoholic family, speaks in retrospect, recalling the agony of his early twenties and his rapid descent into his own alcoholism:

I just drank. That was all I knew. I also realized quickly that something was terribly wrong. But I had no idea what. It was awful.

For many ACAs, the defensive characteristics, the false self, or the unhealthy codependent stance fits very well within a social context. Many characteristics necessary for survival in the alcoholic home are rewarded in the culture. The model child, the high achiever, or the "hero" who has come from an alcoholic home is driven to continue behaviors and relationships that were needed

for survival in the childhood family and are encouraged and reinforced in the adult culture.

Qualities of self-starting and independence are idealized
virtues of the American character, but they are unrewarded and un-
welcomed in many real settings. Few points are awarded for calling
reality what it is. Like the alcoholic family system, many social and
business systems reward conformity and collusion, even when these
behaviors and beliefs support warped or biased thinking.

Adult children of alcoholics seem to experience a deep split.
As children, they identified with both the family's abnormality and
the conflicting need to look normal to the outside world. On the
surface, there may be little evidence that the child or adult is in
conflict; he or she "looks good" and seems to fit in so well. This
"looking good" is deceiving many professionals and it is prompting
them to believe that growing up with an alcoholic parent is an
enhancing or "positive" experience. A facade of competence is still
only a facade, and in ACAs it has been born out of defense, not
healthy development. The competence itself may be real and valu-
able, but the ACA needs an opportunity to experience it as a benefit
and extension of a healthy self, not a peace-keeping requirement for
survival.

THE DYSFUNCTIONAL FAMILY

We've been discussing the abnormality of the alcoholic family
and the short- and long-term effects of a child's realization that
"something is wrong with my family." Popular attitudes and discussion would immediately plug in the term "dysfunctional family" to
describe these situations. After all, don't unhealthy, negative, and
dysfunctional all mean the same thing, with dysfunctional saying it
best? If they do all mean the same thing, we're back to the side-by-
side but separate compartments that were constructed for dependence and codependence, and for alcoholism and coalcoholism
before them. As shown in Figure 4, "functional" would be on one
side, and "dysfunctional" on the other, with a wall between and no
connecting bridge or tunnel—and no middle ground. In that kind of
all-or-none framework, "functional" becomes equivalent to healthy,
and "dysfunctional" is a more elegant term for unhealthy and negative. The two neat-and-tidy compartments simplify descriptions of a

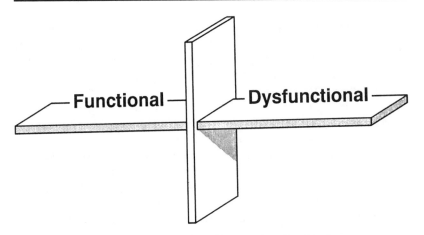

Figure 4.   Using a similar framework to illustrate functional and dysfunctional families.

family by creating two categories that can be popularly compre-
hended. However, as professional counselors know, and as ACAs
find out the hard way, these categories are limiting, naive, and
wrong.

What is not being acknowledged in the popular use of the
term dysfunctional family is that the family is a changing system
and any changing system will experience dysfunction as part of its
natural process of change and growth. The family strives to maintain a balance, and each time it approaches a transition or a new
phase or task in its development, it goes through an imbalance or a
period of dysfunction, before the new situation is absorbed and a
new balance is maintained. Individuals *grow* this way, and so do
couples, relationships, corporations, communities, and even
nations. Every one of us, in the normal and natural processes of
family life, has, in periods of transition and change, belonged to a
dysfunctional family. An organization for the familially impaired
could claim every citizen as a member.

The framework shown in Figure 4 has serious implications for
how people expect life to be. They look for "functional" partners
and a life together, in a new family, that will guarantee health and
"goodness"—positive situations and "things as they should be."
They place themselves on the "functional" side of the framework
and have tremendous resistance to the normal fluctuations and

dysfunctions that are part of a family's changes as years go by. As a result, they become rigid and inflexible about what life should be, and they have an insatiable need for control. Their dilemma would be comical and would invite today's "Get real!" if it weren't so common and problematic.

A system, by its definition, includes an agreed purpose; a team, an organization, or a family has a goal and a shared heritage or belief that has a common internal structure or idea. The system is described as functional when its parts are internally consistent and therefore in a state of equilibrium, or homeostasis. That concept is critical: functional is the equivalent of being at a point of balance, not the equivalent of healthy or having well-being. When its members share beliefs and behavior, and when everyone is bound by a common value or is centrally organized around a particular principle, the system is functional. The system may also be healthy, if the behaviors and beliefs of its members are internally consistent, valid, and appropriate to the members' needs. If the beliefs are distorted, invalid, or based on false premises, the system may be functional but it is unhealthy.

The active alcoholic family is most often a functional family system that also is unhealthy. It maintains its balance by false or distorted premises that are shared by all members of the family: they deny the existence of alcoholism and, at the same time, create faulty reasons to explain it. Because all members of the family tacitly agree to share these core beliefs, they must then develop behaviors and corresponding beliefs that allow the false premises to be maintained. Frequently, these families require another identifiable problem that is agreed upon by all to be the *real* issue (a nagging wife, a delinquent child, or a demanding job, for example). In the alcoholic family, the childhood or adult response is adaptive for *that* system and for the maintenance of attachments within *that* family.

Many ACAs, alcoholics, or other family members feel and behave in a most dysfunctional way, after breaking denial and moving out of the pathological system. Very often, families in recovery are much more dysfunctional than those still bound by active addiction. In recovery, family members are changing behaviors to match new beliefs and are actively detaching from relationships that were unhealthy but quite functional in maintaining denial and the distorted patterns of belief and behavior that were based on denial. A long, unsettling time is needed to learn new beliefs and behaviors that

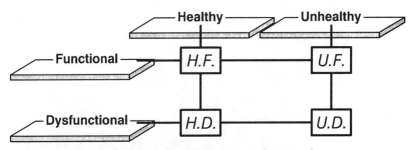

Figure 5. Expanding the functional/dysfunctional framework.

match valid premises and are therefore internally consistent and healthy. Individuals in early recovery often long for the sense of stability and improved functions that they associate with a return to active addiction. It may have been unhealthy, but at least they knew what made the system work. ACAs in recovery experience a strong pull toward returning to old beliefs and behaviors in order to achieve a sense of closer contact, no matter how fleeting or unhealthy.

I propose expanding the concepts of functional and dysfunctional as shown in Figure 5. By adding healthy and unhealthy as modifiers, functional and dysfunctional behaviors become neutral in themselves, or at least can be both positive and negative.

With the addition, in this chapter, of four possibilities for relationships in the alcoholic family—healthy dependence or codependence, and unhealthy dependence or codependence—we have a more comprehensive description of the family's characteristics. Applying the same principles to the family's maintenance of its balance as a system, we have the possibilities of healthy or unhealthy function, and healthy or unhealthy dysfunction. When so much goes on that is disruptive and conflicting, how can the alcoholic family function well? Yet, it does, in many homes. Remarkably, it maintains a point of balance—the homeostasis we discussed in Chapter 3—that allows some patterns to be kept in place. Homeostasis is extremely difficult and fragile, but, through an array of routines and adjustments, it happens. The next chapter examines how.

5

Interactions, Adaptations, and Patterns

One of the most daring productions in theater history is Andrew Lloyd Webber's *Phantom of the Opera*. The original story is an old French classic, produced twice as a movie. In the current musical production, the audience feels threatened, even before the curtain rises, by a huge chandelier that hangs over the orchestra seats; at the right moment in the story, it will ride quickly down a steeply angled wire and crash onto the stage, justifying all their fears. The evil plans of a disfigured, pitiable lunatic-genius are the stuff of the plot. Major scenes take place in a true underworld—the tunnels and river beneath the opera house, and the prison-room in which the Phantom keeps himself as well as his enemies, a nasty place furnished with appropriate props of his twisted view of the world. Yet it all works as sell-out theater. The musical score gathers up the demented Phantom's needs, the grotesqueness of his life, and the constant threat he represents, and creates an unforgettable experience. For three hours in a hushed theater, the world of Webber's *Phantom* is almost glorious. It all *works*.

The first four chapters have proven that the world of an alcoholic family could never be called glorious. Instead, like *Phantom*, it may range from unhealthy to evil; in the most negative way, it is unforgettable for those who experience it. Yet it often stays in balance; it works, even though one or both of its main characters live in an underworld of alcoholism. Let's look at the "score" that gathers up all of its elements and people, and keeps the alcoholic family system in balance.

Like any family, an alcoholic family can vary in its number of members; in having one, two, or three generations under the same roof; and in going through good times, when things run agreeably, and bad times, when everything, but everything, seems to fall apart. These facts can be normal for any family. In looking at what is "normal" for an alcoholic family, and how a point of balance is achieved at any given time, the questions come down to three answers, three elements found in any alcoholic family:

> Interactions—the unique ways the family members give and take with each other and with the alcoholic member;
> Adaptations—the quick responses that the family can make, as a group and member-by-member, when the few good times change to bad without warning and the bad times get to be a way of life;
> Patterns—the tacitly assigned or self-assigned place that each family member has in the routines of the family's day-to-day life.

These elements are the "score" that gathers up the alcoholic family and holds it together. Because of them, the family can function, regardless of its cast of characters and its particular differences.

Naming some common elements does not suggest in any way that all alcoholic families are the same or that all children of alcoholics have had the same experience. Each alcoholic family develops differently; the experiences of children in the same family—the oldest and the youngest, for example, or the sons and the daughters—can be markedly different. Understanding these individual differences among families is important for recovery.

The differences can be traced to several factors. The three we are tracking here are: the time of onset of parental alcoholism (when the drinking began), the severity and dominance of the drinking, and which parent—if one—was drinking, or what happened when both were drinking. The interactions and adaptations involved in each of these factors are woven into the discussion. Then we'll move on to family patterns.

TIME OF ONSET

Some critical questions for all ACAs will have individual, personal answers. At what age in the children's development and at what stage of the family's development did a parent become alcoholic? Were some or all of the children born into a family in which a parent was already alcoholic or parental alcoholism had become the central organizing theme? Is any other situation remembered or is parental alcoholism all that was ever known?

Did a parent make a "turn toward alcohol" later in the children's development, producing a gradual change in the family's relationships and organization? Or, instead of a "turn toward alcohol," was a parent's rapid alcoholism more of a jolt? Did a crisis, an event that suddenly made things different, precede the onset of alcoholism? Did the family go from "normal" and nonalcoholic to alcoholic almost overnight?

Could everyone feel the system going off balance? Did everyone know that something was wrong? Was that something named or unnamed?

How was alcoholism incorporated into the family's identity, the family's "story" or core beliefs, the family's rituals? Was it explained, ignored, or denied?

How did the family adjust to incorporate a parent's alcoholism? How long did it take before a parent's alcoholism felt normal, before the children forgot that once there had been a healthier family environment?

The time of onset is important in determining whether parental alcoholism has been an inherent part of the family's development or whether it has been experienced as a disruption, an intruder that arrived after the family had developed its primary sense of balance and its core beliefs. If the view of "normality" of a family and the individuals within it includes an alcoholic parent, the family members' sense of themselves will be very different from that of a family that experiences the onset of alcoholism as a disturbance, a disruption to a balanced system that did not previously include parental alcoholism.

Toby and Allison illustrate how differences in the time of onset affect a child's experience and development.

Toby and Allison listened as Sherry outlined her family history of alcoholism, including the recent death of her father. Toby was visibly shaken, tearful, and sad. Allison appeared unmoved. Their differences soon became clear.

Allison's father was an alcoholic for as long as she can remember. Her entire childhood was spent worrying about him. He was always at the emotional center of everything, draining everyone, with no idea of the havoc he created. He died in a violent accident when she was 11.

Toby had quite a different experience. He recalled a warm, loving family before both of his parents became alcoholic when he was 13. Since then, he has experienced a constant underlying sense of expectation, hope, and repeated disappointment. He had it all and suddenly it was gone. He could no longer rely on his parents to be parents to the children or to provide love and care. Suddenly, their needs were overwhelming and they were gone emotionally.

Toby's parents stopped drinking periodically and he became excited, thinking they would be available again and the family could return to normal. He was repeatedly overcome with disappointment when they resumed drinking. They are now both dead from alcoholism.

Allison spoke with anger and determination: she had been used and was "closing the door" on her family. There was no loss for her because she never had anything to begin with. Toby spoke sadly in contrast: he had a family and lost it. As a teenager and now as an adult, he wants desperately to find a new family, one he can belong to, warm and close like the one he lost.

Allison is bitter and angry. She believes strongly that she must take care of herself, that she can trust no one to help her or really put her needs first. Toby is sad and seriously depressed. He believes the perfect family is out there, if only he can find it.

Toby and Allison knew the impact of loss, but of a very different nature. Allison's "normal" experience was one of chaos, disruption, drunkenness, violence, and arguing. She and the other members of her family (two brothers and a nonalcoholic mother) were constantly coping with the erratic, unpredictable, dominant behavior of her father. Allison recalls no sense of strength or protection coming from others in the family. They were not a unit. Had they been bonded together, they might have developed a family culture separate from her alcoholic father and strong enough to withstand his disruptions. If Allison had experienced a somewhat healthy and supportive family structure, perhaps she might have negotiated developmental tasks around her father's alcoholism. Instead, Allison felt alone and isolated. Although there were four family members, they felt and operated as if each was alone in response to the behavior of her father.

Toby always thought of his family as a unit, a clan in which he proudly claimed membership. He was close to his siblings and his extended family. Toby's experience of a close, bonded family was shattered when his parents withdrew into serious alcoholism. The children offered tenuous support for one another, but all felt orphaned. As adults, each has become alcoholic, one after another. Toby wonders whether he must become an alcoholic too, in order to find a family.

> Drinking validates my membership in my family. It's the one clear way to belong.

Toby's adult adjustment is quite different from Allison's. The cornerstones for healthy development were present; Toby's parents were emotionally available and positive attachments can be remembered. Toby was able to accomplish the major childhood tasks of development, until they were interrupted at adolescence by his parents' alcoholism.

SEVERITY

Understanding severity is not the same thing as figuring out "how bad it was." That's a tough conclusion to draw and there is no reliable scale from one to ten. Most children and adult children, if they can identify parental alcoholism, will tell themselves and others, "It wasn't so bad." Their assessment usually has nothing to do with reality, but it shields the children or ACAs from the horrible recognition of just how bad it was and it saves them from feeling guilty about betraying their parents. One of the major tasks of recovery is to come to grips with the reality that parental alcoholism existed and that it was "bad" in different ways for different people.

Many ACAs resist seeking help because they are not sure they deserve it and because getting treatment will confirm the reality and intensify their guilt. When they hear others report experiences of violence or incest, they wonder why they should even be considering asking for any help. They "only" grew up with denial, parental arguing, and the stoic facade shared by all family members for the sake of outside appearances. They've yet to realize that the question "What's wrong with this picture?" applies to them too.

Understanding severity means understanding just what the alcoholism was like for this individual in this family. What did the child's environment look like and feel like? What was the context for growing up? Which normal tasks of child development were able to be accomplished and which ones required adjustment or were impaired because of parental alcoholism? How much of the child's life was devoted to or focused on coping with or actively dealing with the realities of parental alcoholism? How frequently did the child experience repeated loss when the parent left home for a hospital or detox center, or when the parents divorced, or when a parent simply disappeared and abandoned the family? How much distortion was required to keep the family system in balance around these events? How much of the child's experience was passive, connected to emotional neglect and deprivation?

The severity of parental alcoholism can't be measured. No one can say that one child experienced a 70 percent loss and another, a 90 percent loss. The important fact to realize is that there may be physical, emotional, and developmental consequences, and all of them must be recognized and addressed.

WHICH PARENT IS ALCOHOLIC?

Determining which parent is (or was) alcoholic is another critical variable in understanding the impact of parental alcoholism on children. The effect on the family system and on an individual's development can be different, depending on whether the mother, the father, or both parents are alcoholic.

Both Parents Are Alcoholic   The norm for a family in which both parents are alcoholic is alcoholism. Because children do not see other behaviors, they cannot appreciate that something is amiss. When they discover, as they grow up, that the drinking behavior of their parents is not typical, intense feelings of shame and humiliation, and a feeling of being a deviant outsider, suddenly develop. With the recognition that their parents are different, the children become more defensive and more isolated from the rest of the world. Mary discovered that she wasn't in the books she was reading:

> I began to get some inkling that my parents weren't normal when I was reading the primary books and learned about the storybook families of Dick and Jane. Nobody had cocktail hours or "situations" in these families. My parents usually missed evening meetings at school, and I had to be part of the excuse. I felt terrible lying to my teachers, and I began to realize that something was different about my home.

Joe's only sense of belonging to his family came from being needed; he had to protect his younger brothers from his violent parents. Deep down, he never believed he belonged to anyone:

> Nobody claimed me. I was an orphan in my family and am now an orphan in the world.

For Joe, the whole question of whether he is healthy, adequate, and acceptable is tied to whether he belongs. Yet, Joe senses great danger in belonging. If he is part of his family, he is like them, and that means he is out of control, violent, alcoholic, and crazy. He's one or the other: he's alone as an orphan, or he's one of them. Joe struggles constantly to bridge these extremes of identity.

Children in a family in which both parents are alcoholic learn that not only is alcohol normal, but it is used to cope with many problems in life. Some parents have no relationship outside the use of alcohol; they drink as a part of every interaction. Children learn that alcohol is a part of the expression of love, sorrow, joy, hate, anger, and all other kinds of emotions. For Patty, it never left the house:

> Nothing ever happened in my family without alcohol. Sometimes drinking was the main event, but more often, alcohol was in the

background, like musak, framing my parents' fights, reconciliations, and everything we did.

When both parents are alcoholic, they may trade off responsibilities, as we've already seen. Or, both parents may be alcoholic and drink together. Their drinking forms them into a closed unit and excludes their children from their emotional awareness. Such children feel abandoned and perhaps constantly frightened about the loss of one or both parents.

One Parent Is Alcoholic   Chapter 4 described unhealthy codependence, the adult's negative reaction to alcoholism, in detail. Let's add some examples here, to illustrate the child's experience with one alcoholic parent and one nonalcoholic parent. Sid knew what it was like to cope with parents who were both caught up in denial:

> In the beginning, I used to remind my father and mother of a forgotten promise, but then I stopped. Too frequently I was told it never happened. My father really couldn't remember, and my mother couldn't stand another reminder of our severe problems.

Penny coped with more than denial:

> I was abused severely as a child by my nonalcoholic mother. None of these episodes was ever acknowledged or talked about by anyone. As far as the world knew, I was a happy child from a happy home. I carried two secrets: my father's alcoholism and my mother's beatings.

Years later, as she attempts to describe what happened, she repeatedly changes her mind and retracts what she has just narrated. Embarrassed, she says at first that it wasn't so bad and she sounds like such a complainer, and then she says she is not sure any of it ever happened.

For some children, the nonalcoholic parent is a source of support, safety, and a more accurate version of reality. That parent may recognize the presence of alcoholism, acknowledge it, and buffer the children from its negative effects. But the buffering may have a down side too. A child may experience a tremendous split when one parent says there's no alcoholism and the other says there is. The buffering may offer support and protection, but the child may feel caught: siding with one version of reality means siding with one parent and abandoning the other. This is a common experience for children of divorce and for children of alcoholism— who may *also* be children of divorce—particularly when one parent steps out of the denial.

When their parents have control of determining what reality is, and there's no way to choose a version that is true without alienating one or both parents, the children are in a no-win situation.

PATTERNS: THE FAMILY DIAGRAM

In working with ACAs for many years, I've recognized the importance of the environment and the central organizing principle of alcohol. Chapter 3 touched on them briefly. I've also stressed the importance of understanding differences between individuals and between alcoholic families. To help represent those differences and to pinpoint particular patterns of relationship within families, I developed what I call the Family Diagram.

In its simplest form, the diagram is a large circle representing the family as a whole, with smaller circles placed inside or outside the large family circle to designate the relationship of family members to each other and to alcohol. I sometimes ask clients in an interview, or therapists in training, to "pick a time in childhood and draw your Family Diagram." When they've finished, I might then suggest that they draw that same family of origin as it exists in the present.

The Family Diagram almost always yields surprising and helpful information that has been known by the individual but never articulated. Normal channels of logic and attentional defenses have to be bypassed, in order to create this kind of spatial drawing. Long-submerged information comes up and floats on the surface. The Family Diagram also provides a base for understanding the roles, alliances, and degree of denial operating within the family.

There is no "right" way to do this exercise. The "correct" family diagram is the one that each person draws. One family may need more than one diagram—a sober family diagram, a drinking family diagram, or even an additional configuration that's "on the way to drinking." Families with binge drinkers often experience a cycle of "anticipation" or "readiness," as the binge approaches. Families with daily drinkers may experience the same sequence in a shorter cycle. Kids know, for instance, that the period of anticipation occurs every day as the time approaches for Dad to arrive home. The ice clinks and the cocktail hour is launched before the ice melts.

The Family Diagram can be adapted to suit any need for information about different times or situations. Drawing a Family Diagram is especially useful for revealing well-hidden or disguised patterns of interaction. Let's look at some general examples of these patterns. (Remember, every diagram will be different.)

Figure 6 illustrates the centrality of alcohol. Our earlier image was of a large bottle of liquor at the center of the family table. In this Family Diagram, the alcoholic is not identified. All family members come together and are organized through the alcohol in the center. Several members have access to one another on the

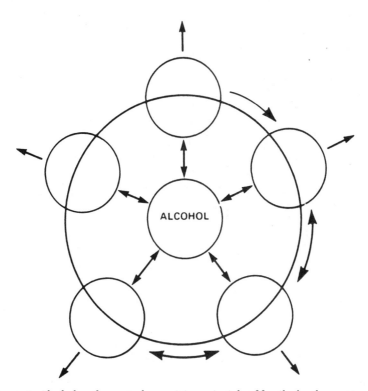

Figure 6. Alcohol as the central organizing principle of family development.

periphery of the circle, in spite of the central organizing principle of alcohol. This might represent a strong sibling relationship, for example, founded on a shared interest in sports or on mutual support. Others in the family have no relationship to one another except through the core of alcohol. These individuals may feel isolated, except when a parent is drinking or when the family must draw together to actively deal with the consequences of someone's drinking. Each family member has a tie to the outside world, although it is not clear what that tie is. Still, the arrows extending outward suggest that all individuals operate outside the family.

The ACA might next label the circles as family individuals, including the alcoholic, and further describe the meaning and the placements of the two-way arrows connecting to the alcohol and the arrows pointing outward from the family.

Figure 7 illustrates a family organized around alcohol but closed off from the world outside. The kids in this family may have

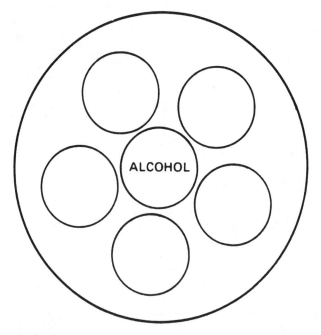

Figure 7. The family organized around alcohol and closed off from the outside world.

been instructed not to talk about home and not to develop close ties with "outsiders." One ACA explained it this way:

> I was never permitted to talk with friends about my troubles at home. We had to keep it all within the family. When my father died, I wanted to tell a few friends from school, but I just couldn't. He died drunk, so what could I say?

This ACA added that everyone in the family is now an alcoholic. The depiction of a closed family system goes on.

The next three Family Diagrams illustrate other adaptations. Figure 8 suggests that the alcoholic and alcohol are isolated from other family members, who bypass both and interact with one another. This family has no center; it is split and fragmented. The parent's alcoholism may be acknowledged or not, but family members have found a means to circumvent its centrality in their lives.

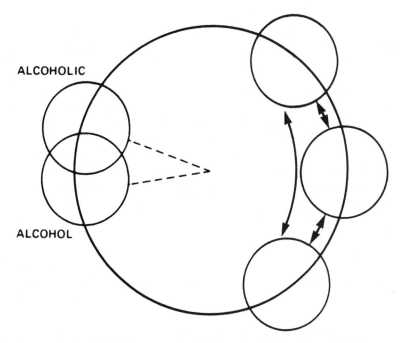

Figure 8. The family that bypasses alcohol as a central organizing principle.

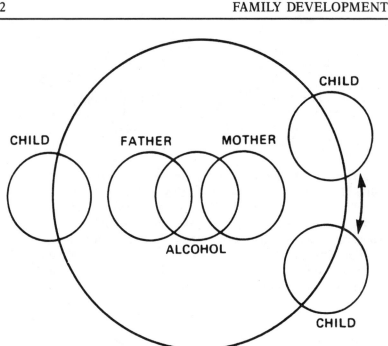

Figure 9. The family organized around the alcoholism of both parents.

In Figure 9, both parents are alcoholic and are centered on alcohol. Three children are straddling involvement with the family and the world outside. Two of the children have a close, mutually protective relationship; the third feels isolated from everyone in the family. Further exploration might reveal that the adults provide little parenting because of their absorption in their drinking and their drinking relationship. The two close children provide care for one another, and one of them actively assumes parental duties for the family. The isolated child feels neglected, helpless, and frightened.

Figure 10 illustrates another variation. The alcoholic, now recovering, is outside the family, having left and divorced her mate while still drinking. The adult who drew this configuration recalled growing up with his mother gone and described a mutually interactive system that bypassed the alcoholic or alcohol. This individual struggles with his sense of loss and with the increasing responsibility he felt as a child, after his mother left the home.

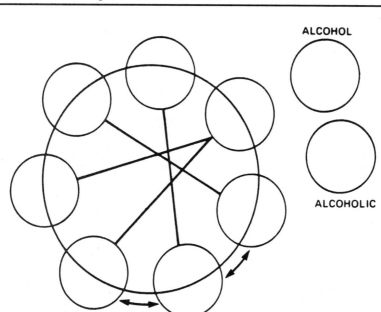

Figure 10. The family without the alcoholic.

These diagrams show some combinations that might appear in an individual's own Family Diagram. A Family Diagram gives an ACA a representation of the true structure of his or her family's organization and pattern. The Family Diagram allows us to move from assessment of the family system to examination of individual development, without losing sight of the interaction between the two.

Part III makes that move, shifting from the family to its individual members.

_____ III

*Individual
Development*

6

A Developmental Perspective

Now that we've looked at the alcoholic environment and the family system, it may be hard to fathom that, for many years, children were widely believed to be *unaffected* by parental alcoholism. This point of view survived even during the years when Al-Anon was born and there was beginning recognition that one person's alcoholism had an impact on others. Those "others" did not yet include the children.

In Part I, we saw what actually goes on when alcohol, or alcoholism, is the central organizing principle in family development—what the environment is like, how the family dynamics work, how a pathological system maintains the alcoholism, denying and explaining it at the same time. In Part II, we continue looking at alcoholism as a central organizing principle, but now we'll be examining its effect on the main tasks of the individual's development—what is supposed to be achieved in each stage of growing up.

The development of the individual is a large and complicated area. Acknowledging all its elements is like sitting in a second-deck seat at the circus and trying to keep track of the action in all three rings on the floor below, the trapeze artists swinging through the air above, the clowns tumbling into the front-row seats, *and* the hot dog vendor. Individual development poses a danger of oversimplification and at the same time requires over-simplification for any understanding of what is happening and in what sequence.

Our focus will stay on alcoholism as an organizing influence. First, we'll look at the general effect of parental alcoholism on some of the tasks the children are supposed to be achieving in the stages of their development. For children in alcoholic families, the important developmental tasks, and sometimes even the simplest ones, require adaptations, made to accommodate the parent's alcoholism. These same developmental issues, we will see, become the focus of difficulties when the children of alcoholics reach the stage called adulthood. Then, we'll move to two specific and critical tasks, attachment and identity formation.

We saw in Chapter 3 that parents, as the first caregivers for children, are also their primary figures of attachment and their most influential teachers about themselves and the world. Ruptures in the early bond between parent and child can lead to later difficulties in establishing close, intimate adult relationships. The essential process of identity formation—literally, the child's answer to the question, "Who am I?"—becomes a serious obstacle to healthy development, for the child in an alcoholic family. In one sentence, we'll be looking at what is supposed to happen developmentally for the child, what actually happens, and what kinds of themes and problems persist and characterize the adult in need of recovery.

I noted earlier that professional therapists are beginning to understand the impact of parental alcoholism on development, from work with ACAs in long-term treatment. Repeatedly, issues of attachment—to parents and to current partners—and identity are critical for ACAs. If it weren't for the popular ACA movement and the descriptions given by ACAs in treatment, we wouldn't even be close to comprehending the developmental issues that are so predominant. The ACAs often look so good, so solid and fully matured, there are no visible clues to their true condition; or, they still have no idea what's wrong but have only an awareness that their view of themselves and of their life, past and present, is not what it should be. ACAs seeking recovery are beginning to echo Matt's question: "What's wrong with this picture?"

The answer leads us back to our central premise about the alcoholic family: the close, primary bonds between parents and child are founded on an unstated agreement to share the family's "story" about parental alcoholism. Members agree to deny the drinking *and* to explain it in a way that allows it to be maintained. Often, this unrecognized pact means that other areas of a child's development will be distorted too. Let's follow this central premise, starting with the general tasks of development.

THE TASKS OF DEVELOPMENT

Experts in many fields of study recognize the importance of a point of view that identifies expected and necessary tasks and stages in the normal processes of growing up. Technically, this point of view is a developmental perspective. Earliest development starts at a simple or primitive base and proceeds later to higher levels that have more complex functions and interactions. In the developmental view, each successive stage, and the tasks identified for that stage, builds on the previous one. Problems at any point along the way may lead to an arrest in development or an adjustment to accommodate the gap or difficulty.

The process of human development has simultaneous multiple tracks. A child "grows up" biologically and physically, emotionally, cognitively (intellectually), and socially. Parental alcoholism may have an impact on any or all of these tracks at various points— or at all points—in a child's development.

We know from the biological and genetic sciences that parental alcoholism may have a profound impact on the child, apart from the effects of the environment or the kind and quality of bonds established with parents. Alcoholism runs in families. It's passed from one generation to the next through a genetic process that is not yet understood. Although this track is very important, we won't be accenting it. Our focus will be primarily on children's emotional development, starting with the primary bond of attachment between the infant and the parent, and on children's cognitive development— their process of knowing, which involves their awareness and their judgment. We'll then look at identity formation, how a child develops a sense of self.

The work of Erik Erikson gives a general developmental frame. The stages of development that he identified are well-known and useful for their combined interpersonal and individual focus.

Basic Trust All human development must start with a very close, dependent relationship. Erikson defines the task of this early bonding as "basic trust." In simple form, the infant cries and the parents attend to its needs. An expectancy that one's cries will be understood and one's needs attended to is established. The process of mutual communication and responsiveness between infant and parent is a predictable part of the dependent relationship. All theorists agree on the importance of certainty, predictability, and stability of the caregiving figures. Disruptions in the accuracy, empathy, timing, and certainty of the response can have serious consequences for all aspects of later development.

The building of basic trust will be disturbed for an infant whose mother is primarily involved with her own drinking or with the welfare of an alcoholic husband. The child whose needs are randomly met because of this preoccupation or absorption with alcoholism will grow to expect inconsistency, inadequate care, and disorganization. Confidence in caretakers and the environment derived from successful bonding and from the building of basic trust will be missing or impaired, and all subsequent development will suffer.

> Betsy drank heavily during her pregnancy and in the early years following Jenny's birth. Jenny's father left the home when she was nine months old, and was replaced by several live-in boyfriends. Betsy believed that she loved her daughter, but she was unable to care for her. Her attachment to Jenny was seriously disrupted by her involvement with her own daily drinking and her intense, violent relationships with boyfriends. Feeding, soothing, mutual attention, and physical needs such as diapering and bathing were randomly performed and with varying degrees of intensity and engagement. Jenny cried frequently in her first few months and then lapsed into apathy and nonresponsiveness.

Autonomy versus Shame and Doubt Erikson's second stage, autonomy versus shame and doubt, also becomes impaired in an alcoholic family. This is the toddler's time of experimentation with issues of control, of "holding on" and "letting go," of negotiating closeness and distance. Many children of alcoholics are already tuned to the primacy of their parents' needs and are therefore unable to begin this process of early detachment. In this stage of development, a child should be able to move back and forth from parents. In an image familiar to many of us, the child delightedly runs away from the mother to explore the nearby world and, just as suddenly, runs back to find the mother standing still, where the child left her, waiting to welcome the explorer back to home base for snuggling and refueling. The toddler may be quite confused and frightened because alcoholic parents are struggling so unsuccessfully with issues of control themselves that it is not safe enough to try out an exploring run. Indeed, a mother (or father) may not be standing still, where the child left her, because of her own preoccupations.

Children also may experience mixed messages. At one time, parents may encourage independence, or even push a child away; at another, they may thwart a child's independent efforts because of their own needs and insecurities.

Initiative versus Guilt The same process interferes with the next stage of development, initiative versus guilt, which is the focus for preschool children. By now, the child in an alcoholic family may be predominantly geared, like the parent, to a reactive, defensive posture and can't risk the experimentation necessary to develop feelings of competence and mastery. Many children grow up with a chronic, deep feeling of fear. They are capable of experiencing themselves only as reactors, never as initiators.

Other children develop a precocious competence; they need it to cope with the family's lack of control and disorganization. The development of deep, internal self-confidence and the pleasure derived from experimentation are thwarted, however. The competence they demonstrate is driven by necessity and anxiety. Underneath the facade of control are feelings of doubt, inadequacy, and responsibility for others.

Frequently, the range of intellectual and emotional development will be limited at this stage. The child will find a niche of apparent competence and control that successfully quiets internal anxiety and fears about the parents' instability. Many adults recall finding comfort and safety in early academic achievements or in the pursuit of one well-defined and therefore controllable hobby.

Although such carefully and narrowly channeled development is adaptive and is positively reinforced in the family and in our culture, it results in limitations and difficulties in establishing both adolescent and adult interpersonal relationships. One of the

most common complaints of ACAs is their inability to develop and
sustain emotionally mature relationships. Not only did they lack
adequate role models, but their energy was invested in defensive
operations in an unsafe environment. There was no possibility for
experimentation.

The interference of denial is critical during this period. To
maintain attachment to parental figures, children must deny their
own perceptions of reality and accept the explanations presented
by their parents. Within the family there may be constant distortion and a shifting reality. Pam alternated between two scripts:

> My mother's alcoholism was the central issue of my life. We had
> two completely different family plays around that issue. When she
> was drunk, we were scared, depressed, and closed to the outside
> world so we could protect our secret. Of course, we didn't acknowl-
> edge that she was drinking either. We just sunk into despair, shifted
> gear, and tried to cope until she stopped again. When she was
> sober, we were the happy family, active in school and community
> affairs. We all grew up knowing both plays backward and forward,
> and easily shifted parts.

As we saw in earlier chapters, the child in this family develops
a hypervigilant, guarded stance as a result of having to repeatedly
assess the environment to determine what reality exists for that
moment and then behave accordingly. A narrow intellectual and
emotional range is required, to keep the child's eyes open and attention focused. Free, unhampered exploration and experimentation,
to discover what the world is like and what it has to offer, are not
even possible options.

Identity Formation   If all goes well for children, these early
stages prepare them for the ongoing tasks of separation from the
close emotional bonds of attachment with their parents and identification, the establishment of their own understanding of who and
what they are.

In an alcoholic family, all does not go well. The children's
fundamental sense of attachment is based on sharing the distorted
family beliefs, the "story" that holds the family system together.

Because the children move toward adulthood unable to challenge the family's beliefs or identity, they acquire and develop their

own "personal identities" by imitating and identifying with the beliefs and behaviors of the parents. In a family in which denial and distortion are the rule, there may be no viable adult figure for children to consciously emulate. They will do so unconsciously, however. They may mirror the alcoholic with helplessness and failure, perhaps mixed with affection and warmth, or with strength and control, reflecting the family's successful denial of the alcoholic reality. The nonalcoholic parent may be seen as critical, depressed, victimized, and more unavailable than the alcoholic. Years later, an ACA still had sharp profiles of both parents:

> Even though my alcoholic father was cruel, I know he loved me. But I can't forgive my mother. Where was she? Why didn't she protect me? She was gone, depressed and helpless.

Development may stop short of separation, for a child who refuses consciously to identify with either parent. If there are no other models available, the child must remain in an arrested state of development, failing to successfully move into an adult identity. To identify with either parent would equal destruction, because both parents are seen as unhealthy, damaging to themselves and others. The process of identification brings the adolescent to a crisis. Bill wished that his calendar pages would stop turning:

> I remember anticipating high school graduation with a horrible feeling of dread. There was nothing I could look forward to about growing up, becoming an adult. I can feel it now; there was such a sense of doom. I was going to be in trouble and I wouldn't be able to stop it. I kept postponing sending in my college applications. It made no sense then, but now I see it was the only way to postpone growing up.

Children with an alcoholic parent may make some offbeat adaptations at adolescence. A child may actively experiment with alcohol and drugs, becoming addicted or delinquent and thereby "joining" the family and taking the focus off the family at the same time. A competent "model" child may begin to drink with the family, developing the same belief in control as the parents. Only later will the drinking begin to interfere with achievement. Adolescent girls may marry an alcoholic, continuing the task of controlling a male alcoholic or making a family well.

Separation   Children of alcoholics most often do not negotiate the final turn and cross the finish line of separation. The accumulation of their previous failures makes a view of themselves as independent, well-functioning individuals impossible. Many adult children of alcoholics recognize that they are still tied emotionally and physically to their families of origin. They feel guilty about having "left behind" their siblings or their needy parents, and, if they seek treatment, they feel equally guilty because they need help to "get out of my family."

For the adolescent in an alcoholic family, separation feels like abandoning the family or being abandoned by them, without the solid foundation of nurturance and belonging from which separation can occur. The adolescent may unconsciously fear survival outside the family. Actual separation may emphasize problems with control, feelings of loneliness and isolation, and barriers to trust and intimacy. Many people in their early 20s report the kind of crisis that is more common at midlife. They become depressed and have a sense that life is meaningless: "I feel so guilty leaving chaos behind. How can I look ahead?"

Their depression often reflects their acknowledgment of having repeatedly tried and ultimately failed to control the alcoholic's drinking or to make the family well. By continuing that crusade with the family of origin, or in a new family, they can sidestep emotional separation and healthy adult development and protect themselves against overwhelming depression.

Problems in identification or separation often bring adults to treatment. The defenses that may have served them extremely well in childhood are now outdated or the wrong size. Many competent, high-achieving individuals have, as adults, serious interpersonal and internal problems. Chronic fear, depression, and excessive emphasis on control are often at the center of those problems.

Long-term treatment may reveal a profound, deep identification with being "out of control" and therefore just like the alcoholic. Many ACAs believe that they are already alcoholic and it is inevitable that they will act out their belief. They realize they cannot will themselves to be different.

All of the developmental tasks and processes covered in this chapter are critically important. Two of them need more of our attention because they involve prominent effects of the alcoholic family. Let's look, in greater detail, at attachment and then at identity formation.

7

Attachment

Attachment is a popular word and a popular concept. It's common in our culture to talk about the importance of close, intimate relationships and of feeling "connected" to others. Attachment is just that: a close human contact; a bond and a relationship. The bond that starts from birth and continues throughout our lives is the base or foundation for all processes of normal childhood and adult development. Healthy development is believed to be derived from a strong, positive core attachment during infancy and early childhood years.

None of us can survive without at least one important early bond to someone who understands and meets our needs. If that bond is faulty or becomes badly frayed, it can be the source of difficulties and unhealthy adaptations in development. Many problems can be traced to early connections between the child and the parents or other primary caregivers, or between the child and other significant figures such as siblings, grandparents, or other extended family.

Humans are social animals who develop and survive in relation to others. Psychiatrist John Bowlby has said that establishing a primary emotional bond with another person is the major goal of life. To support and secure the bond with the parent in an alcoholic family, the child defers or denies its own needs and perceptions. To preserve the closest bonds of human relationship—those of the primary family—the child will join in maintaining the family's denial of alcoholism, or the particular "story" that allows parental alcoholism to be denied and explained at the same time.

Attachment to parents is a critical theme for adults struggling to break the denial pact and "rewrite" their own personal family histories in recovery. For many ACAs, attachment to parents was seen as conditional and often fragile; one of the conditions for them was that they had to deny having a separate self and a separate view of the world.

In this chapter, we'll look first at the early bond and how it gets frayed by the common and serious problem of parent–child role reversal. Then we'll see how this disturbed pattern of attachment affects all relationships and is a central theme for ACAs in treatment.

ATTACHMENT THROUGH ROLE REVERSAL

Role reversal was described earlier as a response, among family members, to the environment; it shows up again as a central feature of attachment in alcoholic families. The experience, as children, of having exchanged roles with their parents is one of the most limiting and serious problems for ACAs who try to establish healthy, satisfying relationships. Let's look at the problem's components.

Parental Narcissism   The road to mature development starts with a very close, dependent relationship. Psychoanalyst Margaret Mahler calls it a "symbiotic" bond, in which parent and infant are like one. Erikson identified the merged relationship and the same period of time in infancy as the stage of basic trust, which we examined in Chapter 6. It is the time when the infant first experiences communication and learns, through close contact with the mother or other primary caregiver, that he or she will be understood and responded to.

Philosopher and analyst Alice Miller has spoken out emphatically about parental abuse and neglect in the primary bond. "True autonomy," or independence, Miller says, is always preceded by the experience of being dependent. She outlines the severe consequences for children, when their parents occupy the center spot of attention and require support from their children to resolve their own problems and conflicts. Miller describes a common but very

unhealthy parent–child bond in which the child exists to recon-
firm the parent's value or point of view, becoming an extension or
tool of the parent.

Parental narcissism, the dominance of the parents' needs at
the expense of those of the child, is an insidious, often subtle kind
of role reversal. For the child, it leads to a loss of self in service to
the parents, rather than to healthy development and ultimate separation. Miller stresses that attachment and dependence founded on
the centrality of the child's needs and the parents' accurate responsiveness to them are essential for healthy development. No one
disagrees.

The importance of the environment and of how the family
works surfaces again in relation to the parent–child bond. The
alcoholic family is organized around the parents' needs—the alcoholic's growing need for alcohol and the nonalcoholic's (if there is
one) need to control the alcoholic. Because both parents are frequently overwhelmed by their own anxieties and needs, they are
inattentive or only marginally attuned to satisfaction of the needs
of their children.

Childhood is short-circuited or nonexistent for children whose
primary needs are secondary to those of their parents. Children
learn to experience and express their own needs only in reaction to
the uncertain or random capacity of their parents to respond. Mea-
suring or controlling one's neediness is another way of protecting
the parent. Kids won't expose parental inadequacies by wanting or
needing what can't be supplied.

How many ACAs remember themselves being described as "a
regular little mother" or "the little man of the house," when they
took charge of chores or responsibilities for their incapable alcoholic parents. When they must take over the role of one or both of
their parents, children may develop a precocious pseudomaturity—
they act older than they are, and they speak, respond, and give support so close to an adult level that other adults tend to forget that
they are children in every way. Typically, they assume responsibility for the parent (including feeding, clothing, and maybe cleaning
up) and for parenting younger siblings. The child reacts to the dominance of the parents' needs *and* assumes a parental responsibility
for meeting those needs.

Attachments in the alcoholic family stay magnetized by the
centrality of the alcoholic and the denial of parental alcoholism. In

Miller's terms, the child exists to confirm for the parents not only that they, the parents, are good, but also that there is no alcoholism. The child must then adopt the parents' logic and reasoning and sustain their double denial: "There is no alcoholism here, and don't talk about it."

Theodore Lidz, whom we met in Chapter 2, outlines a similar theory. He suggests that the parents' struggle to maintain their own fragile emotional balance leads them to shape the family environment rigidly, to meet their needs and to maintain their own view of themselves. Lidz notes that the parents' insistence on altering family members' perceptions and meanings creates a family environment filled with "inconsistency, contradictory meanings and denial of what should be obvious." As we saw in the Family Diagrams, this distortion of meaning can close off the child from the larger culture outside the family.

Like Miller, Lidz points at how the children are forced to put their parents' defenses before their own needs. The meaning a child gives to experiences is related to solving parental problems instead of helping the child to master events and recognize feelings. In addition, when the child must accept contradictory experiences and meanings, a distorted logic results that allows a child to recognize on one level that A and B cannot both be true, and to explain on another level just why they are.

Children must perceive the family as the parents dictate, repressing or denying feelings, and distorting perceptions to fit the family's mold. Facts are constantly altered to mesh with the emotionally determined needs of the parents rather than the child. Lidz elaborates on this entire process, outlining a child–parent role reversal similar to Miller's. Lidz calls it "parental egocentrism."

Parental Egocentrism   Egocentric parents are unable to recognize that the other person, the child, has different feelings, needs, and ways of experiencing. These parents cannot respond appropriately to the child; instead, they require the child to adjust itself to the parents' needs or point of view.

A child growing up with this pattern of relationship may be quite open and sensitive to the needs and feelings of others, precisely because he or she has had to fit in with the parents' needs. But this kind of attachment actually leaves a child extremely vulnerable. Directed by the parents' needs, the child has not invested energy and attention to self-development and is likely to feel quite empty inside. Ironically, the child then needs the parent, to provide a sense of self, false though it may be. The child becomes entirely other-directed.

Children growing up with this kind of reverse attachment will also come to believe that they are essential to their parents' survival. The magical thinking that is a normal part of young children's development leads them to believe that they can affect the parent by their thoughts and feelings—that growing up, or separating emotionally, will kill the parent, for example. Many children believe that they literally keep their alcoholic parents alive. These children may experience nightmares, school phobia, or other signs of extreme anxiety when they are separated from their parents. These fears are not directly for their own safety, but for the survival of the parent.

Lidz's explanation is very useful in understanding the apparent contradiction many ACAs experience: They are extremely important, even the central person in their parents' lives, yet they are nonexistent, not recognized or heard on their own behalf. They are needed and valued to meet parental needs and expectations, but long to have the right to needs of their own. In essence, they long for appropriate role reversal—to be the child with a caring, attentive, responsive parent, the way the roles should have been.

Several ACAs demonstrate how this parental view of self hinders development. Meg recalls the burden of parenting her parents. She cries as she thinks about the overwhelming needs of everyone in her family:

> I had to set limits on both of them. I told my father to leave me alone when he was drunk. I never had a chance to be a child. I wish I'd had an opportunity to be a 12-year-old.

Dan shares a similar memory:

> I can remember planning how to get something I wanted from my father. He was so unpredictable. I'd have to behave very carefully for days in advance so as not to upset him. I always thought I could "manage" my father's reactions to me by being on good behavior myself. When I'm with him the negative pull is so great I lose my good feelings and get drawn in to meet his needs. I can't remember

an occasion when my father felt sympathetic with what I needed or was talking about.

As Dan spoke of "managing" his relationship with his father, Gloria added:

It's like the "marketplace" of human relationships. Everything is bartered to get anything in return.

HOW ATTACHMENTS ARE MAINTAINED

Identification with Parental Beliefs and Behavior   One of the ways children maintain the close bond with their parents and the sense that they are keeping the parents alive is by identifying with the feelings that belong to the parents, but which they—the parents—are not themselves feeling. Intense feelings of anxiety, shame, humiliation, or embarrassment may provide a lifeline to a parent otherwise emotionally unavailable or unresponsive. The child may indeed experience himself or herself as a real savior, providing life to the parent who is out of control or emotionally "dead." Several ACAs identified with behavior, beliefs, or parental emotions that served to sustain the attachment both ways. Sally's deep, intense, and unyielding anger toward her alcoholic father is now generalized toward all men. Although she made progress in recovery, she insisted that she would never relinquish her anger and no one should ask her to examine it. Eventually, Sally could see that her need to hold on to her anger was hurting her:

I realized that my tie to my mother is based on my being angry with men. But it's not my anger, it's hers. I took on the anger and contempt my mother must have been feeling for my father but never expressed. If I stop feeling angry with men, I'll betray her and lose my relationship with her.

Sandra explored her unshakable belief in her badness, expressed and reinforced through constant self-criticism and self-punishment. She began to see that her belief was vital to maintaining her very close, but negative, bond with her mother:

I suddenly had this feeling that if I altered my belief about myself—my badness—I would abandon my alcoholic mother and lose my tie to her in the process. It's impossible. I know how my mother feels in my bones—"I am my mother." I walk in her shoes. I have always felt the criticism that she held toward herself, but constantly gave to me.

Sandra worked very hard to feel better about herself, but was amazed at how difficult it was. She was kind and generous with others, always on the lookout to yield to or take care of someone else, which was appreciated but also challenged by friends. Both the positive regard of others and their challenge only fueled her bad feelings. She began to see that, whenever she was actively attacking and hateful of herself, she also felt much closer to her mother.

Other ACAs share Sandra's dilemma, although in different ways. Harvey's close bond with his mother always boiled down to a battle over which one of them owned him. If he wanted his mother's affection, he had to see the world exactly as she did. There could be no difference in point of view. As an adult, all of Harvey's closest relationships are characterized by a battle over who's going to control whom. If he's not struggling, Harvey feels defeated.

Some ACAs achieve a limited but stable adjustment by consciously refusing to identify with any recognizable aspect of parental belief, emotion, or behavior. This kind of adaptation takes a lot of energy and a major emphasis on defense, to keep inside what is deeply hidden. These individuals may be emotionally flat, using isolation to avoid feeling too much about anything. They may have survived predominantly through role reversal, assuming parental responsibility for parents and siblings. Any feelings of need are much too threatening, bringing them too close to the neediness the parents experienced and to the possibility that they might have needs themselves. This is a very tough position. The ACA must rigidly deny that he or she feels or needs anything, while stifling a deep, painful longing. The individual is likely to end up feeling lonely and isolated, with no way to let anybody in. Mark describes it well:

The only way I feel safe and good about myself is when I'm taking care of others. I can't imagine feeling needy myself, or really letting others care for me. I just have no sense of what that would be like at all, except awful. All my energy goes into proving I'm not like them at all.

Close Relationships   Attachment has everything to do with relationships. According to some experts, early primary attachments serve as the model for *all* succeeding relationships. The child develops a sense of itself both in relation to a primary figure and, in normal development, as a separate individual. Given what we've seen so far about childhood development in an alcoholic family, difficulties in forming close, intimate partnerships that are not based on a denial of oneself, a submissive, reactive posture in relation to another dominant person, or a repeat of the parent–child role reversal can be predicted. The chances for healthy relationships are likely to be lacking, or seriously impaired. A role-reversed child, unable to separate emotionally from a parent, is not able to establish a close, primary relationship, healthy or unhealthy, with an appropriate partner. Because one level of development proceeds on top of another, *continuous* distortion is required to maintain the unhealthy base of relationship formation. The alcoholic couple builds and maintains a partnership based on unequal and unhealthy premises, and they pass this model of close interaction on to their offspring.

The most problematic issues for ACAs often involve relationships: with parents and families of origin, with significant current partners, or with children, born and growing, or yet to be conceived. A constellation of problems is associated with intimacy. The deep meaning attached to being in a close, committed relationship can be terrifying for many ACAs: it automatically signals the loss of self and the dominance of someone else's greater need. Will others be too dependent on them, when they long to be dependent themselves? Yet, the idea of being and feeling needy is much more terrifying than taking care of a needy someone-else.

Being involved in a close relationship almost always brings up issues of boundaries and of limit setting. Because attachment often, paradoxically, means the loss of self, ACAs struggle with how to be involved and still have space. Much important work in recovery occurs as ACAs try out different kinds of roles and patterns in relationship, and experiment with having needs and establishing boundaries and limits with others. Let's look at these themes as they unfold in the process of recovery.

Not Having Needs   ACAs may easily identify with the pseudo-parental role of "not having needs." Disclaiming any needs is a helpful strategy that shields children from the devastation of emotional and physical abandonment, rejection, or withdrawal by a parent. In interpreting her childhood's effects on current relationships, Wendy spoke as a parent who had failed at parenting:

> My mother was supposed to teach me what to say and how to respond to people but, in fact, I had to teach her. The problem is, when I do respond or suggest something to her, it feels so aggressive. If I know something she doesn't, it's a betrayal of her.

Over time, Wendy could see that she could not have any needs herself because her mother failed to meet them and she could not successfully take care of herself because that was a betrayal. But, if she focused on taking care of her mother, she felt guilty. As Wendy said, "Being involved is no-win."

As she worked toward being able to experience herself as having needs, Wendy saw her dilemma: the parent's need is so great, the child is frightened that hers will be just as overwhelming and repulsive to others. That fear was only one of her reactions:

> I alternate between feeling angry and terribly needy myself. I know what my mother must have felt. How can I be angry with her for being so cold and unavailable when she couldn't help it? She was always so needy.

> I remember waking up to hear her sobbing uncontrollably, drunk and begging forgiveness. I felt so helpless in being able to take care of her. You know, I was the child. I was the one who needed care and protection, but I had to comfort her repeatedly and tell her it was OK.

As Miller suggests, the narcissistic and needy parent pays attention to the child in order to obtain reassurance about the parent's worth, not from an interest in or an empathic response to the needs of the child. ACA responses to a 1986 television movie about parental alcoholism ("Shattered Spirits," by Robert Greenwald) provide some insight.

> Sara did not feel sympathetic for the male at any point in the film, till the very end. She had a glimpse that this father cared about his family when he was able to cry and recognize that he was not ready to come back to live with them. Sara said later that she never had any

sign at all that her father cared about her or anybody else. Once again, she felt intense anger at his tremendous preoccupation with himself and alcohol, to the injury of all those around him.

Brad agreed. He noted how much time and energy all the other family members had to pay to the alcoholic and to his treatment. Brad and others wondered when, if ever, the family members get to pay attention to developing their own lives or looking at their own needs.

Ben discusses an upcoming visit and his fears of dealing with his father's needs as a sober parent:

I feel worse about my father being dry than I did when he was drinking. I'm worried about seeing him. He won't be "insulated" by alcohol and therefore he'll be more vulnerable to what I might say. I feel very protective of him and am afraid I'll be destructive or hurtful.

I just want to see what he's like. I'm not interested in "getting" anything from him. I hope I can create an atmosphere that will be safe enough for him to talk and maybe reflect back to my childhood. I'm actually afraid of what I have to learn about myself from a sober father. I was a difficult child who needed a patient father.

Paula also talks about need and the sober parent:

How can you have anything wrong with you or have needs as the child of a sober alcoholic? What do you do when you've been deprived of a parent all your life, and your mother gets sober? You know, it's harder to be rejected by a sober parent than a drunken one, but their needs are just as great.

Often, it is difficult for ACAs to recall or feel the pain associated with never successfully helping their parents to become the functional, responsible parents the child needed. ACAs sharing their experiences often start with a discussion of what they needed as children from their parents, but they inevitably shift to what their parents needed from them and how they failed to provide it. This keeps them in the parental role. The focus of blame and failure stays on themselves.

Having Needs   One of the toughest, often buried issues is "having needs." It's safer to think in terms of meeting someone else's needs, and terribly frightening to allow oneself to feel needy. Past experiences with alcoholic parents cement the expectation that cries will not be heard or that parents are so preoccupied with their own concerns that they cannot shift to paying attention to their kids, small or grown. The adult may struggle for a long time to make sense of the fact that, while the picture looked good to outsiders, an accurate, empathic emotional bond, in which parent was responsive to child, was missing. As Matt got closer to recognizing his own deep feelings of need, he looked at his beliefs and expectations of how others would respond:

> I have a picture of myself huddled alone in the dark. I cry out for help and people look up. But they can't see me. Or, they come, hobbling on broken legs, and can't really help me at all. I'm *always* disappointed by people I thought I could count on.

As ACAs progress in recovery and begin to recognize the depth and reality of their own need—both what they missed experiencing and receiving as children, and what they are missing as adults—they are often terrified. They may act on an impulse to run, to end this uncovering process, and to reaffirm an old belief that they can take care of themselves. They may suddenly wonder whether *any* of this new reality is true. The idea or the experience of "having needs," though appealing at a distance, is repulsive up close. Shirley puts it all in one sentence:

> Having needs makes me feel just like my alcoholic mother, disgusting and out of control.

ACAs in recovery chip away at the defenses that mask their own recognition of need and severely restrict them as individuals. Relinquishing the view of oneself as a parent figure, the person in "control" who must listen for and respond to others' needs, is fraught with anxiety. Nevertheless, a deep need to feel safe, cared for, and listened to exists.

Some deep needs may be paired with counteracting emotions. A primitive wish to be "boundariless" may be quickly countered by intense fear. The notion of "merger" may awaken a sense of danger. Imagined freedom and gratification, sometimes openly desired, may be canceled out by a feeling that relinquishment of control or vigilance to the care and protection of another is not safe.

Their identity as "children of alcoholics" gives ACAs permission to feel their dependency needs, as frightening as that may be. Gloria gives a detailed example of how her own deep wish to be cared for conflicts with the parental role that keeps her attached to her mother:

> My mother did outrageous things but always thought the problems belonged to somebody else and not to her. I was the opposite. I grew up believing there was something wrong with me—I was never quite good enough. It is central to my view of myself. I realize now that I feel like my mother must have felt underneath her anger and outrage. As long as I define myself as the one with the problem, I can feel close to her. It's painful, but feeling good about myself also carries with it a great sense of loss.
>
> Still, I long for someone to care for me, to praise me and cheer for my successes. As a child, I used to fantasize that I was an orphan, adopted by a new family so I could "start over again" or begin a new "slate."

Gloria kept repeating this same cycle: she achieved new insights, felt better about herself—got a new "slate"—but always returned to the "fact" that she was not good enough and really had done nothing at all. Gloria accepted her mother's defenses and definition of reality, in order to have a relationship with her. As Gloria continued her work of reconstructing her past, she experienced a deeper and clearer sense of her close tie to her mother:

> The more I open up, the more I experience myself as the "falling apart mother," which is the role my mother always played. She commanded our attention through her drinking and her dramatics. I don't know how I felt as a child. I felt only my mother's feelings, or the ones she should have been feeling, which were so deep and out of control.

The notion of "leaving" their parents behind—giving up their parent-figure feelings or the negative view of self necessary to sustain the attachment—is a major theme of ACAs in recovery. Gloria described the closeness of the bond with the parent and the difficulty of separating:

> The idea of "leaving" my mother is terrifying. It's like leaving a very important part of myself. My mother is the only source of my

self-definition. I built my identity from her knowledge and view of me, which was always critical and punishing. So that's who I am. When I'm down on myself, I know I exist.

If I feel angry or punishing toward my mother, it's like punishing or doing away with my very own self. I feel so much a part of my mother and understand her so well that to attack her is to attack myself.

Many ACAs can feel need, but only alone:

That's how it was growing up and that's how it is now. You didn't dare feel any need. There wasn't anybody there.

ACAs often return to the painful question: did they ever have anyone to talk to? Many imagined an ideal special family to which they could belong, one that would be honest and normal. Others had the fantasy of being adopted or they openly wished to belong to another family. Along with these wishes came the recognition that they desperately needed someone to talk to and they needed to be heard.

As ACAs begin to understand the function of their parental role and how it covered their own feelings of deep need, they often must face painful truths about their parents and families. Gloria sobbed as she experienced a deep longing and a strong recognition that her parents could not provide for her:

If I gave up the notion that I was to blame, I would have to recognize my parents' inadequacies and I couldn't do it. I needed them to teach me about myself and the world.

Recognizing need also brings up painful themes of loss and deprivation.

Sue describes her mother as childlike and vulnerable, frightened much of the time and therefore unable to model or pass on a sense of safety about the world or maternal protection for Sue. She experiences a constant, nagging, deep loss. When she thinks of herself as a small child, she feels frightened and tremendously deprived.

Rather than accept her right to have her own needs, Sandra wishes they would go away:

My mother was depressed because I had too many needs. If I could
have been better, less needy, then my mother might have been able to
be more giving.

ACAs reject their own dependency needs, to protect themselves against a sense of loss and against disappointment related
to the parents' unpredictability and inconsistency. Many recall not
the loss of what might have been, but the repeated disappointment
they experienced with the emotional withdrawal and detachment
of a parent during a drunken episode. These ACAs can allow only a
measured or controlled need in themselves, and the caregiver must
be constantly monitored for signs of withdrawal or disapproval.

If I am too needy, I overwhelm others who must withdraw to protect
themselves. I end up having caused my own abandonment.

The strong urge to deny any need at all often leads to a false and
rigid "macho" style for both men and women. When Henry joined a
support group, he felt openly contemptuous of needy people:

You have to be able to take care of yourself and you ought to be able to
control yourself too!

As time passed, Henry expressed his envy of the warmth that Bob
and Jim received from others. At first, he believed that people were
against him, felt threatened by him, and actively withheld their
support. Members of the group challenged Henry, repeatedly not-
ing that he was always angry and guarded. He revealed just so
much of himself and then was angry for the lack of response. After
this pattern occurred several times, Henry thought about need:

Being needy equals being out of control which equals being drunk.
My father was so helpless when he was drunk.

Henry realized that he maintained an angry tone to protect
himself from feeling needy or communicating need and especially
to ensure a sense of control. Several weeks later, he spoke about
the consequences of having needs and experiencing them:

My family and I lost at least two decades in our emotional and personal
growth as individuals and as a family due to my father's alcoholism. It

was a tremendous loss to me—an enormous consequence of my father's preoccupation with taking care of his own needs first. I can't imagine putting my own needs first, though I often wish someone else would do so on my behalf.

Over the weeks, Ray listened intently as Henry broke down the barriers he had long ago erected to protect himself. Ray suddenly knew why *he* could not speak up, and could not feel, despite his wish to be able to:

To open up is to have needs. If I reveal myself, I'll be out of control and someone will be hurt.

Having needs highlights another important issue that stands out in recovery: boundaries and limit setting. This theme often emerges as the flip side of the wish for closeness or even for "merger." The need for distance and control in relationships represents the fear of what the longed-for closeness or the ability to feel and be needy will bring.

Boundaries and Limit Setting   ACAs recall the centrality of their parents' needs and the feeling of being constantly overwhelmed by them. The sense of themselves as parent-figures, responsible for out-of-control, unpredictable "children," is often reflected as a constant need to set limits and maintain boundaries in their relationships. This theme relates to two needs: to actively control the parent's drinking or out-of-control behavior, providing limits as a true parent would for a two-year-old; and to be protected from the overriding sense of invasion that characterizes the reversed child–parent attachment.

Martha provides us with a detailed example of this kind of intensely close, disturbed bond.

Neither Martha nor her mother can step out of an unhappy but mutually binding relationship. Martha has been linked and identified with her alcoholic mother since childhood. Her mother directed her childhood, molding and producing the very kind of child she wished: a model of good behavior and deference to her mother. Martha carries on this tradition to this day—she is still obedient and deferent, trying to be a good daughter.

Martha always ends up failing to meet her mother's needs. There is never a situation in which Martha doesn't do her best to please her mother but she still ends up having to set limits which her mother feels as a grave disappointment.

Martha is so locked into feeling inadequate and unsatisfying of her mother's needs that she cannot shift her point of view to see her mother's behavior as the problem. To challenge her mother's authority would be equal to "divorcing" her. She is locked into a view of herself as a daughter who is failing to adequately parent her mother. The need to set limits with her mother is a constant, painful reminder of her failure.

For Martha, alcohol is the binding agent in the attachment between child and parent. Pamela's case emphasizes the problem of boundary definition with alcoholic parents; alcohol seems to be positive, even essential, in maintaining a sense of separateness between parent and child:

I always get through visits with my parents by drinking with them. Alcohol is clearly the tie that binds us, but it also establishes the limits. Boundaries between us could be defined and tolerated as long as everyone was drinking. I am afraid my father will be just as fuzzy, overwhelming, and enveloping with me sober as he was drinking. I get swept up by him and lose my clarity. Drinking always helped. There was something between us that somehow established the limits.

Other ACAs purposely refuse to drink with parents, but still believe they have to respond and be involved with them, regardless of the parents' behavior. These issues are always present, but frequently come to stage center in December, when ACAs contemplate parental visits or "going home" themselves. Patrick speaks about the automatic loss of himself, which he takes for granted:

I feel chronically controlled by the uncertainty of my parents' visits and by their behavior when they come. At first I feel angry and then I get depressed as I resign myself to the fact there's nothing I can do about the "rights of parents." They call the shots about everything. The best I can do is set some basic limits, if only by staying clear of them. Isn't that funny? I'm often baffled as to why I can't feel needy when I know that being alone is the only way to protect myself.

As we see in the examples of Pamela and Patrick, attachment and boundary issues are not simple nor are they the same for all ACAs. Sheila relates how her mother "took up" with alcohol as a way of letting Sheila move away and grow up emotionally. Unfortunately, it only worked on the surface:

> My mother was an alcoholic all my life but I was very close to her. I never could have cut the apron strings had she not become a "drunk." Ironically, my mother did the "cutting" by becoming emotionally unavailable to me as she turned more and more toward alcohol. My mother was such a mess, I left, going away to school as she had wished.
>
> But I never really "got away." How could I leave such chaos and really create my own life? I was constantly on call to pick up the pieces in the family I couldn't leave behind.

ATTACHMENT ISSUES IN GROUP THERAPY

The power of the therapy group lies in its promise to awaken deep issues, through what is called the "here-and-now," so that members will experience inside the group the same difficulties they struggle with outside it. Members join a group with the ironic purpose of developing the same feelings, thoughts, and behaviors that cause them trouble in their lives. The only sane reason for doing this intentionally is the hope for change. The therapy group creates an environment in which individuals work toward uncovering deep beliefs and patterns of behavior that were essential to maintaining early bonds of attachment and family relationships during the child's development. As an adult in the protected group setting, the individual can challenge the validity of these beliefs and behaviors and test them to determine whether they are necessary or appropriate to healthy adult development. This is a long and painful process; it is quite different from deciding intellectually to stop being a caregiver and become a recipient instead—and it's easier said than done.

Let's look at the issues of attachment and boundaries, as they unfold in the group setting. In this particular sequence, members experienced a shared, powerful sense of role reversal and a need for limits in their interactions with another member who repeatedly demanded the group's attention and diverted it onto him.

Members could see that Jake is a metaphor for their most important relationships, past and present. He is needy and demanding of constant attention, just like parents and just like the partners they've chosen as adults. How do they react to Jake?

Mandy sets limits by ignoring him or tuning him out, which is what she does with her mother. Sherri would really like him to leave, but she can't acknowledge this wish to herself or others. To do so would mean giving up her view of the group as a happy nurturant family, the same fantasy she'd always had about her family. So she tolerates Jake's intrusions and feels resentful.

Members recall that they were never able to say that something was intolerable in their first families. As Mandy noted: "I approach all relationships with the expectation that I will fail to get my needs met and I will end up having to set the limits and therefore reject the other person. Then I feel alone and abandoned, which I have done to myself by failing to meet the other person's needs and ultimately drawing the line."

Another member reacted to Jake in a similar fashion:

You remind me of my mother, who was so childlike and vulnerable. Whenever we point out your intrusiveness and your need for attention, you quickly accept our feedback and become apologetic. Then I feel guilty for setting the limits and have to make it better for you, still denying the fact that I feel hurt and needy too and want you to listen to *me*.

In the group setting, the introduction of a new member often brings up issues of boundaries and limit setting, sharply reminding members of the unpredictability and uncertainty of out-of-control parents.

Members discussed their automatic distrust of the new person, who has the power to be out-of-control, inconsistent, and needy, just like parents. Even the therapist is still suspect. Members maintain a vigilant stance, waiting for her to become unpredictable or disappoint them. Sara has been in group for several years and she is still waiting for disaster. She missed her personal development because she needed to have her "eyes open." She needed to be watchful and guarded, because those around her were so out-of-control. It was her responsibility to stop them if she could, stay out of their way, or fix whatever was wrong. A new member means Sara has to put her own needs aside for a while, in the interest of protecting herself.

This example says a lot about the everyday life of many ACAs. Conditions have to be perfect before ACAs feel safe, relaxed, and open. And, conditions are almost never perfect. Novel, challenging, or creative situations and relationships are viewed as threatening. They require a narrowing or a closing down of attention, with a bolstering of defenses, rather than an opening up or a receptive stance stemming from a belief that the unexpected could be enriching. Patrick feels anxiety and panic about a new member:

> "Is there a rule in this group about smoking?" Patrick imagined that the new person would be a "puffing maniac," blowing a smokescreen in his face and engulfing him. Patrick insisted that the therapist set a no-smoking rule before the newcomer arrived. If he could successfully control the new person's imagined smoking, he could reduce his anxiety and feelings of powerlessness about her arrival. The whole notion of a new person sounded the alarm: Patrick was endangered and needed protection.

Connie gives us another reaction:

> I know I'm going to feel inhibited and withdraw. It's my automatic response to anything new. Surprises are dangerous. In my family, there was no room for me. Mother was the important one whose emotions were most prominent and central. Mother came first. I was expected to help her deal with her feelings and felt repeatedly rejected when I tried to get emotional support.

For many, the idea of boundaries and limit setting is purely protective and quite manipulative as well. How can the needs or reactions of another be gauged, to avoid intrusion or attack? Can actions be ordered to fit what others seem to want or expect? Paul established all his relationships from this base of "management." The ineffectiveness of this strategy was evident as he became completely controlled by his need to be able to accurately predict the thoughts, feelings, and actions of another member.

> Paul can't focus on anybody or anything today because he is so concerned about Mary. He needs to ask her how she is because he is

worried about her and because he needs to ward off the consequences of not asking her. If left alone, she will later explode. But Paul also runs the risk of asking her a direct question and having her be angry for the question. There is no way he can assess what she needs from him at the moment that will satisfy her and ensure his protection.

Boundaries, limits, and control evolved as central issues for another member who wished deeply to "belong" but was terrified of "belonging" at the same time.

Bob reported that he was still thinking about leaving. He is intolerant of others asking him questions and of having to listen to others express themselves with words he doesn't like, such as "mushy" or "warm inside." Bob wants a way to shut people off. Someone else's empathy or wish to deepen a relationship with him is threatening, because he has no sense of boundaries or limits and does not feel he can stop the exchange. He can't tolerate listening to people's problems in the group and being unable to fix them or stop them. This is just like his life outside and growing up.

The central difficulty emerges for Bob: he can't join the group and stay detached. But he needs to be detached as a way of controlling his and others' emotions and the degree of involvement. Setting limits is not acceptable for him so he has no choice but to feel trapped and impatient or to leave.

Many of these examples illustrate a paradox: the parents need the child to confirm their view and provide an emotional bond; the child then develops a sense of self as a parent, responsive to the centrality of someone else's needs. At the same time, the child is led to a false belief that he or she is necessary to the survival of the parents.

Occasionally, an ACA will exhibit a strong need to be the center of attention, or at least involved in all interactions, in order to sustain the illusion of attachment. Underneath is the more dominant feeling of "not existing," of being "wiped out" by parental figures—directly, through critical attack and chronic hostility, or simply by the centrality of the parents' needs. The feeling of "not existing" is also an expression of the individual's recognition of the parents' lack of emotional awareness and availability to the child. The need to constantly maintain the illusion of an emotional bond serves to ward off recognition that no bond exists with a primary parental figure.

Today the group focused on Ron's need for constant attention. He must include himself in every interaction or he feels bored or angry. In including himself, he personalizes or overinterprets what someone else is saying, and ends up shifting the focus of the group to him. Ron recognizes he is uncomfortable if he feels left out. It's like he is "not there." Ron can't be quiet though others urge him to try. The feeling of being left out is so intense—it reawakens feelings of being left behind and the loss of all his family to alcohol, which he experienced so frequently.

On another occasion, Ron wondered sadly whether anyone would ever miss him if he didn't keep showing up at the places he belongs.

The other side of the intense need for "contact" and constant engagement is the inability to experience any at all. Many ACAs have few memories of childhood or of feelings of their own, and they may not be able to respond appropriately to the feelings of others. These individuals often seek treatment because of severe interpersonal problems, especially difficulties establishing and sustaining intimate relationships. As Matt, one "unfeeling" ACA, put it:

How do you communicate a feeling of emotional involvement with others when you don't have it or can't give it yourself?

Matt spent a good deal of time in group figuring out the "right" way to respond, since he had no internal feelings to guide him. He felt and was seen by others to be "tuned out." With careful exploration, he came to realize that his emotional withdrawal and isolation were necessary for his survival as a child. It was his way of setting limits. His parents were most often drunk and out-of-control emotionally, demonstrating wide, fluctuating extremes in mood and behavior. Emotional insulation was his only protection against feeling constantly out-of-control himself. Yet, as an adult, his emotional withdrawal is felt by others as a problem.

Further exploration revealed the double bind Matt felt with his mother. She was often upset that he refused to be engaged with her and was so uninvolved and inactive. Yet he was also supposed to be an "ornament," seen but not heard. His mother wanted no part of him.

In the group, Ron got bored or upset if he didn't feel a "connection," which he kept trying to get from Matt. But, no matter what Matt said or did, Ron didn't feel he had gotten what he wanted. Matt remained baffled—he didn't know what it was that Ron was asking for.

Many of us might now express a groan of instant recognition. This dilemma is the prototype for the most common, but serious interpersonal problems that ACAs experience. They want something they can't ever get from others, or they can't understand or give what others want from them. This baffling, helpless state of affairs underscores feelings of loneliness. It took a long time for Ron to see that, in childhood, his withdrawal was literally lifesaving for him, a way of maintaining a boundary. Lifesaving then, it's disabling now. Ron lives with a chronic sense of loneliness, the cost of distancing himself from his intrusive, alcoholic mother.

Let's move on with issues of development as we look at an important partner to attachment: identity formation.

8

Identity Formation

A favorite device of seminar leaders and presenters at business meetings is to write, with wide-tip differently colored markers, each main topic or category of problem on a separate flip-pad sheet and tape all the sheets to walls and windows that everyone in the room can see. The technique has been traced back to announcements of vaudeville acts, but it still enjoys corporate approval.

We're in the home stretch of the part of the book dealing with development—family and individual. Our mentally displayed flip sheets show some key terms, to be remembered and known for what they are: double denial, the family "story," adult children of alcoholics, unhealthy codependence, roles and reversed roles, alcohol as the central organizing principle, the Family Diagram, attachment. Some have been only introduced; others, through connections and examples, have laid down some of the roadbed that will eventually be paved toward recovery. Many of these concepts will stay linked and will join with others, as we move into the next group of chapters. At this point, we're adding another top-line item; we're placing personal identity alongside attachment.

The acquisition of self-knowledge, or what is called a personal identity, is founded on and shaped by the family's core beliefs. In an alcoholic family, as we've seen, these beliefs, which we call the family "story," are based on denial of alcoholism, or—if it is not denied—on the explanations adopted by the family to excuse or disguise it.

In this chapter, we'll first see how children acquire knowledge. Then we'll examine how the defensive need to maintain the family "story" influences the development of the children's own "story" or personal identity.

A PERSONAL IDENTITY: WHO AM I?

Growing up, we learn about ourselves and the world in many varied ways. We acquire emotional, moral, social, and intellectual knowledge through our senses, our instincts, and our developing perceptual and reasoning capabilities—how we relate things to one another and figure out why they happen. This acquisition process begins immediately at birth. We gather facts and develop patterns of knowledge before we can speak or make sense of what we already "know." We acquire knowledge and draw conclusions by testing whether our cries will be heard and responded to. When our development eventually includes language, we begin to construct theories about ourselves and the world, and these theories become the foundation of our developing and emerging personal identity. We will build on that foundation, to know who we are. This kind of knowledge is called cognitive.

In the last chapter, we focused on attachment, the emotional bond between parent and child. Our focus here is on the cognitive, information-processing part of that bond.

Cognitive Theory Leading writers on cognitive theory, especially those influenced by the work of Jean Piaget, an eminent developmental psychologist, suggest that individuals obtain self-knowledge by developing theories about themselves—ways of seeing themselves and describing to themselves what they're doing and why—through their interactions with their environment. These theories evolve into concrete and well-defined beliefs about the self and others, and these beliefs regulate and shape the individual's behavior and his or her perceptions of the surrounding world. Beginning in infancy, the child develops a core of basic assumptions that must not be disproved, if the child is to have healthy progress toward adulthood. These assumptions are essential supports for the further building of knowledge. They *are* the personal identity, because they are the most fundamental and basic beliefs about the self.

Maintaining a solid, stable identity is critically important to a developing child. To achieve this stability, children begin, quite naturally, to be selective in what they take in. Information that is consistent with the developing self-image is retained and incorporated; information that doesn't fit is rejected. Through this process of information selection, the child's way of seeing reality is increasingly anchored in a manner that matches the child's basic assumptions. This whole process of identity construction is self-reinforcing. Basic beliefs, true or false, become the building blocks for answering the question, "Who am I?"

Let's clarify something about the term "the developing child," which keeps reappearing. Every child, unless it has suffered brain damage that makes it totally unaware, is a developing child. Its development continues in every waking moment, every experience, every seen, or heard, or sensed happening in its environment. Some parents may regard a trip to a zoo or museum, the daily dose of "Sesame Street," or a nightly reading session as being for their child's "development." That development goes on every day, in every light and sound, and in every silence.

The child's interactions with its environment, and particularly with the key figures to whom it is attached in that environment (typically, the parents), exert a profound impact on the child's core beliefs. Parents are the whole world, and the only one possible, for infants and young children. The parent–child emotional bond has no alternatives, only substitutes. It is the child's most important source of early knowledge. Is it any wonder that children will automatically adopt the beliefs held by their parents and will cling to the beliefs that are necessary to preserve their own and the family's identity? Children learn who they are, and who they are to become, primarily through identifying with their parents.

In a healthy environment, the acquisition of self-knowledge is an expansive process. The child, free to explore and interact openly with the environment, takes in more and more information, and begins to sort out what fits as "part of me" and what doesn't fit.

In an unhealthy setting, such as an alcoholic family, information gathering is limited by the parents' need for defense, particularly their need to deny the reality of their drinking or its consequences. In this indirect way, parental alcoholism influences and structures a child's developing view of self.

How much influence does it have? In some families, *all* perception and knowledge may be restricted and regulated by the family's defensive needs. In other families, parental alcoholism may be less dominant and much less a central organizer: information gathering may be highly selective and distorted when it relates to alcohol, and more open and expansive when denial is not involved.

Denial Comes Again   The parents' need to exclude certain information exerts a stunning influence on a child's cognitive and emotional development. In an alcoholic family, the denial of drinking or its consequences forces children to reject information from their own senses or revise their ideas, in order to accept the parents' point of view. To the degree that denial is necessary and the family's attachments and perceptions are revolving around it, the children will be in conflict with their own perceptions and explanations.

A mismatch of information throws the family off balance. The family no longer makes sense or has meaning, and is therefore not predictable or manageable. Family members must revise their basic beliefs or omit contrary information and perceptions from their awareness, in order to cope with the disorder. Couldn't children challenge or alter their deepest beliefs, to straighten up their view of reality and provide a different, healthier kind of balance to the family? It rarely happens. The challenge of these deep beliefs is the greatest threat to the child and the family.

The Family "Story"   As Daniel Goleman notes, the family is the child's first model of a shared reality. In many alcoholic families, the shared reality of a family identity that is based on denial of alcoholism becomes more important than the individual self. The child's personal identity or personal story has to be filtered through the family's "story." The shared outlook shapes all individual data collection, and family members must join in, to maintain the family's attachments, stability, and cohesion. As Goleman notes, in an organization or family bound together by distorted beliefs and perceptions, there is nothing worse than a "whistle-blower," anyone who has a different view or who challenges the validity of basic assumptions.

Very young children cannot "blow the whistle." They must accept their parents' point of view and they must develop a personal identity that confirms the parents' beliefs.

Because children cannot challenge basic assumptions, they must refuse incoming data that conflict with them. They begin, like their parents, to develop distorted or illogical explanations for contradictory information.

When information is excluded or distorted, two things happen: the deep beliefs are reconfirmed (the threat to them, from conflicting information, has been removed) and some emotions are blocked out. As one ACA observed:

You can't have feelings about a reality that doesn't exist.

The need for denial and the need to maintain certain key assumptions about the family and its "story" literally shape the child's whole developing view. "Who am I?" becomes limited to "Who must I be?" and to "What must I see and not see, to keep things the way they are?"

The whole process of information gathering can become a restricted, vicious circle. Individuals must narrow and distort their environment until their behavior and perceptions fit. They cannot claim the right to their own viewpoint or keep enlarging their knowledge so that they will later be able to cope with a larger, real environment.

The alcoholic family has too much to lose by allowing an open, expansive, and receptive stance in relation to the world. Too quickly, the information would flood in, to reveal that its deepest beliefs are out of sync with reality.

PERCEPTION, BELIEF, AND ATTACHMENT

The need to define and fit perceptions and information to an already established shared reality is the dominant force in identity formation in an alcoholic family. Hugh Rosen, a clinical social worker and cognitive theorist, states that, when the child's interpretation of reality differs from the parents' explanation, the child will alter his or her view to conform to that of the parents. As we did with attachment, let's look at adults in treatment, to illustrate how this process of distortion works. One group member had an intense need for a nourishing parental attachment.

> Shirley and Peg became very angry, accusing each other of excessive demands and misperceptions of the other's intent. They maintained their anger for one meeting. The next week, Shirley agreed that Peg's view was the correct one and apologized for her misperception and resultant failure to be responsive to Peg. Other group members were aghast, pointing out that Shirley had altered her perception—equally correct in their view—in order to cover the anger and patch the relationship. Shirley couldn't tolerate the challenge: "I felt so alone and isolated after confronting Peg. I began to feel so responsible for her anger and so sorry I had seen things differently. I decided that she was right."

Group members insisted that Shirley look closely at what she was doing: she was changing her view of reality, to stop the anger. Shirley cried:

> I would do *anything* to keep others from being angry with me. It's a much better choice to give up my position and to feel responsible for others than to risk having them be angry.

Following this very important exchange, members concluded that parents did construct a view about the family that was different from the children's, but the parents were always right. As adults, these ACAs have a difficult time trusting their own perceptions or fighting for a point of view. As Mike says:

> It is so hard for me to hold on to my own view or feelings as legitimate. Whatever my supervisor says is automatically the truth. I have to change my view to fit hers and then I feel so stupid. That's why it makes no sense to become angry or disagree. I always have to adjust my point of view to solve the disagreement.

Not surprisingly, Mike held a deep view of himself (at first, out of his awareness) as incompetent. He chose bosses and partners who had strong opinions and a need to assert them. Mike hated to feel dumb, but the alternative was worse. Mike believed deeply that if he held his ground, or tried on the idea that he might not be stupid, he would lose the people he most needed.

The Assumption of Responsibility How do kids cope with such chronic distortion? One of the most common and effective ways to manage it is to accept responsibility for problems that don't exist. Doesn't this sound ridiculous? It is exactly what happens. Children hear repeatedly that there is no problem with alcohol, but they know that something is wrong. Therefore, something must be wrong with them. A child begins to believe that, if she or he were a better, more loving, less demanding, or more responsive kid, then the parents would be available and the world would make sense.

The idea of having omnipotence, or tremendous self-power, is a natural part of child development. We all have it and we all must give it up as we mature. Omnipotence fits perfectly with the child's assumption of responsibility and is very difficult to relinquish. The child may become fixed on trying to be perfect, trying to find just the right strategy to "straighten up" and be acceptable to the parent.

How powerful is this mechanism of responsibility, which may drive children to try to "do better" even when they see that the real problem does not change? Powerful enough that they can't stop trying. They need to protect their relationship to the parents at all costs—to maintain parental approval and to reduce their own unconscious guilt. It is difficult for children to feel they are wrong, but it is much worse to recognize that those on whom they depend are wrong or have become too incompetent to care for them. Taking on responsibility is problematic, but it is also a protective shield against feelings of hopelessness and deep depression that would accompany children's recognition of their parents' unavailability.

When children assume responsibility, they may develop a pattern of self-hatred, self-criticism, and self-abuse, in response to the conflict of having caused the problem and being unable to solve it. Or, they may narrow their range of cognitive and emotional involvement in their environment. They may become knowledgeable high achievers in one well-defined area, for example, but impoverished in their range of exposure and their depth of cognitive and emotional development. Sarah shows us how this works.

A few years ago I saw a movie about slavery. People were marching in a line with each whipping the one in front. I almost fainted and had to leave the theater. Now I suddenly see why. These individuals assumed responsibility for having caused their plight and were exorcising the demons from within and punishing themselves at the

same time. That is how I've spent my life: punishing myself for what I
caused at home and could not fix.

Burt shares a similar memory:

I felt an intense drive for perfection and an inability to achieve it in
my family. On weekends I cleaned the house, moving around my
parents as they sat there drinking.

Burt realizes that he is chronically upset with the loss of control he
feels at work, which reminds him of his family.

I'm always looking for structure, for rules, for something in here.
I'm so anxious about my boss because I can't tell what she's feeling or
thinking. Work is just like my life—a state of chronic anxiety. If
there's a cyclone in Bangladesh, I caused it.

The assumption of responsibility is important and useful to
children of alcoholics. It operates as one of the key defenses they
develop to cope with the family reality and with their relationships
to their parents. It is part of their false self, but no one can tell
them that, least of all themselves.

Let's look now at the impact of perceptual distortion on the
child's developing self view and relationships with the world outside the family.

Socialization   As we saw earlier, children are supposed to learn
the rules of the culture from their families. Most do. What they
learn should be consistent or compatible with the broader culture's
beliefs and expectations, so they can move with relative ease from
the shelter of the family into the larger world.

In a family with an alcoholic parent, children may have difficulty learning any social rules, or they may learn rules that are so
bound up with denial and distortion that they don't match the world
outside.

Children in an alcoholic home gradually recognize how different the world at home is from the world outside. That difference,
which may be vague and unnamed, is related to the dominance of
alcohol, beliefs about alcohol, and drinking behavior. From his adult
perspective, with parental alcoholism now named, Charlie tells us
how he learned about himself and the world.

The children in my family saw and heard an abnormal form of reality. I had no prior experience to clue me that something was wrong. So I developed a feel for what was appropriate in my family, for what was right or wrong in that world, and then I discovered it didn't carry over. As an adult, I found myself lost, insecure, and frightened in the world outside my family. I'm sure that I'm emotionally immature but I don't know what to do about it.

As children realize that the drinking behavior of their parents is not typical, their feelings of shame, humiliation, and alienation may be intense. They may become more defensive and more isolated from the rest of the world, to avoid being found out. A terrible bind—caught between belonging to this family that does have something wrong with it *or* to the world outside that doesn't—follows ACAs into adulthood and is often a source of tremendous pain. To be "normal," to really "join" the grown-up world, is equal to betraying or abandoning the family. Bev recalls being face-to-face with this bind as a child.

When I was about twelve, I invited several close friends to spend the night. I was excited but soon humiliated. My friends' faces registered disbelief and dismay as they watched my parents drink. They had never seen anyone drunk except on TV. They were frightened but giggled to hide their fear.

I felt so humiliated. I was embarrassed by my parents and defensive on their behalf at the same time. I wanted the approval of my girl-friends and to be just like them, and I also was angry with them for laughing at my parents. So I became much more protective and secretive about my family. I must hide the truth. There became an inside world of alcoholism to which I belonged by birth and there was an outside world to which I strived to belong as well. I had to overcome and hide my origin and birth to belong to this normal world.

As cognitive theorists note, the child's developing self-concept is closely connected to the family context. Quite simply, the child develops a view of self that is consistent with the family's description of itself—its "story." As children grow up, they become less influenced by and less tied to parental beliefs and values. Developmentally, they are much better able to construct a personal identity that is independent from the family's "story."

Unfortunately, this puts their attachment at risk. The child in an alcoholic family is bound to maintain denial, in order to keep the child–parent bond. The move to separate and become an independent adult will be fraught with anxiety, because the individual perceives that the outside world operates on a different view of reality and perhaps different rules for behavior as well.

It's here that the adolescent and adult children of alcoholics feel caught between two different worlds and two different versions of reality. ACAs often express the dilemma: they could not join or operate in the world outside the family, without transgressing the family's beliefs. Individuals often struggle with which view is correct. They feel pulled toward familial attachments, maintained by denial and the family's distorted core beliefs, and they feel an equal pull toward separation and independence, represented by affiliation with the culture outside the family. Can they separate and join the world outside, when it means they must betray the family's beliefs and lose their core attachments?

The inability to separate, emotionally or physically, from their alcoholic families of origin is what brings many ACAs to treatment. Some are worried that they will repeat with their own children exactly what they experienced, and they are terrified. Others can't move themselves forward, to really feel or behave like adults, even though they're well into their 20s, 30s, 40s, or beyond. They feel and behave as if they stopped their own developmental progress at adolescence, and they need to know why. The critical factor seems to be identity, the "Who am I?" we've been looking at. For many ACAs, becoming an adult means becoming *like the parent*—thinking and behaving in exactly the same ways. Some do just that, becoming alcoholic or choosing an alcoholic partner and playing out the same patterns of behavior, deep beliefs, and roles that were modeled by their parents. Others stop short of a replay, developing problems or in some way trying unconsciously to avoid doing it all over again. Many of these individuals seek help. In the process of treatment, they return again and again to the central issue of identity.

FORMING AN IDENTITY: "WHO WILL I BE WHEN I'M GROWN UP?"

Experts in child development agree that adolescence is the time when identity formation is at stage center. The child's self-concept begins, at birth, to develop in all the ways we've touched on, but adolescence is the time when the various elements merge into a stable, maturing, and autonomous sense of self. The adolescent tries on various identities and constantly questions, "Who am I?" The adolescent also begins to act like an adult, a very important move from the fantasy or play that gives younger children a window into what it means and feels like to be "grown-up."

Under the best of circumstances, the developmental tasks of adolescence are turbulent: what is learned and felt and expressed has the fluidity of a roller coaster ride. Socialization is more dominant; the child must attempt to integrate the values and the culture that exist inside the family with those outside. There is less black and white, and much more gray. The adolescent masters, or attempts to control, much of the gray—emotional ambiguity and wide inconsistency—through logic and abstract reasoning. These newly acquired, higher-level thinking capabilities help the adolescent to manage a barrage of new, different, and often contradictory information. Complex ideas and discoveries about the self and the environment can be sorted out, simplified, and selected for belief. Emotionally, the young adult can now scan a range of feeling, having gained an ability to determine what is real and a capacity to integrate opposite feelings.

The alcoholic family, constantly adapting to what goes on inside the family and defending itself against the world outside, interferes with the adolescent's ability to progress to these higher levels of development, especially when denial is required of all family members. As we've seen, denial limits what can be recognized, explored, and ultimately accepted as one's own.

By the time a child reaches adolescence, family alcoholism may be well-established, and the defenses against the outside world may be its primary focus. In that kind of family, the adolescent is likely to be poorly prepared for beginning the process of detachment and separation, and may face a severe crisis.

Adolescence demands action toward achieving independent identification; the teen is approaching adulthood, in thought and deed. Many children of alcoholics cannot confront the reality of the family's disturbed beliefs and behaviors. Instead, some teens may put into action their underlying identification with their alcoholic parents and start drinking alcoholically, like the parents, while denying that any problem with alcohol exists.

For several reasons, children of alcoholics cannot negotiate emotional separation. They lack an environment that allows the necessary maturity to develop. An adequate base of healthy attachment, from which maturation and separation can occur, has not been formed. As parent figures to the parent, they cannot leave their real, inadequate, and needy parents behind. When they seek treatment, they feel guilty about betraying their families (by ending their denial of alcoholism) and about wishing to separate. At the same time, they feel a deep longing for a dependent bond, missed or impaired so early in their development.

Many ACAs who experience themselves as the "hero," the model child, or the "survivor" pay a price for those self-complimentary words—often involuntarily—in survivor guilt, which keeps them attached to their original family. Every step forward in their development is met with guilt and self-punishment.

> It is such a struggle for me to be successful. I don't know why I'm the one who got out, but it often feels terrible. I think about my younger sister who was so scapegoated by all the family and I am drawn back in to try to help her. But I never can. Still, I have to try or I feel too guilty getting better myself.

As recovery progresses, it becomes clear that, in addition to all the developmental problems and the guilt that comes with leaving a "sick" family, the major roadblock to adult development is the necessity to acquire an independent identity. Let's look closely at why.

Alcohol and Identity Formation   Figure 5, one of the Family Diagrams in Chapter 5, had a circle labeled "Alcohol" at the center and a ring of circles around it, all enclosed in an outer boundary. Let's borrow the graphic technique for a moment, and adapt that diagram mentally. The middle circle gets labeled "Alcohol and the denial of alcoholism." In the ring of circles, instead of family members' name or rank, let's mentally put some of the elements of identity formation: attachment, cognitive learning, emotional learning, socialization, separation, maturity. The outer boundary stays as before. The completed figure would represent how impossible it is, when alcohol is the central organizing principle, to develop a stable, integrated, independent identity that bypasses the influence of alcohol. Anyone forming an identity asks, "Who am I?" Children of alcoholics, in families where identity formation circles relentlessly around alcohol, add a second question, "Am I an alcoholic?" The question may be unconscious but it is no less real.

In some families, it is possible for alcohol to be one of several issues around which identity formation occurs. Let's see how this diffused focus works.

Imitation and Identification   Imitation is one of the child's earliest activities, and identification with the parents occurs an eyeblink later. Several experts put imitation and identification at the center of the development of one's personal identity. Psychiatrists Vittorio Guidano and Gianni Liotti, both cognitive theorists, are among those who stress that the self-knowledge that constitutes "who I am" is the accumulated result of organizing the knowledge that has been gathered from the beginning of early experiences. Piaget demonstrated how children begin the most rudimentary, early forms of learning by acting on their environments. This action—technically, behavioral orientation—is seen in the infant's imitation and active mimicking of the mother's expressions and actions. Imitation is an early, important cornerstone of attachment and cognitive development.

Identification is a more advanced part of modeling. The individual actively selects some aspects of another person's attitudes, values, and beliefs, and takes them on as his or her own. This process is largely unconscious and occurs throughout development, although adolescents will literally "try on" different models with a conscious intent. "Who am I?" becomes reflected in behavior as well as ideas about self.

One fact is critically important to an understanding of the impact of parental alcoholism: children imitate and identify with parental behaviors and beliefs, regardless of whether they are valid or invalid, healthy or unhealthy. Parents may try to interfere with these natural processes of learning, but children align themselves with the deeper beliefs anyway. Children may loudly proclaim disagreement with parents about everything, but agreement at a deep level is absolutely essential to preserve the bond of attachment.

Thus, as children move through adolescence, they begin to actively imitate and identify with their parents. In an alcoholic family, the imitation and identification are often centered on drinking. Depending on many factors (environment, degree of denial, or location of alcohol in the Family Diagram, for example), children of alcoholics may imitate the alcoholic parents. One ACA said it all:

> Drinking tells me that I have a family.

Many recovering alcoholics who are also the children of alcoholics report that they were alcoholic from the first drink; they never had an internal experience of control. For these young people, behavioral loss of control was immediate.

They also identified with the beliefs and attitudes of their parents. They had to, to maintain denial and secure attachments within the family. As a result, their behavior is in immediate conflict with their beliefs about themselves. They believe, as their parents did, that they can control their drinking. Any evidence that they can't gets explained in other ways. The "thinking disorder" that once had a child-to-parent connection is now used to deny and explain their own drinking. Peg shows us how this works.

> Peg recalls her beginning awareness of an inside world and an outside world in which the rules and perceptions of reality didn't match. For her, the adolescent tasks of identification and separation occurred around the central core of alcohol. As an adolescent, Peg began to drink with her family. She got drunk regularly with them and just like them. But she denied any problems with alcohol. Peg maintained that she, like her parents, had control, a faulty belief that allowed her to hold on to the illusion that she and her family were not outsiders in the world away from home. By identifying with them and imitating their behavior, she could maintain her sense of connection with them and move into the world outside believing that everyone in her family was "normal." As a young adult, Peg drank alcoholically while establishing her "independent" life. She married an alcoholic and both organized their lives around alcohol. They were already severely disabled by their advanced alcoholism, mirroring an identification with and imitation of the advanced alcoholism of all four of their parents.

Not all children of alcoholics imitate the drinking behavior of their parents, becoming active alcoholics themselves. Why this happens is still unknown. A good part of that explanation likely relates to biology and genetics. Another part probably involves the learning theory we've been exploring. Perhaps children have viable nonalcoholic parents or models, with whom a stronger identification is possible. Some reject drinking, fearful of the possibility of resembling an alcoholic parent; they consciously sever the most obvious and central link to that parent—alcohol.

Extensive experience with ACAs indicates that those who do not imitate their parents' drinking behavior may still have identified with their parents' dominant beliefs. A fear of being deeply out of control, just like the parents, is entrenched for many ACAs. They share a conviction that they are barely holding themselves together, or that it's just a matter of time until they "lose it," becoming crazy or abusive. They concentrate their energy and work hard at not becoming like the parent. Sara illustrates the impact of identification that does not include the behavior of excessive drinking.

> Sara idealized her severely alcoholic mother. As she remembered her childhood, she recalled her mother's dramatic flair and her ability to be the admired and envied center of attention. Sara also recalled her mother's angry, critical attitude toward her, which Sara took on as her own. She was compulsively negative and self-critical, engaging in a constant barrage of punitive attacks on herself.

> Sara felt chronically out of control emotionally and completely dominated by her compulsive self-abuse and criticism. Ultimately, she could see that her chronic depression and erratic bursts of emotionality equaled her mother's drunken, out-of-control behavior. She had identified with her mother despite having vowed never to touch alcohol.

Denial of loss of control is an important piece of identification for many ACAs who do not imitate the alcoholic drinking behavior. These individuals either do not drink at all or exercise hypervigilant control over their drinking, lest they become just like the alcoholic. Many of these ACAs believe that becoming alcoholic is inevitable— that underneath their conscious control, they are already alcoholic and just waiting to act it out.

> Michael emphasizes the importance of intellectual and emotional control. He grew up in an atmosphere of constant tension, the potential of violence and chronic loss of control by both parents a constant. His father was a violent alcoholic and his mother suffered periodic psychotic episodes.

In the therapy group, Michael exhibited little tolerance for the expression of emotion and felt immediately responsible to fix anyone demonstrating helplessness or need. As the group advanced, he grew more anxious and exerted more control, obstructing the progression of the group into deeper exploration and emotional expression. As his anxiety increased, he realized that he believed deeply that he was out-of-control. Just like both of his parents, any expression of his feeling would result in his becoming violent or crazy. Any expression of feeling by others required his assumption of responsibility and unsuccessful efforts to fix the other.

When both parents are active alcoholics but deny their loss of control, the possibility of alternate models for imitation and identification is minimal. Children cannot challenge their parents' view of the world if they have no independent model, no alternate figure of attachment.

In families in which denial is minimal, or in which the nonalcoholic parent is a viable figure, children may not imitate the alcoholic behaviorally (genetic factors precluded). They may, instead, significantly imitate and identify with the attitudes and behaviors of the nonalcoholic parent. This identification often involves an excessive emphasis on self-control, maintained by a rigid and narrow range of thinking and emotions. These ACAs righteously believe that people ought to be able to control themselves, and they're terribly frightened that they cannot. Ron identifies some missing pieces:

> My key problem growing up was a lack of role models. My father couldn't cope and my mother just reacted. She was always trying to control someone and would explode when her efforts failed. He's dead now and my mother still doesn't know how to regulate her behavior. She overreacts, can't control her anger or put things in their proper perspective. I'm like her. I can feel that anger in myself, just ripe and ready to explode. I never saw mature, responsible behavior.

It is well established that many children of alcoholics marry alcoholics. They identify with the nonalcoholic and with the relationship patterns modeled by both parents. Often, ACAs will choose a mate who needs to be fixed or "controlled." Many hope to be successful with their own alcoholic partner after having failed to help their parents.

Many ACAs seek help because they recognize that they have chosen inappropriate or disturbed mates, alcoholic or not. In treatment, they realize that they had no examples of mature relationships characterized by a respect for autonomy and interactional, interdependent partnerships. They have no sense of give or take and they continue to perceive relationships as all-or-none—somebody dominates and the other submits; one is weak and the other is strong; one is right and the other is wrong.

As we've seen, the nonalcoholic parent is often viewed by the children as more disturbed than the alcoholic—more angry and out-of-control, with no excuse; or, passive and unprotective of self and children. Identifying with the alcoholic and maintaining a belief in self-control are often the most appealing resolutions to an identity conflict in which there are no viable figures for positive identification and ultimate separation.

Having no viable models is a serious issue that creates a crisis and perhaps a standstill, when identity consolidation and separation approach. Adolescents in treatment and adults retracing their development in recovery are stopped by the belief that, to identify with either parent, alcoholic or nonalcoholic, is equal to ensuring self-destruction. They may see themselves repeating the unhealthy patterns of relationship that were part of their own early attachment or that existed between their parents. Unfortunately, for these adolescents and ACAs, such recognition is usually unconscious. Instead, an unhealthy identification (imitating alcoholic drinking behavior or addictive disorders), a developmental arrest, or a limited and highly defended maturation occurs.

BECOMING ALCOHOLIC: A DEVELOPMENTAL MILESTONE

During my years of work with children of alcoholics, I have seen how adolescents struggle directly with establishing their identities and how adults suffer the consequences of having formed an unhealthy identification or of having warded it off. For these people, there is no way around it: *Alcohol, or being alcoholic, is at the center of their identity formation.*

The Adolescent Struggle For adolescents whose parents have been identified as alcoholic and are already recovering, the significance of the question of "being alcoholic" is clearer than for those whose parents are still denying alcoholism. Regardless of the degree of denial, however, all are struggling with how to incorporate parental alcoholism and/or its meaning into their own sense of personal identity.

Children cannot "not identify." The process of identification is occurring continuously from birth—often unconsciously, as we've seen—and is one of the most important developmental tasks. Children must incorporate or accommodate the reality of parental alcoholism in some manner. Naming the alcoholism is extremely difficult, if not impossible, for children whose parents are strongly invested in denial. To name a reality that is not shared by other members is simply too threatening to the child's developing ego and sense of belonging to the family. As a result, even though there is much greater awareness now, most adolescents in treatment who are identified as children of alcoholics, also have parents who are in treatment. Let's look at how adolescents cope with the dilemma of identification.

Nineteen-year-old Michelle sought treatment in a group for young adult children of alcoholics. Her mother was a recovering alcoholic, sober for six years. Her father, also a recovering alcoholic, had been sober for one year. Her older brother, 24, was currently in treatment for chemical dependence, in an inpatient program that emphasized family involvement in the therapeutic process. Michelle lived too far from the family to participate in the treatment program, but she agreed readily to seek treatment on her own, in response to her parents' suggestion.

In the evaluation interviews, Michelle spoke about the centrality of her parents' alcoholism to her childhood and family life. Her mother had been an identified, sober alcoholic since Michelle was 13, and her father's continuing active alcoholism had been the focus of much denial. The denial could now be acknowledged, because he had identified himself as an alcoholic.

Michelle stated matter-of-factly that being alcoholic was a part of belonging to her family. She already had experienced a turbulent adolescence with her "rebellion" centered on the issue of her drug use. Through her early adolescence, she had maintained that she was not like her parents because she was not an alcoholic and she was not having difficulties with alcohol.

When she separated from her family and her older brother entered treatment, she became more concerned about the centrality of the issue of alcohol in her own life. She maintained she was not like the others, but, as she progressed in treatment, she wondered repeatedly: do I have to be an alcoholic and then a recovering alcoholic, to belong to my family?

For adolescent siblings Kevin and Donna, family issues of dominance, authority, and control were played out around the issue of alcohol. Their father had been in on-again, off-again treatment for alcoholism for seven years and was now severely disabled, suffering from malnutrition and liver disease as a result of around-the-clock drinking. He had been diagnosed a "failure" and was believed to be dying.

In describing his unpredictability and erratic behavior, the children denied any emotional impact or difficulties themselves. They agreed to talk to someone only if they could come together.

The children presented a history, corroborated for the most part by their mother, in which their father's alcoholism had been *the* central problem in the family for many years. The parents ultimately separated and divorced because of the father's drinking. Custody was awarded to the mother for the same reason. However, following the divorce, the father became sober. After a year, he successfully won visitation rights and, later, alternating custody. Recently, he had begun to drink again, and the children's living arrangements now fluctuated according to whether their father was currently sober.

The children insisted that the unpredictability of this arrangement and their father's erratic emotional and practical availability did not bother them. They had, in fact, rejected all previous attempts to acknowledge the existence of a "problem" and seek help for it. They now could label and speak about their father as an alcoholic, but they refused suggestions to attend Alateen. To seek help for themselves was, for them, equal to abandoning their father. In the course of treatment, Kevin and Donna both demonstrated a strong identification with their father's role as the failure in the family. Both bright, they were failing in school. Donna was also using drugs and sleeping during the day—behavior similar to her father's when he was on a binge. Both denied vehemently that they had any problems with drugs or alcohol or any fears that they might have problems in the future. Yet, their roles in relation to others, in the family and school environment, were just like their father's role in the family—the failure. Kevin and Donna both rejected a conscious identification with their father, but imitated his drinking behavior with a symbolic substitute.

Both staunchly defended their father. They dismissed or explained away any acknowledgment of pain, loss, or damage. Their failures represented their attachment to their father, which they could not yet give up or change.

Paul, 15, was referred by his parents, both recovering alcoholics, for behavior problems. In the first interview, Paul indicated that the realities of his parents' behavior while drinking (they had been sober for five years) could not be discussed in the family, although their identities as recovering alcoholics and their involvement with A.A. could be talked about and, in fact, were a source of pride for all.

Once in treatment as the child of alcoholic parents, Paul began to talk about what really happened to him when his parents were drinking and about his own fear that he was going to be just like them. He stopped his destructive behavior, but remained terrified that ultimately he would be out of control himself.

As several years passed, Paul struggled with an eating disorder and then with his own drinking. Of four children, he always had been seen as the "strong one," much like his aggressive father, whom he greatly admired. He wanted desperately to be in control of himself in a way that his father had failed to achieve. Years later, in recovery for his own alcoholism, Paul noted:

> I always knew I was going to be an alcoholic. There was never any question.

The Adult Struggle: Identity Issues in Group Therapy   Issues of identity formation stand at stage center for adults in treatment. ACAs, whether they have themselves become actively alcoholic or not, share the symbol of alcohol as a central theme that directs their own identity formation. Let's look at two important issues that arise in group therapy.

The first issue is *belonging and being alcoholic*. ACAs talk about "belonging" a lot—in the group, in one's family, and in the world. When a new person joins the group, members frequently compare family data, trading facts about which parent was alcoholic, whether that parent is still alive, and what it was like. Sometimes this evolves into a discussion of whether they belong in the group. Ray and Patsy had this dialogue:

> My father didn't start drinking until I was a teenager, so my primary image of him is not as an alcoholic. At least I hold on to memories of him before he got bad. So I wonder if I really belong here.

> Me too! My parents' poor marriage, lousy communication, and alcoholic drinking were always there but never publicly acknowledged till I was out of the home. Do I fit?

Others in the group nodded a vehement *yes*. Sonia said that she has a deep image of herself as coming from a bad, sick, alcoholic family and that children in families like hers carry that identification in a very deep way.

Ray continued to wonder whether he belonged and actively resisted "joining." He always had explained his father's alcoholism as a "minor" matter, only slightly interfering with his very positive image of him. "Belonging" to an ACA group threatened to disturb his whole view. Couldn't he deal with the realities without having to feel, or to change his picture of, what life was like?

Bonnie suggested that Ray might be denying some major difficulties or feelings. After all, he had joined a group explicitly for adult children of alcoholics; that had to mean something. Bonnie knew about the issues of belonging and denial herself. It took her a year of being in group before she could figure out a way to belong and still not have to be sure whether her mother was alcoholic. What a dilemma that had been! If she decided her mother *was* an alcoholic, then she had to be one, too.

Bonnie was surprised and confused when her mother stopped drinking. Bonnie had been so firm in denying that her mother had a "serious" problem with alcohol that she couldn't explain why her mother would need to stop. According to Bonnie's accounting system, her mother never fit her idea of what an alcoholic was, so the alcoholism never had to be true. Bonnie used a whole range of mental maneuvers to make reality fit her needs. Her mother's decision to stop drinking was a great threat to Bonnie's denial of her own drinking and to her inability to decide whether she was alcoholic.

For a while, Bonnie fluctuated, deciding that she was an alcoholic, then drinking, after deciding that she wasn't a "real one." When she was drinking, she was also more confused about her identity and her feelings and perceptions. Finally, she decided drinking was not good for her—just as it had not been good for her mother—and she stopped for that reason. She no longer needed to determine once and for all whether she or her mother was alcoholic. Months later, Bonnie could see that she was driven by a single goal in life that she had not been able to recognize or name: not to be an alcoholic like her mother.

Being alcoholic is also linked to issues of dominance, control, aggression, or simply an active stance in relation to others. Sandra illustrates:

> I have tried desperately not to be like my mother, who was so passive and depressed. But then I must be like my father. When I think of myself as aggressive, I also wonder about the possibility that I might be alcoholic like him.

Andy, who had also been struggling with belonging and commitment to the group, has an identity struggle with polar opposites. He describes his severe difficulties with integrating two opposite internal views of himself. One is the quiet, passive, self-protective person and the other is the free, expressive, active, successful man who is also an out-of-control, violent drinker. His difficulties belonging to the group reflect his fear of choosing one side over the other. Not taking a stand and feeling like "nothing" is the only way to avoid choosing a negative, harmful identity, no matter which of the two views is true.

Andy's indecision and conflict are reflected in his choice of career and his commitment to it. He had always dreamed of being a professional athlete, but a back injury stopped his chances, when he was in his late teens. Next, he envisioned himself as an entrepreneur, successful and hard-driving. Now, in his 30s, he still has fantasies of himself as an aggressive executive. In reality, he has chosen other jobs that have no career track and no competitive components. He feels that he's marking time until he "goes after" his real goal.

Whenever Andy describes his internal conflict and career dissatisfaction, he also wonders whether he is really alcoholic and just waiting to act it out, whether someday he will let go of his control. Andy missed several meetings after straining his back in a recreational game of soccer. When he returned, he related the following:

> For many months in this group I have left in tears, longing to feel closer to my father but terrified. I started going to A.A. meetings and listening carefully to older men, hoping I could identify with what my father would have been like if he'd ever stopped drinking. I even had the crazy thought that I might become a recovering alcoholic before I go through being alcoholic myself. I didn't feel too differently from the alcoholics at A.A. One night, I left a meeting and started drinking. I drank for three days and couldn't stop. I didn't even want to. Being alcoholic is there, waiting for me.

Sandra listened to Andy and sighed:

> My father was the alcoholic and the active one. The rest of the family waited for his next act or for the consequences of his behavior. The alcoholic identification is the more active and therefore more appealing. Identifying with action gives me a much greater sense of control than the reactive, passive, and protective stance of the nonalcoholic.

Following months of discussion of belonging and identification, members agreed that they often feel stuck in growing up, despite the fact that they are adults. Still, they hold on to a sense of themselves as "not yet there," of waiting to *really* grow up, because it protects them from having to act out a destructive adult identity, the only option modeled by their parents.

The second major issue that arises in group therapy is *the longing to know.* As group members struggle with polar, negative choices, they are also looking for something positive, something to hang on to and identify with, something that isn't so harmful. ACAs outline a need to fill in the holes or gaps in their personal identities that represent the self-destructive or abusive parent. As adults struggling for healthy self-development, ACAs must come to terms with the "bad" parent, so long warded off, and must find acceptable parts of a "good" parent to align with.

> Brad spoke of his admiration for his father and his fear that he will be a "souse" just like him. By piecing together bits of early family history, Brad has determined that he had two talented parents. But

all he saw was withdrawal, depression, and a sour attitude toward the world. Brad cried, feeling a deep sense of loss for what he didn't know about his parents, for what was covered up by alcohol.

Matt saw a picture of his father as a child, splashing with the garden hose. It made him sad to think of him as a spontaneous, happy child. Matt saw him only as emotionless and withdrawn. He worries that he is like his father—not someone others could find likable.

Ultimately, Matt could see that he spends all his energy trying not to be like his father, which means he can't grow up.

To get out of this bind, ACAs begin to fill out their views of their parents. They actively search for positive qualities to identify with, qualities that might allow them to feel good about themselves rather than bad. Penny feels her search is worthwhile:

I've been looking around in antique stores lately, thinking about what I might collect. My mother had a wonderful collection of porcelain figurines which gave her much pleasure. I remember how closely she guarded her figurines and how much care she took in cleaning them. Through all the battles and all the broken dishes, I never saw a broken piece of porcelain.

The message is clear: underneath all the destruction, Penny's mother could protect what she most valued. Maybe Penny can, too.

We've explored the general topic of development and the impact of parental alcoholism on the two major developmental tasks of attachment and identity formation. What are the results of all of these factors? What are the consequences of growing up in an alcoholic family environment and family system, and what is the impact on a child's development? How do children cope? As we move ahead to look at consequences, we'll see how all the pieces of the alcoholic family puzzle come together in coping and defense.

IV

Consequences

9

The Effects of Trauma

What happens to children who grow up with an alcoholic parent? What happens to kids whose lives are shaped and influenced by the environmental context of alcoholism and the distorted thinking so necessary to preserve the family's defenses and bonds of attachment? We've already examined what the environment looks like and feels like, and what happens. We've looked at the family system and the impact of alcoholism on developmental tasks. We've traced the themes that arise in group and individual therapy back to the central organizing principle of parental alcoholism. Let's look more closely now at ways of adapting and at consequences.

First, it's important to emphasize again that no two families are alike and no two people will respond to parental alcoholism in exactly the same way. The particular meaning a child gives to the experience will depend on many factors, including the child's own innate endowment (genetics, biology, and temperament, for example); the specific environment of *this* alcoholic family (what it was like and what happened in this particular home); the nature and quality of the child's relationship with parents, siblings, or other significant people; and the organizing influence of parental alcoholism on attachment and identity formation.

No formula can spell out predictable consequences that will hold true across thousands of different families. But consequences can be examined in a more general way. In this group of chapters, we will explore some common effects of living in the traumatic environment of the alcoholic family, and the development of strong defenses to cope with this reality.

We will see that kids are adaptive. They learn what is necessary to survive, sometimes at great cost. Kids adjust themselves and their thinking to fit the demands of parents. Much of this adaptation might be viewed as resourceful coping, the healthy response to life's particular circumstances. Yet, as Daniel Goleman notes, the line between an early coping mechanism, which is healthy, and an early defensive maneuver, which is unhealthy, is thin. We'll look at how the coping strategies of childhood become the much more rigid, defensive traits that create tremendous problems for children and adults in the world outside the alcoholic home.

What goes into surviving? As we've already seen, in many alcoholic homes, the need to cope is an all-absorbing family preoccupation. As one ACA put it:

> All my energy went into surviving. There was no room for development separate from survival.

Trauma was introduced earlier, in discussion of the environment. Let's now look at trauma in more detail, as an entity that has its own consequences.

THE TRAUMA OF PARENTAL ALCOHOLISM

Until recently, it was widely believed that children could grow up relatively undisturbed and unaffected by what went on around them; that children could somehow remain insulated from abusive or otherwise unhealthy environments, and free from the effects of parental beliefs and behavior. "Do as I say, not as I do" was still the favored, reassuring admonition.

As a culture, we have developed the same thinking disorder and denial that characterize the alcoholic family. We constantly look for ways to explain many childhood emotional problems and behavioral disturbances as something other than alcohol-related. We continue to ignore the fact that alcohol and drug use are widespread and culturally acceptable, and that we have a remarkable tolerance for a level of drug use that is actually abuse.

Psychiatric researchers have long recognized the link between unhealthy environments and problems in childhood. They've long known that poverty is one of the most serious causes of emotional disturbance and that racial and ethnic minority groups suffer negative developmental consequences directly related to discrimination.

In 1980, the psychiatric community officially recognized a new diagnosis, called post-traumatic stress disorder (PTSD). Still utilized only for adults, this diagnosis was finally sanctioned to deal with the reality of the trauma and aftermath experienced by Viet Nam veterans.

To apply this new diagnosis to children was a short, but earth-shaking step. Again, psychiatric researchers and clinicians led the way, examining the impact of war, crime, and natural disaster on children's adaptation and development. No one identified the effects of parental alcoholism as akin to PTSD, however, until the popular ACA movement.

Those effects *belong* in the PTSD classification, even though it means that much of what we consider normal in our culture may, in fact, also be traumatic.

Psychiatrist Timmen Cermak has likened the experience of growing up with parental alcoholism, including the adaptations of unhealthy codependence, to PTSD. He lists the following symptoms of PTSD as relevant to ACAs:

1. A tendency to reexperience the trauma through obsessive thoughts about the family and compulsive reemergence of behaviors and feelings in response to symbolic equivalents of the trauma;
2. Psychic numbing, with a sense of isolation;
3. Hypervigilance (anxiety);
4. Survivor guilt (depression);
5. Intensification of symptoms by exposure to events that resemble the original trauma, such as withdrawal by others.

In clinical work, professionals have found that PTSD is one part of a larger spectrum of consequences that includes traditional psychiatric diagnoses of anxiety disorder, panic, phobias, and depression. Let's take these terms one at a time and look at them in more detail.

Trauma Psychiatrist Henry Krystal defines trauma as the "overwhelming of the normal self-preservative functions in the face of inevitable danger. The recognition of the existence of unavoidable danger and the surrender to it mark the onset of the traumatic state."

Many people think of trauma as a single event or episode outside of the "normal" pattern of events and relationships within the family. This description fits what are called acute disasters, such as fire, flood, or earthquake, or a single episode of rape. In abusive and/or alcoholic families, the trauma is frequently chronic; a state of unpredictability, terror, and abuse is the norm. Episodes of acute trauma—violence, incest, arguments, psychological and physical abandonment—may also occur within the framework of chronic trauma.

Other researchers have described the cumulative effects of living with trauma. Psychiatrist Joseph Sandler suggested, in the late 1960s, that the accumulation of potentially traumatic experiences could lead to a state of "mounting vulnerability." This notion of vulnerability is central to current research: what kinds of experiences lead to what kinds of consequences; how much of this experience will lead to that result; what experiences for which kids create the greatest risk? We have no answers yet, except in general terms, but personal accounts are pouring in.

It's important to understand both the "normal" chronically traumatic environment, or "life context," of the alcoholic home, and the acute traumatic events that can occur within this context. This is where an understanding of the environment and the system's pathology becomes so important. Whether it's in the background or the foreground, or both, *the context is traumatic.*

Krystal suggests that psychological trauma may make an individual particularly vulnerable to intense emotion. The person will respond excessively and in ineffective ways, and will rely tremendously on defenses such as repression, rationalization, and denial of the trauma. In an extreme case, the person may be able to feel only a sense of being "dead." Severe trauma may result in a paralyzed, overwhelmed state; victims may be unable to move, withdrawn, disorganized, and lacking their former personality traits. The most common consequence is a mixture of depression and anxiety.

The need for such extreme defensive measures leads to impairments in memory, imagination, association, and problem-solving abilities.

Psychiatrist and researcher John Bowlby describes "defensive exclusion," the ability of children to exclude, redefine, or distort information or events. Bowlby suggests that the consequences of such distortion include chronic distrust of other people, inhibition of curiosity, distrust of their own senses, and a tendency to find everything unreal. An ACA who grew up in an atmosphere of chronic tension, frequent violence, and constant criticism describes his sense of awareness as an adult:

> I look at the world—people, events, and feelings—through a filter. It's like a haze, a cheesecloth, that mutes the intensity of what's out there and what's coming in. I couldn't tolerate my feelings without this filter.

Anxiety Disorder and Depression   Anxiety disorder almost defines itself. It is periodic or chronic fear, tension, or stress. Sometimes, it is accompanied by feelings of impending doom and depression. Panic states, marked by intense anxiety; unrealistic, life-threatening fears; and different kinds of phobias are other members of this group of disorders.

Many theories, from different schools of thought, have set out to explain the origins of these disorders, but no single theory is widely accepted. The cognitive theory, which we looked at in the previous chapter, is based on an information-processing view: individuals selectively take in information from which they construct theories about themselves and the world. Disturbances in cognition lead to disturbances in feelings and behavior, and vice versa; corrections in thinking result in improvement in feelings and behavior. This linkage is important in the process of recovery: the break in denial and the process of "making real the past," which is the next step, help alleviate the source of anxiety.

Psychiatrist Aaron Beck, widely known for his research on anxiety disorders, suggests that symptoms of anxiety set off a kind of survival alarm network that is directed by the cognitive defenses of denial, rationalization, and projection. These are the major defenses used by the alcoholic and by unhealthy codependent parents, to both deny and maintain the drinking behavior. Beck stresses that psychological disturbance occurs when there is a mismatch between the child's or adult's perception of the environment and the environment's actual characteristics. A "mismatch" is exactly what can be found in the "normal" environment of the alcoholic family. Everyone is working hard to keep from seeing what must not be seen and from knowing what must not be known.

The defensive processes may become severely overtaxed. The resultant stress might well be expressed as an anxiety disorder in which the person feels totally vulnerable, in grave danger, or deeply depressed.

Beck outlines symptoms of a "thinking disorder" in anxiety, most of which characterize the "normal" state of the ACA. The individual's attention, concentration, and vigilance are bound to concepts of danger or threat. Cognitive capacities are "used up" by constant attention to the environment. We saw earlier how ACAs describe being "on duty," hypervigilant, and responsive to the threat of danger and to cues from others. For many ACAs, the hypervigilance involves a search for signs of approval or disapproval from others. The unhealthy reactive stance reinforces the significance of the external environment and the dominance of others. Sherri had no sense of being safe:

> Isn't it amazing how pervasive the threat of danger is? I know it's not real—there is no danger out there—but I feel it nevertheless. It comes from within me and is always there.

Another ACA describes her behavior in a new intimate relationship:

> I can't believe how I'm behaving. I want this relationship more than anything, but I am pushing him away. I'm acting like I must be terrified, but I don't feel it. I just feel awful about my rejecting behavior and the way I turn off—just literally freeze up emotionally—when things get too close or too good.

In addition to an "alarm system," Beck describes the loss of objectivity, and catastrophizing (reacting to every ripple as though it were a tidal wave) as symptoms of anxiety disorder. Many ACAs fit right in again:

> I am constantly on guard. Life consists of waiting for the next disaster and then surviving it.

Beck adds three more symptoms, all relevant to an understanding of ACAs. The first is *selective abstraction*—taking a particular piece of information and drawing conclusions out of context, so that the fact or perception may be correct but the meaning is wrong. ACAs are particularly prone to this distortion, because of their hypersensitivity and vigilance. It is common for ACAs to pick up a single clue or detail from the environment and give a whole situation the wrong meaning. This kind of selection often confirms and reinforces deep, distorted beliefs that hold the family together.

Next is *dichotomous thinking*—the all-or-none, right-or-wrong approach. This type of thinking is a major defensive characteristic of ACAs.

Finally, Beck notes *lack of habituation*—not learning from experience—as a third symptom. People are not reassured, even when their fears and distortions are proven wrong. ACAs tend to experience a controlling center that exists outside of themselves. Because that center is unpredictable, inconsistent, and likely damaging, the individual functions in a state of chronic vulnerability, and the potential of danger or harm is a constant.

These symptoms surface in the group setting, when individuals filter out cues, signs, and information that validate their sense of danger or reinforce their deepest, worst beliefs about themselves. ACAs often deal with the anxiety of treatment by looking for rules or formulas to guide their perception and behavior. Jack would have liked a how-to manual:

> If I can figure out what is required here, I can behave accordingly and make the appropriate response.

Jack continued to believe that the key to understanding his interpersonal problems rested in his failure to "figure out" the "right" answer. It was extremely difficult and very anxiety-provoking for him to realize that there wasn't a "right" answer waiting "out there," that he would have to learn to use his own judgment and perceptions, to give meaning to his experiences. Why is this a frightening realization for ACAs? Because their own judgment and perceptions are exactly what they have been unable to trust, or what they had to reject years before, in favor of seeing the world from their parents' view. Recognizing that they must unravel old perceptions and deep beliefs *adds to* anxiety!

As the core of anxiety disorders, Beck emphasizes vulnerability, which he defines as the person's perception that he or she is subject to internal danger with no sense of control or safety. When the person is caught in this danger "mode," formal thinking is impaired; the individual then interprets all information from a negative or endangering slant. Unfortunately, the anxiety and distorted thinking reinforce each other, sometimes making it impossible to get any relief or to sort the truly grave dangers from the smaller, manageable threats. One of the best aids, to get out from under this circular process of distortion, is to talk to others—to get reassurance and support about the reality or absence of danger, and then to begin to make corrections in thinking.

This may sound like a simple process, but it is not. The distorted beliefs and patterns of behavior are deep *and* they have long served a very important purpose: maintaining an attachment to parents. In long-term work, the sense of connection is sometimes revealed as centered on anxiety; the ACAs false sense of "security" is tied to maintaining a self-critical, frightened stance. Challenging or changing one's deepest beliefs and feelings (weakness, vulnerability, and fear) feels like a betrayal that will surely result in the loss of attachment.

Beck sees anxiety disorders as closely related to interactions that carry a risk of being dominated, devalued, rejected, or abandoned. All of these risks have to do with people and relationships, and all are frequently experienced by ACAs. Many ACAs experience difficulties in their intimate relationships; they have problems forming or maintaining close ties; they fear having children. Many describe a measure of limited security and adjustment that they've achieved by living alone or carefully controlling the degree of intimacy they allow into their lives. Others maintain relationships with alcoholics or with drug-abusing or otherwise disturbed partners, with whom intimate bonds are not possible. Peggy had emerged from that tunnel:

> I've never chosen a healthy partner. I blamed my loneliness and problems on my boyfriends, who were always drunk. As soon as I picked a healthy partner, I lost all my confidence and began to have anxiety attacks. Now I see myself as the problem.

A longing for closeness or a desire for more intimacy may prompt individuals to seek help. A decision to step out of the security of one's isolation and defensiveness often triggers anxiety. Ironically, the move toward a healthier sense of self and a less distorted world view may at first feel much worse than the familiar, and therefore strangely safe, "cheesecloth filter."

Other Consequences   As we saw earlier, in our review of research, children of alcoholics may suffer from nightmares and sleep disturbances, and from all kinds of emotional problems. They may also experience tremendous difficulties with trust—fear of trusting others and a chronic mistrust of their own perceptions. As kids and adults, they may have trouble feeling and expressing anger and may experience guilt if they do *not* repeat the family pathology.

The issue of surviving or doing well while leaving an unhealthy family behind is one of the major themes ACAs must reconcile in recovery. Survivor guilt serves many functions; for example, it allows the ACA to maintain an attachment and it assures the individual of roots, the seeds of identity, as unsatisfactory as they may be.

Still, many ACAs can't do well, or they're afraid to do well. They may feel arrested in development and unprepared to cope as adults, and most of them have trouble maintaining close, intimate relationships. The building blocks weren't there. The defenses required to cope and then to survive take on a life of their own, producing a rigid attentional style. Let's now look at the four major traits or mental maneuvers that cross the line from coping to defense.

10

From Coping
to Defense

Throughout this book, in our discussions and in their own words, we've seen how kids cope with the trauma of parental alcoholism. Unfortunately, the ways in which they cope become a big part of the problems they develop as adults. Let's first review coping strategies and then see how much of coping turns into defense. In this chapter, we'll bring together the various pieces of the alcoholic family puzzle that we've explored separately.

COPING STRATEGIES

Roles   Widely accepted in the popular movement as authors of the first classifications of ACAs, Claudia Black (*It Will Never Happen to Me*) and Sharon Wegsheider (*Another Chance: Hope and Health for the Alcoholic Family*) described several roles that kids assume as ways of coping with parental alcoholism. Black outlined three types:

1. The responsible child, the one who takes charge, who cares for needy parents and siblings;
2. The adjuster, the child who is on guard to rapidly accommodate behavior and thinking to whatever is required by each situation;

3. The placater, the child who tries very hard to please, or to take the focus off whatever is happening. (Comics, or kids with lots of problems, could fit this third category.)

Wegsheider added four similar types: the hero, the mascot, the lost child, and the scapegoat. These early labels helped many COAs and ACAs to begin rethinking their version of family life and seeing their adaptation within the family in a new light.

Although they are very useful, character typings like these are not unique to alcoholic families. In any system, individuals will develop roles and patterns of interaction that maintain the system's balance. As we saw earlier, the balance may be healthy or unhealthy, and the roles and behavior may be flexible and broad or rigid and narrow. The unhealthy alcoholic family is narrow and rigid in its roles and patterns of interaction.

It's difficult, and maybe even impossible, for anyone who is in a system not to have a role. Someone who is in a system has a part in its operation and is expected to act and react to keep his or her part of the operation going well. In an alcoholic family system, a way to cope with the reality is to develop a role as an unhealthy codependent—to mold oneself to fit whatever reality and explanations of reality are demanded, even if distortions in thinking, behavior, and beliefs about the self are required to keep the denial part of the operation intact. The narrow and rigid alcoholic family system has two pathological choices of roles: the dominant aggressor, usually the alcoholic, and the passive victims, the unhealthy codependents. In a healthy system, dominant and submissive roles might well be healthy and interchangeable, with lots of flexibility and range between individuals.

Beliefs We saw earlier how children cope by developing very deep core beliefs, about themselves and others, that will support their parents' view of reality and their parents' defenses. In the alcoholic family, children often create very negative ideas about themselves, to protect their ties to unhealthy parents. The kids are likely to believe that they caused the problems that aren't supposed to exist, that they are the cause of the "real" problem, which Mom and Dad drink over.

A belief that they are deeply flawed, or bad, and that they are completely responsible for all that goes wrong, is a very important way for kids to cope. It's easier to say "This is all my fault" than to say "My parents are out of control and can't take care of me."

Psychologist Lewis Engel, part of the Control-Mastery Group led by Joseph Weiss and Harold Sampson in San Francisco, outlines the critical significance of beliefs to every aspect of development. In *Imaginary Crimes* (coauthored with Tom Ferguson), Engel asserts that most emotional difficulties can be traced to deep, faulty beliefs formed early in development as a response to parents or the environment. These beliefs are the foundation of the individual's view of self, even though they do not match reality.

Kids develop all kinds of deep, faulty beliefs and explanations, to preserve an idealized view of a parent and what might also be a precarious emotional tie. Later on, in recovery, as ACAs unravel the stories of their past and challenge the validity of these deep beliefs, they struggle constantly with feelings of loss and abandonment. A change in the family "story" plus a change in deepest beliefs about self equals no more family.

Loss of Self   One of the most serious consequences of growing up in an alcoholic environment is a virtual loss of self. Instead of a separate, healthy, independent self, the child develops what many theorists call a false self—a personal identity shaped, by the quartet of defensive maneuvers we met earlier, to match the needs and demands of others and the environment. We'll see soon that at the heart of the process of recovery is a breaking down of that false, defended self and the building—sometimes, seemingly, from scratch—of a new, healthier self. Serious challenge of the past and of all the deep, faulty premises on which attachments were built is required before the healthy identity can be constructed.

From Coping to Defense   In the unhealthy alcoholic family, much of the coping we've just reviewed becomes defense—very pathological defense. Role assignment, patterns of interaction, and the sense of false self are rigid, narrow, and stuck.

Denial, projection, or rationalization have their place as thought processes and can be a source of healthy coping. Trouble looms when the individual must rely on these defenses to repeatedly distort and deny a more objective reality. Alcoholic parents and their kids must resort to distortion and defense on any issue, feeling, or behavior that threatens to disturb the turf of alcoholism.

The child in an alcoholic home learns the family "story" and the particular defenses that successfully maintain it. Then, as Goleman notes, successful defenses becomes habit and habit molds style. The alcoholic family limits the bounds of thought, feeling, perception, and action, in order to feel secure. Ultimately, this defensive style becomes what psychoanalyst Wilhelm Reich calls "character armor"; the self adopts the family's defensive style as a shield against anxieties produced by a threatening world.

Goleman suggests that defensive style is more than a shield, that it shapes a person's entire way of being. This path, from coping to the family's defensive style to the individual's defensive or "attentional" style, leads us directly to the defensive traits of the ACA.

DEFENSIVE DIMENSIONS
OF ADULT PERSONALITY

The alcoholic family's defensive strategies are not just "defenses," mechanisms used to ward off emotional or perceptual clarity. They emerge in adulthood as deep traits—they become an individual's "style" and they color all aspects of development. Many of the major issues or problems ACAs experience—depression, anxiety, or problems in forming close, intimate relationships, for example— are related directly to these defensive maneuvers. Acquired in the service of survival in the family, they are now a severe impediment to mature development. As we'll see, for many ACAs, the defenses themselves, including the rigid attentional style, become the core problem. Ted, a 23-year-old adult child of an alcoholic father spells out these issues, accenting the double childhood tasks of surviving and maintaining the parent–child bond.

> Ted feels the burden of alcoholism falls disproportionately on children. His mother didn't learn her behavior from his father or model from him. But the kids—he and his sibs—know nothing else. They learned only how to see and behave unsuccessfully.

> Ted is extremely worried about what he calls his own lack of control and inability to regulate *his* behavior. He is hyperexcitable and overly happy, emotions used to cheer up his depressed family. He has no idea

what behaviors go along with loving someone and, if he can't predict the reactions of others, he is always unsure how to behave. Ted feels tremendously insecure socially and especially in developing close relationships outside his family. He is certain he is just as moody and lacking in emotional controls as everyone in his family. So he maintains a vigil on himself just like he did with his family. Constant monitoring offers the only hope of preventing disaster.

Ted feels terribly young—young at least in the world outside his family. Ted says matter-of-factly that his father's drinking interrupted his development in the fifth grade. He had to think and behave just like an adult for his survival, even though he wasn't ready to think in grown-up terms. It meant tight control, so he missed what he calls the jumble of emotions of adolescence. Now, out of the family and an adult by age, he often feels like a beginner, a small child, terribly needy, very emotional, and lost at sea in an adult world.

Ted reflects that up until now he has had no choices. His relationship with his father and his father's alcoholism were all-consuming. He and others did whatever their father wanted. There was no thought of opposing him. He had to respond to his father or desert him. Now, his struggles are his own.

Like Ted, many ACAs feel frightened, inexperienced, and underexposed to the real world. They have no sense of anything beneath their defenses and therefore cannot step out of these automatic responses, to reflect on or alter them. Their defensive adaptations—denial, all-or-none thinking, an emphasis on control, and a sense of responsibility—are enduring and highly resistant to change. They shape interactions with others and they structure the development and interpretation of self-knowledge. They once permitted childhood survival; now they severely limit the adult. Sally sensed that limitation:

> I have a deep sense of myself as needy and vulnerable. But I have an entirely different "face" I present to the world. That "face" of competence, strength, and even defiance isn't real, but I rely on it anyway. The facade is my bricks and mortar—my support of myself.

We've already met these defenses in different guises. Let's look more closely at each of them, focusing on examples of adults in treatment so that we can see the defense and the process of change in action at the same time.

Denial Denial, a gatekeeper for the alcoholic family, dictates what can be known, acknowledged, and incorporated into the individual's view of self and family. Earlier, we looked at denial as an organizer of the family's knowledge about itself. We also looked at the wide range of denial that exists and at its impact on both the individual and the family. Let's now look at denial as a key defensive trait for the ACA who is grown up and out of the home. This is an embedded denial that has outlasted the experience of the first family's focus on alcoholism. This denial has become habit, or armor—a way of being and seeing that dramatically influences the individual's view of self and world.

Denial of parental alcoholism includes denial of perception and of the feelings that would match up with the truth. Denial also necessitates an illogical or faulty explanation of what has been denied, which reintroduces rationalization, the sidekick to denial. Together, denial and rationalization block incoming data and alter reasoning processes, to explain what supposedly didn't get in.

This faulty reasoning frequently involves the creation of another problem. Someone or something outside the family, such as a stressful job, gets to be the cause of strife—the "real problem." Sometimes a spouse or child must absorb all the feelings that really belong to the alcoholic or the alcoholism.

Maintaining this kind of denial requires that cognitive and emotional ranges be narrowed. The developing view of the self then becomes distorted. One ACA said it always felt to her like she was suffocating—there wasn't any room to breathe, in this closed-in, vise-like family space.

Whatever has to be denied cannot be consciously incorporated into one's view of reality or one's sense of self. When a lot of denial is required, there will be big blanks in awareness, or very strange explanations to account for the reality that can't get past the gatekeeper. This is what denial is: a failure to register what's coming in. Jim shows us how it works within the group.

> Angry and exasperated, group members finally confronted Jim about his behavior. Either he is the center of attention or he's "asleep," sitting through the group with his eyes closed. Surely he must be very anxious.
>
> Jim always denied feeling anxious. This time, however, he wondered if it might not be so. In reading the summary every week, he realizes

he has missed important things in the group. Sometimes he wonders if he's received the wrong summary.

Ultimately he could see that reading the summary filled in the empty spaces he experiences each week in group. Indeed, he is so anxious he must exclude a great deal from his awareness.

Months later, Jim could see that his anxiety and his denial were related to the "realities" of family life that were being painfully reconstructed by other members of the group. Jim couldn't "see" yet, so he had to drop out.

Sometimes, denial is obvious to others who are not invested in protecting family attachments. Group members will have no trouble assuring a newcomer that the latter's home life was "bad enough" to warrant membership, even though the new person may be quite unsure that childhood experiences were severe enough to deserve entry. Many ACAs entering treatment bounce back and forth between a clear picture of family alcoholism and no idea why they're here—everything was great at home!

Denial is a tough nut to crack, especially when it's not obvious, or when it's misinterpreted, as it was with Jim for a long time. Group members saw Jim as uninterested and lacking any sense of give-and-take. If he wasn't the center of attention, he'd be "gone," tuned out and distracting others. He gave the impression of being quite self-centered, which angered everyone. Not until it became clear to him and to others that Jim was frightfully anxious because his denial was threatened did his behavior make sense. When it did make sense, group members could be much more understanding and could challenge him directly about what it was he couldn't yet know.

Breaking denial is hard, because it feels like a betrayal. The whole sense of the family's stability is tied to sharing its "story." To tell a different story looms as an aggressive, hostile act against the parents, one that will ensure rejection.

Denial is also preserved by inattention or a pervasive sense of confusion. Individuals literally "can't see" or, if they do, they can't sort out or separate the figure from the ground. To follow the confused person's reasoning or reconstruction of a particular event is often very hard, because *nobody is supposed to get it.* Toni was sounding like a tape of who's-on-first.

Toni once again tried to describe the details of an event, but only got the group confused. As often happens, people got upset because they couldn't follow her. They stopped her, asked questions, and reminded her that she kept using pronouns without ever naming anybody or anything. People lost the point of the story or it got so blurred they gave up trying to get it.

Today, Toni felt just as bad and inadequate as usual because she can't be clear. But suddenly she saw that if she made her story clear, she would name a truth she's not supposed to know: that the crazy reasoning and confusion in her family didn't make sense; that it covered the truth about her father's alcoholism.

Like the child who never utters a word and then, at three, comes out with full sentences, Toni suddenly had many pieces of her puzzle together. She now had to face deep feelings of pain and loss, instead of denial, confusion, and inadequacy.

In a beginning group, members talked about the impact of denial. Sally still has to maintain the family's charade with an elderly aunt, who frequently reminisces about the wonderful times shared by all at family reunions. In the group, Sally clutches her chair and wishes she could smash the old images:

I am bursting with the need to say how it really was.

For many weeks, Sally was preoccupied with denial and her need to break it.

Sally stared at the floor and then jubilantly exclaimed that three of the women had on the same shoes. Members then questioned what it must have been like to be able to notice so much growing up but not to be able to see it at the same time.

All-or-None Thinking This all-encompassing, persistent defense also functions as an organizer, sorting incoming and outgoing perception and feeling in a way that minimizes ambiguity, inconsistency, and uncertainty. Unfortunately, it narrows and distorts as well.

As we saw earlier, dichotomous, or all-or-none, thinking is consistent with the primitive defense of denial and is a symptom of anxiety disorder. However, it is more than a symptom. It becomes a cognitive style that reduces anxiety as much as it stems from it.

Dichotomous thinking insists that there are rules—there is a right and a wrong, a good and a bad—and the problem lies in finding the right or the good in any particular setting or situation. Dichotomous thinking does away with the need to deal with grays— vague, uncertain, or unpredictable perceptions or feelings. It eliminates the need to make sense of apparent opposites or complex ideas.

All-or-none thinking reinforces extreme polar positions and great rigidity. Ironically, this kind of thinking is used to gain a sense of control, although it actually reduces it. ACAs become locked into the view that the parent was good and the child was bad. Until this polarized position gives, the individual cannot begin to see any shades of gray or hold the notion that the parent was both good and bad.

The dichotomous frame is often the age-appropriate cognitive level for the child who is trying to make sense of parental alcoholism. The child determines that the parent is good and there must be something wrong with the child. As we've seen, it is usually too threatening to a child to recognize that the parent has problems, or, in the opposite frame, that the parent is bad and the child good. The child must also see that reality, deep pain, loss, anger, and feelings of abandonment and depression must be dealt with.

Many ACAs grow up clinging to the view of themselves as bad, in order to preserve the attachment, or illusion of attachment, to their parents. No matter how problematic, that illusion covers the more painful recognition of isolation and aching loneliness.

After many years of struggling with his sense of being bad, Ted says, matter-of-factly:

> How can a child feel anything else but bad? The source of the problem? It's the only way to make sense of brutal parental behavior.

Another ACA struggling with the same awareness reported a series of dreams:

> I am always in a crowd but have no interactions with any of the people, who occasionally notice me but most often do not. In another dream, I reached out to touch these people and found they were encased in plastic, transparent cocoons that shielded them from contact with each other and me.

Months later, she began to explore her feelings of deep loneliness:

> My parents were encased by their need for alcohol and their denial.
> They were bounded by the beliefs they constructed to preserve these
> illusions. As long as I thought I was bad, I could deny the plastic
> covers and hope to be good enough so they would respond.

The all-or-none frame relates back to issues of attachment and
identity formation. Penny described her family as a "true clan,"
with strict rules for inclusion. There were friends and enemies,
insiders and outsiders, good and bad, all rights and wrongs, and
never anything in between. She was faced with tremendous anxiety in the group when members refused to fit into such tight categories and encouraged her to see areas of gray. Penny realized that
seeing gray interfered with her certainty and security *and* represented a betrayal of her family:

> I either go along with the family's beliefs or I am alone. There is no
> alcoholism or there is and I am out of the family.

This strict cognitive frame maintains a major conflict for the
ACA—whether and how to belong. As we've seen, most ACAs feel
orphaned and alone in the world, standing outside with a yearning
to belong and a deep fear of joining. Hal found the aloneness overwhelming:

> I need a family to come from and belong to. Drinking is my ticket in.

Lori agreed:

> I am always lonely, isolated, and dying to belong. But I just can't.

As she traced her deep desire, Lori realized that "belonging" in
a relationship or in a group implied the loss of herself. "Belonging"
also meant that she would become alcoholic like her father, or depressed and victimized like her mother.

> Lori often emphasizes her wish to belong to the group in some kind
> of middle way. She is provocative or angry or she simply reacts to
> what is directed by others. Either way feels extreme.

This pattern of thinking is so deep and so much a part of the individual's defensive adaptation that it affects all levels of self-knowledge and interpretation of others. Often, ACAs will make great progress in bringing their past and present problems to light, but they get stuck trying to make changes. The rigid, dichotomous set prevents exploration or risk taking in small, incremental steps. This set also restricts insight, the ability to see something in a new way. Michael Mahoney, a cognitive theorist, points out that our deepest core beliefs, or the cognitive frame that shapes them, actually limit what and how we see. We can't begin to deal with complexities and contradictions from such a concrete set. A rigid, all-or-none view stops progress.

> Brad feels frustrated. He recognizes that he cannot integrate the exchanges that have occurred because it is not within his framework to understand how two people can have a difference of opinion and not resolve it. Somebody has to be at fault and you cannot put the issue aside until blame is determined. The group's growing ability to tolerate areas of gray and increasing complexity is foreign to Brad and a source of great anxiety. He keeps wanting to demand resolution while others are tolerating their differences.

Months later, Brad returned to the idea that his "thinking" was a problem:

> I always have relied on my own observations to guide me. Mostly it's turned out well. But then I never know what could have been, because I never know what it is I don't know. All of my thinking is bounded by the parameter of my world view. I can always feel confident and in control because I assess everything in a way that fits my beliefs. I can't trust myself to expand my vision and I can't expand it anyway, since I rely only on my own counsel. I feel safe and sure while I'm missing a lot that would open up my world.

All-or-none thinking arises repeatedly, as a limiting factor, around the issues of intimacy and dependency. One ACA gave a typical description:

> Being involved with someone means I lose. I automatically become wrong or selfish if I don't want to give what the other person needs or demands. It's all or none. There's no such thing as negotiation—only

right or wrong. I'm getting my needs met and I'm selfish, or the other person is using me. There is no such thing as equality or compromise. If I empathize or am sympathetic with another point of view, I lose my own or have to be wrong. There can't be different points of view without my losing in the end.

As these examples illustrate, this defensive framework has a tremendously negative impact on interpersonal relationships. With an all-or-none set, people are allies or enemies and any in-betweens must be denied or explained away. Mike could not deal with normal disagreement:

To hold a different opinion, to express it and to have disagreement is equal to being bad, rejected, or abandoned. The other person has to completely agree or there is only loss. I simply can't trust that there is such a thing as "working it through" to a new ground on which we can agree.

As we've seen, the all-or-none cognitive set is relied on for basic survival in a dangerous world, a world without options or flexibility. Yet, it is not a carefully selected strategy that the individual calls on from a range of options. Unlike the union bargainer who decides to hold a firm line after much exploration, negotiation, and even collaboration with management, it is a limited view that renders a false security and greater isolation. Because it is deeply rooted, the individual can't "see" it, and thus can't simply decide to add shades of gray. Moving from a strict dichotomous mental set to an expanded view that has room for gray is a central task of the long-term process of recovery.

Let's look now at another key defense, one that goes hand-in-hand with the rigid cognitive frame: the need for control.

Control   Much of the popular literature of the past 10 years identifies the need for control as a central issue for ACAs. From a professional vantage point, I agree. In fact, in my very first ACA group, I was amazed at the repeated emphasis on control, which was labeled as a problem in its own right and which was clearly visible as a severe impediment to healthy interpersonal relationships. Many of the issues we've explored—the chaotic, out-of-control environment; the rigid family system; attachment; and identity formation—are closely linked to the theme of control.

Individuals recognize that emphasis on control reflects a need to ward off anxiety and fear and a need to deal with the chronic danger of calamity in relationships. Emphasis on control also wards off recognition of one's *own* uncontrollable impulses. Underneath the rigid defenses, the ACA believes:

> I am just like my parents—out of control and dangerous.

The need for control is supported by the all-or-none view and is often also equated with autonomy—being one's own person and not needing anyone. Together, these form a powerful defense against feelings of vulnerability and dependence. Many ACAs shun reliance on others:

> I take care of all my own needs. To rely on anybody else is to lose control and ultimately be harmed.

The irony is that being in control and taking care of one's own needs also results in harm and self-destruction:

> I have always satisfied my deep longing by eating. It's lucky I never liked alcohol. I've got all the traits to be an alcoholic.

The need for control is always there. It's present in worries about losing control—being too open, too needy, too aggressive, too angry—and in fears about being controlled by someone else's openness, need, aggression, or anger. It's a lose-lose proposition with constant danger, and the only safe ground is being alone.

For Jake, the need for control was a central issue. For everyone in his group, it represented a deep longing for the safety of a family in which parents could turn their attention away from themselves to focus on the child:

> "I still want to invite my mother to my graduation but I've just heard from my brother that she is drinking again. I feel devastated." Jake then described an intricate pattern of recent behavior. He had been consumed with trying to arrange for all members of his family to be present at this important day, while also being able to control them. As a child, Jake recalls that his family could never accommodate to his wishes or let him be the center of attention. He is trying desperately to

orchestrate just that, for one occasion, and he is overwhelmed with anxiety.

The group then spoke about the impossibility of controlling others, and urged Jake to examine his behavior and his unrealistic expectations. Patty's approach would have been totally different:

> If it were my graduation, I'd go alone. It's the only way to insure it's really for me. I always lose because I need to control everything. Any interaction with others means getting through and surviving it—enduring.

As we saw earlier, in relation to identity, the issue of control is symbolized around the theme of alcohol. "Am I an alcoholic?" is a central question to *all* ACAs. Many are already recovering alcoholics who have identified parental alcoholism as an important factor in their own alcoholism and recovery. Others are not sure. They have identified concern about their drinking as a problem that they wish to examine in the context of their identity as children of alcoholic parents. They may have struggled with some drinking or drug use and they may continue to be troubled over whether they are "alcoholic." Identifying oneself as the child of an alcoholic offers the door to explore both.

Many ACAs identify themselves as "not alcoholic," in the initial interview. On closer inspection, it becomes clear that they are indeed "not alcoholic," based on their drinking, but they are "alcoholic" in their core view of themselves.

These individuals either do not drink at all or they exercise a vigilant control, permitting themselves to drink only under certain circumstances and in very controlled situations. As one individual stated:

> I know I would be alcoholic immediately if I ever stopped watching myself.

In the course of the group's work, these individuals, whether on record as "alcoholic" or "not alcoholic," reveal a deep belief that they are out-of-control:

> Life consists of constant vigilance, measurement, and evaluation, with the hope of not "losing it."

The focus on control creates a serious dilemma for most ACAs who enter treatment. The need to be in control has become a major defense and it is also one of the most serious obstacles to achieving close relationships. When preoccupation with control is intense, there can be no such thing as interdependence, negotiation, or the idea of "giving a little." Someone is in control and someone is not. There is a winner and a loser.

Being "out-of-control" is associated with being weak, needy, dependent, and abused, or, on the flip side, being dominant, demanding, aggressive, and abusive. Individuals enter the group believing that the only way they can protect themselves and others is to maintain control: they cannot permit themselves to experience any need or vulnerability. Yet, many seek treatment precisely because they do feel needy, deeply so; or they experience need simply as the longing for a close relationship. The byproduct of the need for control—loneliness—is as painful as the feeling of not having it. Seeking treatment produces an immediate bind:

> I have based my entire sense of self—of precarious esteem—on the importance of control, and now I am coming here every week to let go of it. No wonder this is unpleasant and I so often question if any of this is helpful.

The unconscious link between being out-of-control and being drunk or alcoholic is enduring. Following a meeting in which he revealed himself more than usual and was seen as "spontaneous" by others, Ted reported:

> I felt great after the meeting, but then more and more uneasy. It wasn't long before I actually felt hung over. I then experienced all the shame and remorse I used to feel after drinking.

Group members recognized that the deepening of interactions carried the risk of the group's feeling out-of-control, just like their families. Not only will they "find themselves drinking," which was Ted's experience, but they might act on sexual or violent impulses if sex and violence were discussed.

Feelings   Closely related to the issue of control is the notion of "feelings." Anger, need, love, fear, and shame are named almost instantly, but feeling good or bad about the world belongs on the first roll call too. Many ACAs maintain a rigid, negative view of the world, expecting the worst. Life always turned out worse than their most negative expectations, so why hope for anything positive?

> The negative view provides a sense of control. I can't be taken by surprise or risk having my hopes dashed. You don't get hopeful in the first place.

> Whenever I'm feeling good, I open myself up for disaster and immediately feel vulnerable, terrified, and anxious. When I'm feeling inadequate and self-critical, I don't experience the terror. So I've learned: feeling good just means being out of control and ultimately harmed.

Feelings are a mystery and a source of great concern. They are also an important gauge of control. Group members recognize that they want to open up, to discover their feelings, even to find out what a feeling is, yet they are terrified of the first glimmer, rumble, or sweaty palm.

> Something is coming up and I don't know what it is. I can't label it, explain it, or control it. But I know it's there because of the rumble in my stomach.

As feelings start to come, the all-or-none frame gets in the way and strengthens the emphasis on control. The "rumble" feels more like a blast. To open up, to feel just a little bit, will be overwhelming. There are no little "in-betweens," no gradations, and no way to stop feeling, once it starts. Most ACAs express a belief that, if they once begin to need, to feel anger, or to cry, they'll never stop.

Ben challenged this deep belief in the group setting. His was an important example, because it illustrated the difference between thinking about change while still maintaining control, and actually changing—doing or seeing something differently as a *result* of relinquishing control. This is one of the toughest distinctions for people to grasp, but it is most fundamental and necessary to real change.

> Ben became anxious and insisted again that his feelings would be "overwhelming" if he began to open up. But as he said this, he continued, opening up to the very experience of feeling that had been

taboo. Suddenly, he had the profound recognition that his "universal truth" about feelings was not true. He realized that he could feel very deeply and no one would get hurt. He always thought feelings, if unrestricted, would automatically be "bad." But these were not. He was safe and so was everyone else. From now on, he knew his version of the truth didn't hold.

The rest of the group was as amazed and thrilled as Ben. All recognized that his ability to be completely surprised by his feelings in group and allow himself to have them was an exceedingly important step.

Ben's example also showed the power of core beliefs to influence one's perceptions, thinking, feelings, and interactions. Ben believed not only that feelings were bad (he had lived with explosive, violent parents), but that, if he had them *himself,* he would be bad, out-of-control, unprotected from the violence of another, and violent himself. By feeling, he opened himself to become the victim and the aggressor at the same time. Only by not feeling, and carefully controlling all interactions, could he manage his anxiety, protect himself, and protect others from him.

Anger and Need ACAs struggle with all kinds of feelings, but anger and need stand out as dominant, or most threatening. For many ACAs, anger is dangerous. Feeling it and expressing it will result in destroying the very individuals one would like to rely on, the very people whose approval must be sought and won—those whom one needs and must control at the same time. Recognition of anger also threatens to destroy one's self-image as kind, generous, and caring. And, anger threatens to reveal deep feelings of need.

For some ACAs, anger is the only emotion safe to experience. It predictably creates distance when necessary, establishes limits and boundaries, and covers deeper feelings of sadness, loss, and need. Openly angry individuals may become the "alcoholic" in their relationships; they are potentially harmful, unpredictable, and out-of-control. Because they dominate and control others through their anger, they are often viewed as the source of continuing tension when their personal and work relationships become, in reality, "just like my family."

The individual who uses anger as a defense must ultimately relinquish it, to be able to see and feel what it covers. This ACA likely will have to face deep feelings of fear, loneliness, abandonment, and need, and the experience of allowing oneself to feel dependent.

Other ACAs are terrified of anger. They have organized their entire view of self and world to keep it out. As Shirley showed us earlier, she would alter her perceptions of reality and change her view to match her opposition's, in order not to feel angry or have anger directed at her. ACAs report their willingness to tolerate tremendous insult and distress, rather than feel or express anger. To assert one's opinion, to take the initiative, or to take care of oneself may all be experienced as hostility toward others. This position barely masks the reality of just how much the ACA needs the other and sees the other as all-powerful. Yet, that need must be denied because to feel it would result in disappointment or damage. The ACA desperately needs to depend on another, but is terrified of doing so, because such dependence is seen as destructive.

The task for the ACA in recovery is to begin to feel all the feelings, whatever they are. The rock-solid focus on control is then challenged directly. Individuals begin by challenging their all-or-none thinking. This opens the way to imagine such a thing as gray, a middle ground that, by definition, is modulated, moderate, and "under control." ACAs have little sense of what a middle ground could possibly be. As it becomes an idea, and then an experience, the individual begins to know what letting go of control is all about. Larry shows us how this process develops over time.

> From the first day Larry arrived, he focused on figuring out the rules—the rights and wrongs—expected. He quickly demonstrated a limited and rigid perceptual range based on a view of himself entirely as a reactor. He assessed others only in terms of "expected" response.
>
> He was quickly challenged about his emphasis on rules and his all-or-none view. He couldn't imagine any other way of viewing people and situations, although this extreme categorical frame was full of danger, especially when it came to anger.
>
> The first time anger was expressed in group Larry became frightened. The next week he said it was all he could do to sit still and not leave. It was harder to come back. His first impulse had been to duck—he actually had sat crouched in his chair.
>
> This experience brought forth a flood of painful memories about anger—in his home it meant violence, flying plates, broken glass and

screaming—a regular part of the family's dinner hour. The most Larry could do was take his plate and go upstairs. Last week, it was all he could do to "stay at the table" and not leave the group.

Larry was terrified of anger, everyone else's and his own. Not long after this event, he observed an "angry" interaction between the therapist and another member that served as a grounding point for his work over the next several years. As he said many times: "I knew Stephanie was angry because she said so. But she didn't *sound* angry or behave in an out-of-control manner. I didn't even have the impulse to duck until it was all over and I realized what had happened. From that point on, I knew there was 'something in between' and I wanted to find it for myself."

Again, this example illustrates the difference between thinking about change and experiencing it. Not until Larry could actually feel the gray, and know he was in it, or had been in it, could his all-or-none view and need for control begin to diminish. In the beginning, the idea of gray and the first experience of it are usually negative. Because of the lack of certainty or clear boundaries when dealing with conflicting feelings or ambiguous situations, gray is too murky, too undetermined, too wide open to danger or misunderstanding. It's hard at first to value the ability to let the meaning of a situation or relationship "unfold," or to make decisions a step at a time. Most ACAs don't want to start anything without perfect certainty and total control.

Self-Blame and the Assumption of Responsibility   A deep sense of responsibility shows up in every aspect of ACA development and adaptation. We've seen it as part of role assignment in the family, as a way to maintain a precarious attachment, and as a cognitive mechanism for explaining what doesn't exist or can't be acknowledged. Now, we'll look at the assumption of responsibility, which serves all of these functions.

Kagan tells us that all children need to believe that their parents are good and they will be taken care of. When reality disproves these basic beliefs or places them at risk, a child quickly alters how it sees the self and the world, to preserve a belief in parental integrity and to deal with the disparity between what is seen and what the child is allowed to know. In effect, the child says, "If there is nothing wrong in this family, then there is nothing wrong with my parents. But there *is* something wrong, so it must be with me."

This sense of responsibility, of being at fault, allows the child to feel needed and provides an illusion of security about the parents' well-being and availability. The child experiences the absence or loss of parental attention as a *response* to something bad about the child. The child then gets busy "fixing" himself or herself—becoming perfect. Maybe then "I won't be making them angry, or sad, or crazy. Maybe then they'll have time for me."

The need for rules and for certainty seems to offer a perfect route for that kind of "fixing." If the child or the ACA begins to see gray and to relinquish control, the parent might then be seen as bad and as feeling bad. Holding on to an all-or-none view and to a need for control helps keep intact the deep feelings about who is bad and who is responsible.

It rarely works. There is too much else to be accountable for, such as having survived.

> Sara is struggling with the pain she experiences whenever she longs to have a good life; whenever she determines to go after what she wants for herself. But when she imagines what it would be like to have a good life, she begins to cry. She shouldn't want what her family didn't have. To be successful and to feel good about herself means punishment. It also means leaving the family behind, because feeling good separates her from all the problems and sorrow that bound everyone together.

Sara could see another dilemma related to survival. If she made it, she would then be *really* responsible for everybody else's misery. This conclusion leads to the dead-end belief that the only way to cope in such an intolerable, unfixable situation is to take responsibility for what is wrong.

Survival guilt interferes with feeling good about oneself. After being the focus of admiring attention from friends, Patty felt guilty and frightened:

> I loved the attention but immediately felt sorry for Grace and Janet. I should not be making progress if they're not. And if I'm getting the attention, it means automatically that they're being criticized. Positive strokes for me equal implicit negatives for them. I'll have to pay for this.

Carl adds another piece to the dilemma of survival:

> I can't detach myself from feeling guilty and responsible for my
> family. It's guilt for being OK to begin with and for failing to take
> care of everyone else. I just keep punishing myself for leaving and
> failing to help them. You know, I was just trying to save my own
> neck, but I keep paying for it.

Bob sees another dimension:

> Never mind this stuff about assuming responsibility. My mother told
> me I was to blame. How could I have grown up thinking anything
> other than I was bad and doing it wrong?

ACAs speak about their inability to step out of the feelings
and beliefs they learned about themselves as children, from parents who felt very bad about themselves. They may recognize
eventually that feeling responsible and bad is a protection of their
parents.

This sense of responsibility and badness extends to present
events and relationships. Grace describes how her deepest feelings
about herself always come up whenever she gets involved:

> I am so lonely. Being alone is a reminder that I have failed, but it is
> also the only time I feel good about myself. I long to have a close,
> loving relationship. But that's just a fantasy. As soon as I'm with
> someone, I feel wretched about myself. It's a sense of not being good
> enough. No matter what I do, my bad breeding shows. It's a constant
> source of humiliation because I don't know what it is I don't know
> and it's all my fault.

The issue of responsibility also relates back to all-or-none
thinking and the need for control. Several ACAs struggle with what
to do about their "differences":

> Intellectually I can see that we all have differences, that we don't
> have to see, feel, and think the same. But it doesn't hold up for me in
> reality. Having differences means I'll lose the other person, if we
> can't resolve them.

Jake shakes his head vigorously in agreement:

Differences will result in abandonment. Plus, I can't tolerate the loss I feel while waiting to resolve the difference. It's better to patch it over and take the blame. Then at least I've got the relationship.

Chris understands this thinking:

How can two people have different reactions to the same event? I always thought I could predict how people will feel, so then I could gauge my behavior according to my predictions. If two people can react differently, my theory is destroyed and I don't have the power and control I'd like to think. Suddenly, the world becomes frightening again.

For the ACA, the world is indeed frightening; a great deal of energy and attention must be directed to the task of survival. The family environment of alcoholism demands so much distortion, such constant accommodation, that the emphasis on defense becomes the main event. Normal developmental tasks must be accomplished within the constraints of defense.

We've seen that ACAs rely heavily on four major traits: denial, all-or-none thinking, a need for control, and a sense of responsibility. Recovery involves challenging these defenses—not an easy job, or one that is quickly completed or ever totally finished. In recovery, the ACA takes a stand for truth, a personal truth. The ACA will break the pact of denial and will begin a process of rewriting personal history to finally include the reality of parental alcoholism.

Let's move to recovery.

V

Recovery

11

An Overview
of Recovery

We've come a long way since page one. We've looked at the impact of parental alcoholism on children from many angles. We've examined the environment, "what it was like," to get a good grasp of what kids actually live with day-to-day. We've asked what it feels like at home: what's the atmosphere, the tone, the mood? We've seen that, for many children, living in an alcoholic family means living with chronic trauma.

We've taken apart the system's dynamics so that we could map out the roles and patterns that maintain a very unhealthy family balance, a balance that allows alcoholism to be denied, but, at the same time, explains it in a way that allows it to continue. We've seen that the family system is very powerful—so powerful, in fact, that children and adults will alter their perceptions and beliefs to match the family's "story."

We've learned that they do this because the need to maintain the parent–child bond of attachment supersedes any other needs or versions of reality. We've looked at developmental issues, especially attachment and identity formation; throughout, we've accented the centrality of parental alcoholism as an organizing factor. We've understood that children are dramatically affected by their parents' drinking and by their own efforts to cope with it and to deny it. The effects of the entire experience settle in the very core of the child's being. The sense of self, of "who I am," is tremendously influenced by the realities of the alcoholic environment, the needs of the alcoholic family system, and the quality of the child's relationships with parents.

Finally, we've looked at coping and defense. How do kids survive and what price do they pay? What is an adaptive response to such a dominant force as alcoholism? What responses are unhealthy, rigidified defensive reactions or become embedded as a defensive interpersonal style? We wound up Part IV by exploring four major defensive traits that characterize the ACA and eventually may lead the individual to recovery and, perhaps, treatment.

We've now come full circle; we've gathered up what we need to know and understand to be able to approach the book's goal: the process of recovery.

What is recovery? What happens? How long does it take? What is treatment and who needs it? Does it mean feeling poised on the edge of the highest diving board ever built, ready, but terrified, to make a first freestyle dive? Or is there permission to use the ladder into the pool, entering slowly so that the shock of the cold water is less sharp?

The move into recovery begins with a break in denial of parental alcoholism. Whether it's a sharp and stinging jump, or inch-by-inch, careful exploration and testing of how it feels to know the truth, it's a shock. No matter how fast or slow, the break in denial and the process of recovery that follows are a shake-up, an inside-out, upside-down challenge to everything ACAs believe and know about themselves, their families, and the world.

For some, the break in denial seems to come suddenly. A previously airtight lid of denial pops open and the ACA faces the truth that's always been there, a stored but unacceptable version of reality that now makes complete sense.

For others, recovery starts with a suspicion, some puzzle pieces, a willingness to consider a parent's drinking, or a hint that alcohol played a more significant role than was ever suspected. The suspicion becomes an investigation, and the evidence mounts. Eventually, the ACA can know and speak the truth he or she has always known deeply: "I am the child of an alcoholic parent."

The break in denial is an alarm that wakes the sleeping guard dogs. It marks the beginning of a process of redevelopment that will involve realigning one's deepest beliefs and perceptions and challenging a personal identity that has been built on maintaining attachments within a very unhealthy family system.

Recovery is a process of rewriting family history. ACAs will question and probe, and will literally write a new version of what happened. The mission of recovery is to tell a different story. What could be more basic, more earth-shaking, or more threatening? No wonder so many ACAs, just breaking denial, feel like the ground has ruptured beneath them, or that the rug's been pulled to reveal a foundation held together with adhesive tape.

Recovery is not a simple matter of repudiating the past, nor is it a simple decision to see and do things differently. The ACA will open the family album to challenge every portrait and every snapshot, to look beneath the family ideology, and unravel the complex web of factors that combined to hold the family together.

The process of recovery is developmental; each step builds on the step that has come before. For some, it means starting over, virtually challenging everything. For others, it's less encompassing, more of a repair job. What recovery is like and what it entails depend, to a great degree, on what the alcoholism was like and how central an organizer it was.

Over many years of work with ACAs, I've come to think of this developmental process of recovery as one of "growing up, growing out, and coming home." The ACA breaks denial and then figuratively returns to childhood to "grow up" again, this time with senses, mind, and emotions open to take in and recognize the reality of alcoholism that always existed, but couldn't be known.

We'll see the importance of the perceptual defenses and the thinking disorder that I've stressed so far. In recovery, the ACA is going to blow the whistle on a closed world; some things will be seen and known as if for the first time. An active process of focused attention will be organized around the new identity as an adult child of an alcoholic. The ACA will challenge old defenses, reconstruct the family history to "make real the past," and construct a new, healthier identity in the present.

None of this happens simply. The break in denial implies a breaking away as well. The ACA beginning recovery faces rejection, loss, abandonment, separation. The ACA believes intuitively that to tell a different story is a betrayal that will result in the loss of the core attachment to parents. Seeing clearly, putting the puzzle together, will destroy the family. At the door to recovery, it seems

all-or-none: a challenge to the lifelong story means losing everything.

Individuals don't easily jump into the recovery pool. They
don't actively pursue treatment or a program of recovery unless
they are literally pushed against the wall, unless they now have
everything to lose by *not* acting. ACAs seek treatment because of
depression, anxiety, fear of growing up, fear of marriage, fear of
having children, severe difficulties establishing and maintaining
intimate relationships or dealing maturely with authorities. ACAs
seek treatment because they *have* to know. The popular movement has made it much safer to know. To catch the ACA who has
tumbled off the high wire by breaking denial, there's a net below,
held firmly by other ACAs, and there's a global "ACA story" to
identify with.

ACAs begin the process of "growing out," when they remember and take in more and more of the realities of the past, and move
away from the distorted, pathological thinking and behavior that
maintained their bond with their parents and family. Growing out
is a painful process, because every move forward also feels like a
great loss. It is very difficult to sustain this forward–away movement without a base of strong support.

With denial broken and recovery launched, the individual
may feel a lot worse than ever before. The anticipated loss of attachment is sad and frightening; so too is the recognition of such a
weak foundation. The ACAs quoted in the book talked about their
lack of knowledge about the world and their inability to function in
healthy ways, because they had no models, no exposure or invita-
tion to a positive view of self, and no mature interactions. The ACA
often feels like an "adult child": a grown-up by age, but stuck some-
where earlier in cognitive and emotional development.

Recovery is a long process; it's probably never totally finished.
The alcoholic may give up the alcohol for good, but the ACA doesn't
typically "give up" the parents in the same way, though it may feel
as though that has happened. Most ACAs hope that they can break
away from the pathology, challenge the family "story," develop a
healthier identity, *and* establish some kind of relationship with
parents. Whether this is possible depends, like everything else, on
multiple factors.

ACAs who have made the separation—"made real the past"
and achieved a much healthier adult identity—will close the old

family album by "coming home." Mostly figuratively, but some-times literally, the ACA writes the final chapter. In it, the ACA declares the truth about the family and makes a commitment not to collude anymore, not even for the sake of maintaining an illusory bond or a lingering hope of rescuing a drowning parent.

Let's now stay alongside the ACA through the stages of recovery, a developmental process similar to what the alcoholic in A.A. experiences. Although our continuing focus in this book has been on adults, we're also going to look at what we know about the experience of recovery for children. Because we've looked closely at the childhood experience of living with alcoholism, we should not skip the little we know about the childhood experience of recovery. We can at least hope that, in the years ahead, there will be many, many more recovering families and recovering children and fewer untreated or unknown (to themselves) adult children of alcoholics.

The stages of recovery are organized around the centrality of alcohol, and define loosely the major tasks and stumbling blocks along the way. I have identified them as:

- Drinking and transition: preparation for recovery
- Early recovery
- Ongoing recovery.

As we look at each one, we'll include available information on the child and then focus on the adult.

12

Drinking and Transition: Preparation for Recovery

The phase of alcoholism, or family alcoholism, in which denial is intact and is operating as the central organizing principle for the child and ACA is called the drinking phase. It is all of "what it was like"—the entire experience of growing up with one or two alcoholic parents.

While the actual drinking phase is going on, there is no story of alcoholism. There is denial, there are appearances to be kept up, and there are behaviors and beliefs that support the whole situation. A defensive posture begins to solidify, and the main focus is likely to be on sheer survival.

The task of recovery in this stage is to challenge denial. Let's look first at the child.

DRINKING: THE CHILD

We know that it is extremely difficult, if not impossible, for the young child in an actively alcoholic home to challenge parental denial or the distorted beliefs necessary to maintain it. The child develops his or her concept of "reality" from the parents' point of view. For the young child, the world is the home and the family. Not until school entry, and not fully until latency or adolescence, does the child learn about the larger world outside the family. The parents' reality becomes the child's reality, no matter what the degree of mismatch to the child's own perception or experience. Faced with a mismatch, the child will alter perception and belief to make them fit the parents' view. Young children attached to disturbed or healthy parents will learn from them, consciously and unconsciously, through imitation and identification, who they are and who they are to become.

Adults, reconstructing the stories of their childhood to include their parents' alcoholism, tell of their efforts, first direct and then indirect, to challenge the parents. They recall asking Mommie not to drink so much and being told that Mommie scarcely drank at all; or asking Mom to help control Dad's drinking so the teen party at the house wouldn't be spoiled, only to be criticized or punished for saying such a thing. Eventually, the child stopped trying.

The denial of children can be successfully challenged only with the help of an important "other" who validates the child's perception or helps the child to recognize the reality. Until recently, most important figures, such as extended-family members, teachers, ministers, and physicians, have failed to see the reality themselves, either because the drinking is too well hidden or they don't want to see it or deal with it. Because much of society would rather not see it, there is tacit collusion with the parents' point of view. Goleman describes this societal collusion as an uneasy alliance of inattention. "You know that unstated problem? Well, we still agree that you don't tell and I don't ask."

Fortunately, there are exceptions. Many adults recall a nonparent figure—an older sibling, an aunt, a teacher—who *knew* the reality and knew the child needed help. Even if this knowledge took no active form, the child knew and felt an unconscious bond with another version of reality. This knowledge may have provided an important means to cope with and survive the constant distortions in the home.

A nonalcoholic parent may acknowledge the alcoholism of the spouse, thereby validating perceptual reality for the child. But that parent may not be able to alter any other behavior or beliefs. All family members are then caught in the painful bind of knowing that a parent is alcoholic but continuing to behave in a reactive manner that is self-defeating and self-destructive. A young adult explains:

> Even though we all knew my mother drank, we couldn't go to Ala-teen because that would be too much of an embarrassment. When I finally did go, I felt terribly isolated and lonely because the rest of the family didn't really support me.

Young children require the *active* help of an adult to move into the process of recovery. If that adult is *not* the parent, an extremely difficult task faces the child, in stepping out of the denial that holds the family together.

The young child can move into recovery with the help of a close adult whose own denial is broken and who can alter behavior and beliefs and does. Many parents can serve this function for their children, but usually only after many years of active, unhealthy codependence based on maintaining denial. These parents can facilitate and support their children's break in denial and their subsequent treatment and recovery, but the split in the family's view of reality may be difficult for all to accept.

The cost of stepping out of the pathological system of denial is perceived as high, for a long time. Many partners delay stepping out or choose not to intervene because of the dangerous split it will cause in the family. "What will happen to my marriage, to me, or the children, if I give up my denial?" Most partners feel that the results will be abandonment and loss. The child or adult child feels: "I have to see things the same way as the alcoholic, in order to preserve the relationship."

Prevention   We have a belief in our culture that we can stop, alter, reshape, or prevent anything, through education and a change in values. Some validity has been given to this view with action against cigarettes. As smoking has shifted in public perception from glamorous to unglamorous, many people are now embarrassed by their need to light up.

A tremendous emphasis on prevention of drug and alcohol abuse through education now includes acknowledgment of parental alcoholism and important advice to children about how to get help. Education plants a seed for children who cannot yet see their parents' situation clearly; for those who can break their denial, it reinforces the message that they are correct in their perceptions and that they are not alone.

But something very important is still missing in concepts of prevention: the understanding that drinking is the link to attachment and identification. Julie pulls no punches:

> Drinking is *the* way I become an adult like my parents.

The strongest educational message may pierce through denial, causing anxiety. Children may know sooner, rather than later, that their home is not like others, and that their parents aren't "normal." But they may not be able to use this information to alter their own beliefs or behavior in the present or the future. The natural processes of development—attachment, imitation, identification—may reveal to children that a parent isn't normal, and they may intuitively *know* that they aren't normal either.

> I was 16 years old and I had not yet taken a drink of alcohol. But it didn't matter. I knew deeply that I was out-of-control just like my father and that I was going to be an alcoholic just like him.

Regardless of whether a child is going to grow up to be alcoholic or not, education is critically important. Increasing knowledge and/or anxiety may make young people visible to outside helpers who will intervene, or the children may more readily try again themselves to talk with someone. The next time they try, more people may be willing to listen.

Intervention   What can those outside the family—teachers, doctors, ministers, relatives—do? They can recognize parental alcoholism when they see it, or when the signs are present in the children. They can refuse to join the collective denial of society or the family, and name the reality of alcoholism instead. Next, they must carefully consider what active intervention might follow. All potential helpers must recognize that accepting a new reality about the family is very dangerous for children, when the children and the parents still have everything invested in denying it. Parents confronted too directly may respond with anger, removing a child from treatment or from school. Careful individual assessment is required to determine the next appropriate step that will enhance receptivity rather than frightening parents and children into strengthening their defenses.

Medical doctors who treat the parents or the children hold the most accessible and authoritative position for challenge of denial. The medical profession as a whole must see as its responsibilities the early assessment and diagnosis of alcoholism within the family and some level of active intervention or counseling. Some children do move into recovery, but we don't know yet what this whole process entails. Because these children have not completed their development, the impact of parental alcoholism, and thus the tasks of recovery, will depend very much on the children's age at the onset of parental drinking *and* at the onset of treatment and abstinence. We don't know what to predict for such children or what needs repair. The children we know about in recovery are those who have parents in recovery.

As the parents break their denial, they begin to construct a new story for themselves. They also begin to model new behaviors and beliefs that support a new family "story" and new identities for all family members. If a child is in formal treatment or attending a children's self-help program, he or she will be learning about the realities of alcoholism and, most importantly, will be told that the child did not cause those realities. Children will also learn what to do and how to get help, from the recovering parent or from someone else, if either parent should relapse—deciding, for example, that there really is no alcoholism after all. The child will be encouraged to maintain the new view of reality and the new identity as the child of an alcoholic, regardless of whether the parents continue in their own recovery. This is incredibly difficult for the child. It's very important for at least one parent, or one significant figure, to hold on to recovery, so that the child can maintain an attachment to someone who represents and supports the new beliefs and behaviors. The importance of that *one* other person who is a link to the truth can't be overstated.

THE ADULT CHILD

What Is It Like?   ACAs who are still bound by denial may be experiencing a wide range of recognized problems, or they may be unaware of any difficulties at all. The latter group is not likely to break denial or seek treatment until problems are experienced. Both groups, however, are still bound by the central organizing principle of alcohol and the need for denial in their first families. They will be guided by patterns of behavior and relationship established and modeled by their parents and by a view of the world directly influenced by the defensive needs of their first family.

The ACA may be tightly constrained by an unconscious fear of "becoming an adult," which, in his or her view, equals repeating the parents' pathology—becoming alcoholic, or identifying with the beliefs and behavior of an unhealthy codependent parent. There's no surprise here; how could an ACA's view be expected to be different? Children cannot develop a healthy sense of self and a positive view of the world without models to teach them how and give them permission. An amazing number of children appreciate this fact; they know that they need better than they've got. They turn to after-school programs, community or church groups, television, literature, or the parents of a friend, and literally "adopt themselves out" to healthier models.

Many ACAs with no conscious awareness of parental alcoholism, or of problems of their own, will proceed into their adult lives repeating all the destructive patterns they learned growing up. Generations of children may become alcoholic like an admired grandfather, or generations of children may marry alcoholics, to repeat the patterns of unhealthy codependence. As one ACA recalled:

> All the men in my family, through four generations at least, were alcoholics. I knew what was in line for me. I grew up listening to the women complain about the men who were out carousing, fighting, and getting drunk. I have tried so hard not to be an alcoholic, but I don't know any other way to be a man.

The fear of repetition or the reality of repetition is often the trigger that begins the process of breaking denial.

Breaking Denial The child usually must break the denial of parental alcoholism while still a member of the alcoholic family. For the adult, the break is possible independent of the family's active drinking behavior—and the denial and beliefs that support the drinking. Still, the break is difficult.

Adult children will break denial when they can no longer maintain the status quo, when they recognize, often unconsciously, that they will be worse off themselves by maintaining it. Often, they are experiencing severe problems in their adult lives, with no improvement through their own will or through therapeutic intervention. They may be drinking themselves and concerned about it, drinking themselves and someone else is concerned about it, frightened of their attitudes or behavior with their children, recognizing similarities between themselves and their parents, or frightened of having children because they might automatically reenact the destructive behaviors they experienced.

Severe interpersonal problems, with symptoms of anxiety and depression, may be another signal. These adults may also be aware of a strong need for control, to permit any relationship at all, but they don't know any other way. There is tight control or nothing; tight control or disaster; tight control or emptiness. Interpersonal difficulties may also be occurring in their workplace.

Often, the break in denial is preceded by their own "hitting bottom," the profound recognition that they cannot will themselves to be different. In essence, they come to recognize a loss of control, the same "truth" the alcoholic must finally see in relation to drinking. No matter how hard they try, no matter what the strategy, they cannot make it better for themselves. This acknowledgment of loss of control often leads to a request for help, as Sandra describes:

> I began to get really scared as I watched myself become less and less tolerant of my four-year-old's healthy anger. After all, four-year-olds blow up! They scream, and pound and want it all! But I couldn't stand it. One day I realized that I was reacting to my child's natural feelings as if he were my drunken mother, so demanding and explosive, angry at what the world wasn't giving her. It's then I knew I was in trouble. No matter how hard I tried, I couldn't change my reaction.

Resistance to Breaking Denial Many individuals who seek aid from ministers, teachers, counselors, physicians, and professionally trained therapists will need help in recognizing the reality of parental alcoholism and in unraveling its role in their difficulties. They may bring forward a wide range of valid complaints, including anxiety, depression, sleep disorders, eating disorders, problems with close relationships, marital or sexual problems, suicide attempts, or serious mental illness. They may feel a sense of chronic discontent, a kind of low-grade depression or numbness to feeling, and a sense that life is passing them by.

In talking about these difficulties, they may deny, avoid, or minimize parental drinking. An uninformed counselor, or any listener who is afraid to hear the true problem named and described, may easily miss the central organizer, parental alcoholism, thus adding to the ranks of significant adults who collude with family and cultural denial, agreeing not to ask, if the subject isn't mentioned.

More and more, professional helpers are now informed and able to help people who have not been identified as ACAs break through their barriers of denial. A helper may gently prod the ACA's denial or the explanations that support it, in the same way that one would challenge the logic and behavior of the alcoholic: Does this thinking *really* make sense? The helper might also provide pamphlets and suggestions for books to read, as a way to become more comfortable with the idea of rejecting denial. A suggestion to attend an Al-Anon group or a 12-step group for ACAs is also useful, as a way to gather information and to "try on" the ACA label. How does it feel to hear others talk about their childhood experiences? What would it mean to think of oneself as an ACA? The answer to this last question is often at the heart of resistance to breaking denial.

Many ACAs are no longer stuck hard and fast in the family's denial. They are ready and waiting for the "right" moment, the safe place, or the person who can validate the reality or offer a new "attachment" or environment to replace the one the ACA is betraying, simply by knowing the truth.

The break in denial signifies the shattering of illusion; it challenges the beliefs and defenses that have sustained a false sense of security, attachment, or family unity. Often, the deepest fear underneath denial is of a discovery that the child was not really loved; just a notch above is fear of a recognition of the reality of parental pathology, immaturity, and inadequacy. The chronic anxiety and frequent terror experienced by adults during the long process of recovery are often reflections of these fears or the related facts that have been unearthed.

The key question for the person struggling with the break in denial is: "What does it mean if I think of my parent as an alcoholic or an unhealthy codependent?" The next questions are: "What does it say about me? About my childhood?" Individuals in treatment give us some examples as they attempt to answer these and related questions:

> Will such acknowledgment destroy my lifetime image of a good childhood? I liked my family and always believed we were normal.

Will acknowledgment validate underlying perceptions and deep feelings of being bad?

> I really knew Mom was alcoholic but it was so hard to tolerate. If she was alcoholic, it had to be because of me. Whenever I accept the reality, I feel worse about myself.

Are other realities strongly denied?

> If I say my parent is alcoholic, I have to say I am too. It's too much to deal with.

Carl, a recovering alcoholic, echoed this dilemma as he struggled, in therapy, to determine whether his parents were alcoholic:

> I have accepted my own alcoholism as an adult and "rewrote" my story to include my drinking. But what does it mean if I accept my parents as alcoholic too? I don't want to believe that alcohol was so central to my whole life. Can't it be just a little detail? If I recognize my parents' alcoholism, I will have to rewrite the story of my whole life, and if I take away the alcohol, there will be nothing there. I'm afraid to look beneath the alcohol that bound us all.

As he explored further, the same theme continued:

> I've considered going to an ACA Al-Anon meeting but never quite manage it. I just can't stand the thought of spending the next decade unraveling my parents' alcoholism. Still, I know alcohol is central— it was like an anchor. It was my context, my reality.

Over the months of treatment, he vacillated between concentrating on his own identity as an alcoholic and his own story of drinking, and arguing against the need to include his parents' alcoholism. He found that he had to challenge his denial of his parents' drinking, in order to accurately accept the *real* story of his own. He couldn't keep them separate—one version of truth for childhood and a different version for adulthood. Faced with this split, he spoke about his deep fear of beginning a "family reconstruction":

> I am terrified that if I look backward I'll lose my new view of reality. My parents' view of the world was so strong, so airtight. I'm not sure I could challenge it. I'm afraid I will find myself back in the same house, so to speak—with the same logic that made it all seem perfectly reasonable. I don't know if I can trust myself to know what I know. Will I return to lying and lose it all?

Over the weeks and months, Carl opened up his family history, challenging the logic and the story he had grown up with. But he felt lost, guilty, and alone. Finally, he wondered sadly:

> What is more important, the photo of the party or the party itself? The picture is a reliable source of pleasure. The picture made my history and proved I was happy. How can I look more closely at the party and challenge the photo?

Becky further illustrates the anticipated sense of loss and loneliness that comes with the break in denial.

> I went to an ACA meeting and was shocked by the instability of my own perceptions. My knowledge of the "facts" of my childhood would vanish if I went home now. I can remember feeling that I was about to betray my mother. She was always afraid I would be brainwashed. She must have been afraid that her drinking would be discovered.

> You know, I never believed that people lie. Now I know they do. I wonder what else isn't true. If I go down this ACA road any further, it's going to take me away from feelings of closeness to my family. I wonder if I'm not making up feelings and perceptions about my parents.

Becky fears losing what Goleman calls the "shared self" or "family self." The family's collective reality makes sense of the most illogical and even absurd facts and behaviors, and defines what is pertinent and what is not, within the family and outside it. Becky has an intuitive sense that changing her view about certain "family truths" would lead to a loss of her "connection" to this "family self" and that tremendous feelings of isolation and abandonment might overwhelm her.

The Decision to Seek Treatment Adults seeking treatment recognize that they are bound to the family of origin. Many know intuitively, like Becky, that, because they learned an "abnormal form of reality," they are not able to function as adults in the world outside their home. Or, they're aware of deficits in their development—holes covered by defensive adaptation or by the family's false "story." Most speak of role reversal, problems with identity formation, and an inability to separate. A feeling of emotional unrest, a failure to "become an adult," protects against being like the parent. The ACA is stuck, unable to go forward or back.

Let's follow ACAs who are getting unstuck, as we shift to the transition stage.

TRANSITION: THE CHILD

We've seen that the child cannot alter defensive patterns, beliefs, and behaviors without causing a constant threat to the self and the "integrity" of the family. At the very least, the young child breaking the pact of denial of parental alcoholism must have one significant figure who supports the new view of reality. If more than one important, older figure joins in challenging the family "story," more permission is given to the child. Just one other pair of hands can strengthen a person's hold on a different view of reality. Even two young children can have a supportive influence on each other, by sharing the same view.

Still, going against the crowd is difficult. One of the toughest dilemmas is the split that results when one parent challenges the "story" and the other holds tight to the old view. Children caught in between may experience an all-or-none bind. By choosing one parent's view of reality, they automatically betray and reject the other parent. Children in treatment who are asked to confront parents about their behavior often feel hopelessly trapped; denial is better than having to take a side. Not surprisingly, the ACA or the nonalcoholic parent often agrees. Shattering the family myths is too dangerous to contemplate.

As with the drinking phase, children who are moving through transition to a new family "story" have parents who are in treatment and who are also moving in transition toward recovery. The parents are going through the family album, rewriting the captions, and encouraging children to do the same. The young may be understandably leery. Is this history the final version? Is this the one I take as my own? Or the child may pick up ambivalence from the parents. One parent may be resistant, giving the underlying message to the children not to join the other parent in the new version of reality and the new beliefs that support it. There may be underlying pressure by all to return to the old ways only because they were a known quantity and the new reality is terrifying.

Adolescents have a tough time with this kind of major change. Struggling with separation and formation of views of their own, they may resist any pressure to join the family in its new venture. Adolescents who feel unconsciously that this "progress" is not progress at all, but a severe setback, may fight any pull to join. Any new idea based on relinquishing control—in reality or as an abstract concept—will invite adolescents' resistance. Adolescents may also be preparing to become like their parents, which may include becoming alcoholic or choosing an alcoholic partner. How in the world can the family change its whole view of reality *now!* The shift in family "story" is a very threatening erosion of the youth's foundation of identification, as unhealthy and precarious as that may be.

Some kids will feel just the opposite. What a relief to have the veil lifted, to come out into the world of truth, and to join the parents in their journey of recovery! The kids need to be given room and support, so that they can adjust at their own pace and in a way that matches their own developmental level and needs.

TRANSITION: THE ADULT

The transition phase involves thinking about family alcoholism all the time, and questioning the old values and beliefs. What was the meaning and role of parental alcoholism as an organizing principle for the child and the family? Books, articles, and self-help groups are very useful to reinforce the new reality and to offer support during this time of radical change. The individual tries on the new identity as an ACA, assesses its "fit," relinquishes it, then tries it on again and again, until it begins to feel like "truth." Each new try is painful, because the ACA feels guilty of the crime of betrayal.

This is not a go-it-alone venture; it's a time for seeking help. Services that focus on education and support through lectures, short-term groups, and books; ACA 12-step and ACA Al-Anon groups; and the National Association for Children of Alcoholics (NACOA) offer an introduction to "what it was like" and "what it means," with an implicit validation for uncovering the reality and the new "truths."

Individuals need help in learning how to detach and disengage from old behaviors and beliefs. Again, this is not a go-it-alone proposition. It is extremely difficult and painful to hold on to a new story that betrays "everything I know and everyone I love." Dylan Thomas wrote poignantly, about death, that we were not to go gently into "that goodnight." The move into recovery feels like death to many ACAs, and instinctively they follow Thomas's admonition.

The major task for the adult child in transition is to move from denial of parental alcoholism to acceptance of its reality. The individual accepts that a parent is (or was) alcoholic and, at least implicitly, identifies himself or herself as the adult child of an alcoholic. The ACA may be able to accept loss of control at this point, by realizing that no matter what he or she did, said, or thought, nothing worked to fix the parent. More likely, the recognition of parental alcoholism activates a sense of responsibility to do something about it:

> I could never acknowledge that my parents were alcoholic because then I would have had to get involved. If I acknowledge it now, I'm afraid I'll have to confront them and try to convince them to change.

It's terribly hard to grasp that acceptance of loss of control carries with it a recognition that the individual ACA is powerless to manage, control, or change the alcoholic or nonalcoholic parent. Accepting the loss of control is an ongoing struggle that is probably never complete for anyone. At this point, it just hurts too much to acknowledge, deep down, that "nothing I did mattered."

Some individuals may therefore accept the label ACA, but their purpose in seeking help may be to find the "right" approach to finally "fix" the parent. They will learn that recovery involves not only accepting the reality of alcoholism, but also altering one's established patterns of behavior in response to it. Detachment and disengagement mean new beliefs and behaviors.

Sound easy? No way. Carl shows us how hard it is:

> I realized I have not changed anything. I need to stop nagging my parents about their drinking and put the focus on myself. I can see how controlling I've been of everyone around me. It's so hard to see clearly when you're in the middle of it. I feel different now, on the "outside" and afraid. This new reality doesn't feel normal.

As Carl proceeds in recovery, he keeps bumping up against one question:

> If I change the way I see the family and stop behaving in my usual way, I'll lose my place. Who and what will I have to come home to?

This question plagues countless other ACAs who are embarking on recovery. "Who will I come home to?" is often at the heart of resistance to progress.

Resistance   Resistance to accepting the reality of parental alcoholism, the loss of control, and the tasks of detachment and disengagement is often centered on the "pull of attachment." Each new insight, each new challenge of belief, and each successful shift in behavior threatens the core of attachment to parental figures. Indeed, ACAs often express a feeling of having orphaned themselves by breaking denial. The threat of loss of attachment—akin to death, for many—triggers a pull-back into the beliefs and behaviors of the drinking phase, even though they supported and solidified an unhealthy reactive position. ACAs lose their new identities, their new perception of the past and present, when they revert to old beliefs and behaviors that validated the parents' view of reality. Dan wavers on whether the old way was so bad:

> Sometimes I struggle so much with this new reality. I feel so lonely. I know I must detach and hold on to my new way of seeing things, but sometimes I just can't. I long for the sense of closeness, or just contact, no matter how brief, that comes with deciding I'm wrong about the truth.

Resistance to breaking denial and accepting loss of control is related to loss of attachment and to the very basic issue: "Who am I?" ACAs are constantly faced with the threat of what it means to be an ACA, which is often squarely centered on their distorted view of themselves. Angie finally says it with exasperation:

I don't want to be an alcoholic and I don't want to be unhealthy, but that's who I am. I grew up in my parents' shoes and I walk in them now.

Ginny agrees:

I can't stand the idea that my boyfriend is an alcoholic. I grew up with it and now I've chosen it. What's the matter with me? If I really say he's alcoholic and really *see* it, I'll be such a loser, and then I can't count on him to rescue me.

Resistance also shows up when individuals try to change behavior. It's terribly difficult to put one foot in front of the other, when these seemingly simple steps lead away from the home base and there is no new firm ground to stand on. Mike illustrates:

I realize I must no longer run over to my parents' house or call them periodically through the day, to make sure they're OK. I realize I cannot save them and I must stop trying. Still, it is hard. Often, I can say these words while my feet are headed over there. Changing behavior is hard. I feel so guilty not taking care of them.

The individual may struggle in "fits and starts," because the threat to attachment and identity is strong and there are no ready alternatives. Sally, whose bond to her parents was tied to a reversal in their roles, said it plainly:

If I am my mother's mother, how can I refuse to come when called?

Months later, Sally has a better understanding of the pull:

I think I understand my difficulties detaching and changing my behavior a little bit better. Feeling responsible for my parents and going over to check on them gives *me* a sense of contact. I think I really long for them to check on me, or at least ask me how I am or show some *real* interest or concern. I often feel very empty when I'm there and sad when I leave. The only thing that makes me feel good is the sense I've been a good daughter.

It's hard to let go, even with support. ACAs involved in self-help groups or therapy may receive a mixture of support for making tough choices, and confrontation for continuing denial. Mike laughs as he recalls his early thinking in recovery. Nothing could shift him away from the following logic:

If only I could find the right way, or be a better son, I know my parents would stop drinking.

Another recovering ACA may have gently reminded Mike to put the focus back on the self:

The only person you can change is you. It's hard to give up the idea that you really can find the solution that will make it all right for everybody. Recovery is all about just that: giving up the idea and getting on with your own life.

Individuals who belong to self-help groups will learn the new language of Al-Anon or ACA 12-step group recovery programs, which revises the past and develops a healthier identity in the present. ACAs cling to objects, such as books, articles, and pamphlets, that represent the new view and allow the individual to relinquish the unhealthy bond to parents. Whether there's a *healthy* bond to be built remains to be seen and depends on much more than the ACA's deep wish for one.

The popular movement and the support groups "catch" the ACA who is coming to terms with a new reality. Julie recalls:

You just can't change your whole view of your life overnight. It's like jumping off a cliff or jumping into a vacuum. You've got to have a net to catch you.

Jim adds:

You also need new parents to model everything you missed learning.

Transition is "fits and starts." It's running home to see whether it was really so bad, or wondering, "How I could think such awful things about my family?" But the awful things still come creeping in.

The move from transition to early recovery means more "starts" and fewer "fits," but the same issues prevail. Moving ahead in recovery means changing every belief and behavior. It means abandoning a family and feeling orphaned. But, what seemed like an impossible price to pay for the truth in transition begins to feel worth it in early recovery.

13

Early
Recovery

WHAT'S IT LIKE FOR THE CHILD?

When a child has named parental alcoholism and is beginning to change its own versions of the family's past and present, what happens for that child? Mostly, we still have to guess, because we have so little information about children and the recovery process.

A child in a formal treatment program, in therapy, or perhaps in a group at school, receives education about the disease of alcoholism and guidelines about how to cope with still-drinking or now-recovering parents. Older children may be attending Alateen, where they share experiences with other teens and learn to develop a "program" of recovery of their own—to identify as children of alcoholics and detach themselves from the pathological beliefs and behaviors that bound them to drinking families.

We know that children can't make these kinds of changes without a very strong, supportive person, typically an adult who is also challenging the status quo. For many children, their own parents are those supportive persons, if the parents are moving into recovery themselves and are beginning to model new behaviors and ways of thinking. Members of the family may all remain in treatment during the first year of sobriety, which is a difficult period of adjustment. The parents are so often anxious and preoccupied with developing their own programs of recovery that the child may feel that nothing has changed. The supportive adult often feels that the situation is in as much turmoil as before, and instinctively stays close to the child, to help it through this rough time, which seems as bad as the active illness. All members of the family may be relieved that the alcoholic is now abstinent, but uncomfortable with the loss of the family's former point of balance and uncertain about what the new "normality" will be. Will parents be more available? Will reality continue to change? Will home be safe?

The transition phase was marked by radical change. Early recovery is a settling-in, the beginning of a stable, ongoing process of reconstruction of the family's whole "story," its history in the past and its new identity in the present. This is a big shake-up for most families and a time of great chaos and uneasiness as old beliefs, roles, and patterns of behavior are challenged and revised.

What's it like for a child to grow up with one version of reality, the one that maintained denial, and then suddenly be told by parents, the same people who enforced the old version, that there's a new version that is to be accepted by the child right now, because the parents say it's so? The child may have been punished or abused emotionally or physically for this same now-right view, and having the family turned upside-down may be an utterly baffling, frightening situation, one that is not easily trusted. For some children, the turn away from active drinking may be a great relief. Still, the children are likely to feel anxious and wary, not readily willing or able to grasp this turn of events and the double emphasis on the immediate behavioral change that is being required of them and on the drastic historical revision that now dominates their daily life.

The family may be as fragmented, upset, or traumatized during the process of change as it was during the drinking. An atmosphere of tension and uncertainty about the future may prevail. Who's joining the recovery bandwagon and who's staying behind? Is anyone taking sides? Children may require additional support to deal with the continuing or increasing instability of parents who are themselves coping with early recovery. Chances are that children will feel more anxious, even more terrified. Which situation will win out, the old or the new, and how permanent will it then be? They may resist invitations to be involved in treatment, or they may cautiously become involved. Children in a treatment program or in a peer group such as Alateen or a school education group may find the experience exciting and join in more willingly, to hold on to the new views.

WHAT'S IT LIKE FOR THE ADULT?

The task of early recovery for the ACA is to strengthen the new identity as an adult child of an alcoholic by solidifying new behaviors that support it. The task is similar to the transition phase, in its continuing emphasis on breaking denial. The main difference is a feeling of greater distance and less need to act on the impulses left over from behaving or thinking in "old ways." But this difference can be misleading. The ACA may indeed feel and behave in a way that is more detached from parents, but may still be struggling with long-standing, severe problems tied directly to early childhood experiences and an unhealthy environment. The "work" of recovery is an unraveling of all that was experienced and learned as normal and adaptive. How can the ACA not "look" and feel more disturbed, when denial is removed? Take away denial, and it feels like the bottom has fallen out and the whole container of self can hold nothing, and has nothing to hold. It can be a very scary time.

Early recovery is quite similar to the transition phase in its focus on "fits and starts." An alcoholic in recovery relinquishes the substance alcohol; the ACA may or may not entirely relinquish disturbed relationships. The process of recovery, or detachment, involves giving up the pathological patterns of relationship—ending the disturbed dependency while not necessarily relinquishing the person or the relationship depended on. The definition of "abstinence" or recovery is far less clear-cut for ACAs than it is for alcoholics.

Individuals in stable early and ongoing recovery punctuate their continuing challenge of denial with forays back "home"; they periodically abandon the new story to reclaim old beliefs and behaviors. They may wonder whether the parent was *really* alcoholic or whether they've made this whole thing up. ACAs in early recovery will doubt a lot; they'll question the validity of their new view and their right to perceptions of their own. It's a time of beginning separation from very unhealthy bonds to parents, of challenge, and of testing the experience of seeing things differently. The ACA typically feels great anxiety—a mixture of rebellion, guilt at abandoning the parents, fear of being rejected by the parents, relief at getting out, and guilt about surviving.

Very often, the ACA moves back and forth between the drinking stage and early recovery. The ACA challenges denial, changes behaviors to facilitate detachment, and begins to uncover the core beliefs that have maintained disturbed attachments. But then the individual, feeling anxious, depressed, and guilty, retracts it all, decides it isn't so, and figuratively "runs home" to reestablish the unhealthy tie. Quite normally and understandably, the ACA gets scared. For a time, it feels like there is too much to lose by holding on to these new, radical views.

Self-help or therapy groups provide an essential "holding" base while the ACA is moving back and forth. Through the sharing of experience and advice, group members offer support for opening up the past and the present, and a safe haven to cling to when fears get too strong or feelings of loneliness, loss, and grief become overwhelming.

THE WORK OF EARLY RECOVERY

The focus in early recovery is on alcohol, even though the ACA may resist and may want to get as far away as possible from this now-named subject. The tasks of behavioral change, reconstruction of the past, and construction of a new personal identity as an ACA in the present require the focus on alcohol.

The process of reconstruction involves "making real the past," uncovering a family and individual history as it really was. For many, this will be a long process, finding the holes and blanks in one's childhood history and filling them in with facts.

Lagging far behind, for most ACAs at this point, are the deep, painful feelings that match the recalled realities. Instead, the ACAs are likely to feel anxious or guilty about the possibility of losing the parent–child bond. Feelings about what really happened must wait.

Most ACAs beginning to know the real "story" will still be well-defended. They are going to peel this "onion" of their past one layer at a time. Their defensive maneuvers of denial, control, all-or-none thinking, and responsibility are intact and on-call. The ACA, ironically, experiences a tremendous need to control all aspects of this process of "letting go." The experience of regression, really feeling what it was like as a child, is equated with a terrifying loss of control and is warded off. Yet, many individuals actively read the popular books or seek a 12-step group or a therapy group specifically labeled for adult *children*, because they want permission to open the closed history and feel what couldn't be felt as a child. The desire and the danger go hand-in-hand.

The process of construction and reconstruction, as a whole, is a threat to the security of the ACA's attachments to parental figures and to adult partners as well. It represents an attack on one's entire sense of self, false though that sense may be. The move toward health and freedom often feels like a loss and is accompanied by depression, resistance, and anxiety.

> What's going on here? Shouldn't I be grown up and becoming *like* my parents? Shouldn't I be ready to run with the torch of maturity and adult status passed on by them? Why am I afraid to become an adult?

In early recovery, ACAs begin to see that the torch passed to them is unhealthy and dangerous; its fuel is a deposit of destructive beliefs and behavior. They don't want to continue carrying it, but seem to have no choice.

CORE ISSUES ARISING IN EARLY RECOVERY

The process of recovery is not limited to one kind of treatment, one helping person, or one point in time. Many people benefit from a variety of therapeutic interventions at different points during the long recovery process; these may include a combination of 12-step work and professional treatment. Not everybody seeks help, but it's very difficult to "go it alone," because of the struggle and pain involved in challenging the family's view of reality.

In developing a specialized treatment program for ACAs, I emphasize the therapeutic value of the long-term, interactional group. I have used the same emphasis in this book, illustrating major points with examples from ACAs in treatment. One of the advantages of group therapy is its immediate recreation of "family." ACAs often idealize the therapy group, seeing it as the healthy replacement family for the one they are betraying. Or, painful issues arise immediately, because the label "adult child," and the setting, invite the ACA to open up. We'll continue to "listen" to people who are in group and individual treatment, but it's important to remember that there is no "right" way, and no "right" time, to express or resolve problems or reactions.

As we look at the major issues that arise in early recovery, we'll see that they are focused on growing up, becoming an adult, and separating from early childhood bonds. They are common, as far as we know, to all ACAs who challenge the foundation of their development by questioning who they are and how they got there. These same themes characterize, at least in Western culture, the process of normal development: intense early dependency on parents or caretakers, with increasing separation as the child matures and finally develops an independent sense of self. Challenge and rebellion are assumed to be normal aspects of this process as well.

Long-term recovery is also a developmental process. ACAs in early recovery will "go home" to childhood, to revisit and rethink that family experience. They will intensify their emotional attachment to their parents, as they open up the closed and secret family history. Going home is frightening, especially to the ACA who has gotten some distance and perhaps some safety in adulthood. Why in the world would anyone want to "go back home?" Because the secrets and the continuing denial are literally killing the ACA now. There is no way around the past. It has to be opened up. The alternative is to stay stuck—closed off from normal adulthood and locked into painful, unhealthy beliefs and behaviors.

ACAs try, sometimes again and again, to separate from the pathological bonds that tied them to their first family. All the issues that we've identified with living in the environment of the alcoholic family gang up when the ACA tackles the difficult process of "breaking away." They arise as real-life concern and they come up in the group setting, in relation to what we call "family transference," the tendency to see, think, and feel in the ways that belonged to one's early family but are not appropriate to the present setting. The carryover of old patterns that don't fit current situations is the source of enormous difficulty for the adult. The therapy group becomes a replacement family in which conflicts and old patterns are reenacted and then challenged. When this occurs, the ACA is face-to-face once again with deeply troubling core issues. There's no turning away now; it's time to open them up.

The "Pull of Attachment"   In challenging denial, changing behavior, and reconstructing one's story, individuals recall "what it was like," recreating the reality of the environment and the dynamics of the unhealthy family system that supported the alcoholism. The ACA asks what really happened and what it was like to be in this family. And, the ACA begins to answer. Individuals may determine what role or roles they played and recognize similar patterns in their adult relationships.

As we've seen, the issues of early recovery often center on what it means to break denial and to identify oneself as an ACA. A major focus is on belonging: "Do I belong here, do I qualify?" "Is my parent *really* alcoholic, was my childhood bad enough? And if I do belong, what does *that* mean?"

Individuals may be struggling to hold on to the new identity and behaviors. Swamped with feelings of betrayal and guilt, they may be literally "pulled" back "home," where old beliefs and behaviors might reinstate a sense of attachment to their parents. Group members refer to this longing as a deep desire for a "connection," a sense of union and of being heard, that many never had, or, if they had it, couldn't count on.

The issue of belonging, feelings of need, and discussions of "family" may activate old "impulses." Visits home to parents may renew childhood memories and feelings, especially the longing for a parent who "cared."

Visits home also reactivate denial. A return to the old environment and to the dynamics that maintain the unhealthy patterns of family interaction pulls on the visitor like a powerful undertow. Many ACAs say that no one can go home and only be an observer, staying outside of the family circle with new beliefs. Anyone who wants anything from a visit home has got to be sucked into what goes on inside "home."

The dilemma of needing very deeply, but being terribly afraid of what it will cost to meet that need, is central to the recovering ACA. Individuals often experience the pull toward old beliefs and behaviors as a craving—a yearning for something missed. They speak of it as a pull toward an old attachment that looks positive but is actually harmful, not unlike the pull of the bottle for the alcoholic. ACAs speak of the loneliness and isolation of their new beliefs and the strong lure to "get sucked in," if only for a while.

These are critical issues for an ACA breaking an unhealthy emotional bond with parents; they are also absolutely central to the ACA's difficulties with current friends and partners. The "old environment" and the pull of "home" symbolize old beliefs and behaviors, and a "promise" of reunion. It is a strong pull, when individuals are struggling with feelings of abandonment, emptiness, loneliness, and fear in the present. Ted thinks that pull could win out:

> I will give up my new beliefs, if it means losing my wife. I would rather see things her way.

Bart, a recovering alcoholic anticipating a visit home, spoke about his fear:

> I am terrified of acknowledging my own alcoholism, because it will embarrass my parents. They won't want me to go to A.A. because somebody might know them. My parents don't want me to be an alcoholic and don't want to be alcoholic themselves. I have altered my beliefs about myself and about them, and everyone is frightened. I don't know if we have any neutral ground. What scares me the most is that I'll lose my awareness. Being home and listening to them will convince me I've got it wrong. It's hard to hold on to my new views and not get pulled back in.

After the trip, he thought about the schism he believed he had created:

> By choosing sobriety for myself, I've created an unbridgeable gulf between me and my family. I've got to let go of the idea that they will join me in sobriety. I can't argue them out of their thinking, which is now so different from mine. When I try, I get confused about what is real. The power of their logic is so strong. Several times, I longed for a drink. I knew it would let me reconnect and have a family again.

These examples illustrate the important concepts of "group think" and collusion, which Goleman relates to the functioning of an unhealthy system. The demand for complete agreement occurs frequently in groups that are bounded by a particular belief or ideology. Even minor disagreement carries the threat of expulsion.

For the ACA, expulsion means the severing of the bond with parents and the loss of clan membership. Unfortunately, the threat is often realized. More than a few ACAs report being "cut off," disinherited, or disowned, after challenging the family denial. Charlie shows us how strong the family rules can be:

> I told my mother I was in a group for adult children of alcoholics, and she was angry. She told me that my father is not an alcoholic and I should know that; that he can stop drinking whenever he wants. She kept going, yelling that I had no legitimate reason to be in this kind of group.

> This reality is mine alone. My brother phoned to tell me to stop upsetting my mother. She said I'm a trouble-maker.

These calls took place prior to a visit home. Needless to say, Charlie grew more and more frightened, as the time of his trip approached. If he couldn't raise the issue on the phone, what would happen at home? He began to feel very anxious, terrified that he could not hold on to his new view of reality. The group gave him many concrete suggestions to help him retain his lone dissenter's view in the complete absence of any support.

> Ginny suggested that Charlie stay in a hotel. Danny offered a different kind of driving plan, so Charlie could arrive during the day, when his father would still be sober. Donna said she always took a friend home with her, which was upsetting to her parents, but absolutely necessary for her. Other group members suggested that Charlie take their phone numbers and call when he needed a reminder about what reality was, or to call the local Al-Anon office for the same kind of support. Others told Charlie to take his group summaries, to remind him of these discussions and his wish to keep his distance.

These examples illustrate the power of the "pull" and the need for very simple, concrete behavioral actions, to hold on to the new reality. Some people scoff at these kinds of simple moves, or think they apply only to the weak-willed or less intelligent. Most of us like to think that we know our own minds and can maintain our point of view. We tend to be amazed that the alcoholic in recovery could "forget" so easily, simply deciding that it's OK to drink again, that it "won't hurt anything." It's very upsetting to learn first-hand how pliable our perceptions really are. It's tough to see that we'll give up or change our view immediately, under pressure and a strong need for approval, and that this has nothing to do with will or intelligence. For this reason, it is very difficult to sustain recovery alone, without support or help.

Reality forms the link between beliefs and perception. Martha, a new member, accented these themes as she spoke about her growing awareness:

> I'm angry at my recognition of the depths that I've been influenced by my family's drinking. Every one of us is alcoholic. I heard in A.A. that recovery means you have to stop drinking and change your way of seeing the world. It's like turning everything inside out and starting over.

> My parents didn't know anything about alcoholism, especially that they had it. So they sat there watching us march forth and do it too. How can a parent watch a child become an alcoholic?

> I'm so afraid to trust my perceptions now. I have always given responsibility to others to keep track of reality and give it meaning for me. How can I trust myself to do it now? How can I know what it is I don't know?

> I spent long years in therapy believing I wasn't alcoholic and that nobody in my family was either. I looked at my whole life through the filter of denying my alcoholism. How do I know this version of reality is any more real or honest?

For much of her early work in the group, Martha insisted that this therapy would be merely a process of "fine tuning":

> I am terrified of having to reconstruct my whole life around the acceptance of my parents' alcoholism and the fact that their reality included denial of alcoholism. I'm going to have to choose between my new preferred view and that of my family. It's too painful. There are two worlds, each with a well-developed fabric of logic. Yet, these worlds are completely contradictory and I can't have them both. But they are equally compelling. It makes me sad. I want to be loved by my mother but I can't afford the cost of rejoining her version of reality.

The Threat of Loss   When the pull of attachment is strong and the stability of new beliefs is wobbly, the threat of loss is largely to blame. In early recovery, loss is often a constant, tied to the break in denial and the construction of new beliefs. Among the losses is the attachment to the first family, an attachment that secured a sense of belonging or an illusion of belonging, but that also guaranteed that destructive behavior and relationship patterns would be repeated.

Visits home awaken both the intense longing and the anticipated failure to make a "connection" with parents. Group members often deal with this conflict by reverting to the hope that they can change the parent. This belief gives the ACA time; it's like a delay in sentencing. The ACA can see it as not really betraying the family, not taking a stand directly against the parental party line. Instead, the ACA hopes to gently steer the parents to a new view, a stance that allows the ACA to maintain a sense of attachment while changing beliefs at the same time. However, the stance reinforces the defensive maneuver of responsibility and the patterns of role reversal. ACAs who adopt this stance are often mystified and hurt, when parents resist pressure to break their own denial and are not supportive of the ACAs' way of seeing things.

> I keep hoping that my parents will give up the idea that our family life was so great. I need my parents to change their ideas so I can feel close to them. I need my parents to think like me now. Otherwise I can't be around them. Their thinking is crazy and it's my old way.

Charlie says he feels a deep sense of vulnerability when he's home.

> I feel totally undefended. I want to hold on to my view, but I haven't got any tools to do so nor any right to do so in their home. There were no "opinions" in our house. There were only "rules" and my father set them all. Any different "opinion" means you're out.

These issues and conflicts come up in treatment, when members begin to experience the group in ways that are reminiscent of their first families. When this "family transference" occurs, ACAs are face-to-face once again with loss. They're not challenging only their parents' reality! If they *really* challenge the validity or appropriateness of their beliefs and behavior in the present, they'll betray everything past and present and they'll be alone.

Carla explains how this works:

> You and this group have become my new interpreter of reality, since I am giving up my parents' viewpoint. I hope to use this group and

this version of reality to combat the weight of my mother's denial. Maybe I can still have a relationship with her.

But sometimes the group feels too much like growing up. I feel small and helpless and want to curl up in someone's lap. Often, that longing is connected to a strong desire to drink, so I can really be close to my mother. Then I want to push you all away—turn my chair around or not come for a while. I get scared because, how will I know what reality is?

In the group and in her adult life, Carla experiences repeated problems in establishing and maintaining intimate relationships:

I keep searching for a parent to keep me grounded, but reject finding any because they might have a different view of the world. Sometimes the longing is unbearable.

The Issue of Trust Difficulties with trust never, *never* seem to go away. Too much has gone on and gone wrong; ACAs cannot muster any feelings of trust from deep within. Adding to the difficulty is the unrealistic expectation that trust will come quickly and automatically within ACA self-help or therapy groups. This fantasy may bring initial disappointment. Members often talk about their wish to be able to trust and even test each other, to establish a beginning level of safety, but it takes a very long time to really feel confident, secure, and safe enough to trust another in the same way. However, the small steps—challenging one's rigid rules or perceptions, saying a little more (or a little less!) than last time, or coming back again and again, even when it hurts—are ongoing, and the gains are impressive.

The issue of trust, which is closely related to the longing for attachment, appears early in the group's work and continues as a barometer of resistance and danger. In the group, it may be reflected as a refusal to "join," speak, or become vulnerable. Or, individuals may simply maintain a position of never trusting anyone, which solves all immediate problems. Lack of trust was the only defense possible for Jerry:

Growing up, there was no such thing as trust. What for? It was all survival.

Eventually, many ACAs seek treatment because the price tag for this resolve has been marked up too high. In the group, Jerry maintained a vigilant stance and expressed his suspicion of the motives of others. For many months, he watched; then he spoke of loneliness, his closest companion. He said he was in group because it's not worth it anymore to be so suspicious and defended. Another member considered the link between attachment and trust:

> I never wanted to drink but I couldn't let myself be a nondrinker. It just wasn't an option. I had to become an alcoholic first, in order to become a nondrinker. Now I am obsessed with images of being helpless, injured, and left behind. I've orphaned myself by no longer drinking, but I can't trust anybody or anything to show me a different way. If you can't trust your family to teach you, why would you trust anybody else?

> I feel helpless because I can't even trust myself. For all those years I believed, just like my family, that I wasn't an alcoholic. There must be other beliefs that are just as wrong, still lurking.

Issues of trust arise in day-to-day situations all the time. Penny gives an example:

> My parents insist they want to pick me up at the airport, which seems, on the surface, so caring. But I can't get a flight early enough to get me there before they start drinking. Isn't this the way the world works? You have to take into consideration your parents' drinking before you can let them take care of you.

Other group members laughed and shared instances of how they have to "arrange" visits or contact, to make sure their parents will be sober enough to "parent" them.

> I have a simple rule—call home before 10:00 A.M. Usually, they're still sober and might remember the conversation.

Another group member expressed the irony:

> It's OK to trust, as long as you've got control.

Role Reversal   In early recovery, as we saw earlier, role reversal emerges as a theme related to attachment. But role reversal is also a defense that is very difficult to challenge. For many ACAs, there was no other viable stance: they had to assume the responsibility for others, particularly parents. Feeling responsible or parental provided an illusion of control in a very unsafe, out-of-control environment. Feeling responsible was also the main antidote for feelings of helplessness and need. One member of the group recalls:

> I was always an advisor for my mother. By age three, I was supposed to *do* something to make it better for her. I would try to rescue her from my father's rage or comfort her when she cried. I felt good about this. But then she made up with him and did it all over again. I couldn't fix her or him or anything.

Members of the group quickly feel responsible for each other. They assume the "therapist's" role and support others in the unhelpful endeavor to cover up or deny feelings. They do exactly what was done to them, in the mistaken belief that helping others *not* to feel is being a good "parent." When this comes up in the therapy group, they have an opportunity to observe themselves and to wonder whether this attitude helps anybody. Then they get to see what it feels like to listen to others instead of "fixing" them by making bad feelings go away. Sometimes, the listening is overwhelming because it may remind them of out-of-control parents who were feeling all the time when drunk. Or, it may awaken deep feelings within them that feel unmanageable and frightening. Holding on to a feeling of responsibility and role reversal remains protective for some time. Bart explains:

> It's better to be the helper than the helpee. It's much less vulnerable, even if it's a cover. If you give up the responsibility and caretaking, you open up to being vulnerable to others. It's all-or-none, of course. What others say then becomes the truth. It's their reality and their rules. If I allow myself to be helped, I buy the whole package.

Another ACA, a helping professional in her career and a helper in the group, mused sadly:

> I mothered my mother, myself, and now others in the group. It's all I know. As much as I long to be mothered, I can't allow it. To let anyone

teach me anything is to identify with self-destruction. Knowing it all is my only protection.

Other group members eventually saw this individual's need to take care of others as an obstacle to the deepening uncovering work of others.

You want to take the pain away and make it all better, but that's not what I need. Yes, it feels bad, but it's time to feel it.

Over time, the helper was able to shift the focus off of taking care of others and onto herself, but only with great difficulty:

I'm constantly wondering what the difference is between taking care of myself and self-centeredness. What's the difference between acceptance and compliance, between acceptance and taking shit?

The "Old Environment" and Trauma   Remembering what it was like is a very important theme of early recovery. ACAs begin to tell a different story, when they say out loud what happened and how they felt about it. For many, it's difficult to recall much more than the layout of the house. For others, the true story comes pouring out, once the silence has been broken. ACAs describe the chaos, inconsistency, unpredictability, arbitrary and unclear roles, and atmosphere of tension and shame. The context of daily life is retold and reshaped to more clearly resemble reality. After some time, ACAs can use the group and the family transference to explore the impact of the traumatic environment on their development and adaptation. Julie shows us how this works:

Whoa! I finally realized I was having a hard time coming home in the evening to find the house in disarray. I saw that I was expecting my husband to have everything picked up because he got home first. It was driving me wild. Then I realized that coming home to clutter reminds me of coming home to my childhood family, where everything was in constant disarray. There was always a crisis or action that I was drawn into. If there was a quiet moment or a space, it was only a break in the action, not any open time or space for me. There was no room for me at all. Either I had to be drawn into the clutter or the crisis, as a way of having a relationship, or I would be abandoned and all alone.

Ironically, after Julie spoke about this new insight, Tammie began to talk at 90 miles an hour about the current crisis in her family and how she could not avoid being pulled in. Julie had the same reaction to Tammie's description that she has to coming home: "Listening to you talk is just like walking in to clutter, chaos, and disarray. I have to shut you out or get completely caught up."

Some ACAs tell a story of horror and wonder why everyone else is upset. The individual has learned the facts now, but does not have the feelings that match them. The listeners can more easily identify with the feelings that belong to the reality being described; but these same listeners might have just as much difficulty experiencing the painful feelings that match their own stories. For most ACAs, the history comes first and the feelings don't come until much later.

For some ACAs, however, the feelings come first, during a time when the facts are still blocked out. This can be a painful, terrifying experience: the ACA feels anxiety, panic, depression, or perhaps chronic fear, and no revised family history is yet accessible for making sense of these feelings. These individuals are likely to have been involved in therapy for these problems before they or their therapists identified the centrality of parental alcoholism and the impact of this trauma on their development. In early recovery, with the ACA label in place, the sleeping dog wakes up.

Identity Formation We've seen the importance of parental modeling to all aspects of child development, and we've looked at how kids learn who they are through the developmental processes of imitation and identification. Against that background, it's unrealistic to expect that kids can bypass the impact of a traumatic context, a narrow, rigid pathological family system, *and* parental disturbance. There's no way they can come out of such a family feeling fine about themselves and their life, no matter how much they tell themselves "fine" is exactly how they feel. The work of recovery involves challenging the picture of how "fine" they are, not how "fine" they say they are. As the uncovering begins and the history unravels, the ACA asks the tough questions concerning identity, beginning with "Who am I?" The answer almost always links in some way to alcohol.

Rick could pinpoint a moment when he felt the question was answered for him:

I remember visiting my grandparents as a kid and watching my Dad talking and drinking with them late at night, after the kids were in bed. I had the strong feeling that something important was happening and I didn't like feeling left out. Kids don't like to be told to shut up or go away. They want to feel like they're right there, a part of everything.

Many years later, I remember sitting around talking with my father late at night. One time he offered me a drink. I knew right then I would be an alcoholic if I accepted. I would join my Dad. I said no and have said no since then, but I also feel an acute sense of loneliness and something missed.

Not long after this recall, Rick mused about "being alcoholic":

At 19 years of age, many of my friends are already alcoholic. It's amazing. Maybe it has something to do with identity. You know, wanting to be just like your father. Mine is committing slow suicide with alcohol. What can I do? I can't throw out his bottle—that's behavior for an eight-year-old. But I sure hate to watch. And sometimes I want to shout: Give me something better to grab onto; something better to become!

Brad nodded in agreement:

I am always afraid I will give up my new knowledge of myself as an alcoholic. I have such a need to have my parents accept my being alcoholic, but they can't because it challenges their beliefs. If my parents don't agree with me, then I can't hold on to what I know. They define reality. Why does alcoholism have to be such a big identity thing? Alcoholism is a master status issue, with the rest of the world revolving around it.

For many ACAs, identity formation is not enacted by becoming actively alcoholic, although being alcoholic is still a central issue. Reconstruction of one's "story" spotlights the centrality:

The more I think about my life growing up, the more I see that alcohol was the central metaphor for everything, even problems in identity. Nothing was exempt. When I think about my relationships with boys, they all involved drinking, and sex did too. I've always been attracted to drinking men and the drinking life-style, even though I don't like it much myself. But I can identify: I've always had problems with food.

In the group, members experience the danger of relinquishing new beliefs in order to return to old ones that signify attachment or safety. A group member struggled for months to challenge her consistently angry, bitter view toward the world. She would not give it up or even consider questioning it, because to do so would make her vulnerable to abuse by someone. She staunchly resisted Al-Anon, but finally agreed to try it. After several meetings in which she felt quite skeptical, she experienced a turnaround. She felt calm, less angry and guarded, and less susceptible to the influence of others. In the group, she spoke about her new sense of herself and her fear of losing it.

> I think of myself as the old Gail and the new Gail. They're so close, I can feel them both as very real. It's wonderful not to feel so bitter and hateful, but I'm constantly afraid I'll lose it. The new Gail, with new beliefs and attitudes, will just slip away and I'll be back to the safety of my anger and isolation. These feelings are no problem for me—that's who I am—an angry, mean person.

Identity concerns are also related to issues of "normality." A group member had long thought of himself as destructive, the bad apple of any basket. In his early months in the group, he demonstrated the strength of this self-view, establishing himself as the "problem" in the group. He and others were able to recognize and label his developing role as the scapegoat of the group, and all agreed they wanted to change this group dynamic that was unpleasant for everybody. But it was difficult. Members were amazed at how closely they had to watch themselves, because negative responses toward Jason had become so automatic. Jason, too, had to actively alter behavior patterns that were part of his "normal" sense of himself.

After a number of months with changed behavior patterns, the group congratulated itself on its progress. The experience had taught them all how painfully difficult it is to challenge deep beliefs and the behaviors that reinforce them. Jason reflected:

> It's so strange not to feel defensive, on guard against attack or criticism from all of you. I have to be constantly watchful still, or I'll

revert to old ways. I have to remind myself that it's important to come and to come on time or else I set it up to be criticized. I'm not used to this new "normality" and my new sense of myself as one of the team.

The theme of new beliefs versus old beliefs reappears continually through the work of the group. In early recovery, the new identity is still "shaky" and frightening. Resistance and the pull to return to old beliefs remain constant threats. Often, members feel caught, or even "stuck," because the pull backward is so strong.

I'm biding my time. The "old frame" is just too powerful right now. I need to focus on holding on to the new knowledge of myself and not trying to change too much else right now.

Separation   As members first embark on recovery, the issue of separation is often at the forefront. Separation is also central to why people join a group. ACAs realize they are still emotionally attached to their families of origin in self-destructive ways. They are bound by denial and by the beliefs about the family and themselves that were constructed to preserve these bonds. To change as adults, they must challenge the premises on which their core sense of identity has been constructed. Implicit in the entire process of recovery is ultimate emotional separation from parents, whether alive or dead. ACAs seek treatment because they recognize intuitively that they cannot decree such a separation or step out of the self-destructive patterns of behavior acquired through parental attachment and development.

The ground for separation is neither firm nor healthy. Individuals sense they have no choices and are threatened by the prospect of becoming an adult. As we've seen, they are guided and defined by defensive processes that they will transfer to new relationships.

Separation entails "becoming like the parent," acting out an identification that is already well formed. For many, this involves becoming actively alcoholic. For others, it involves an unhealthy codependent stance: identifying with a reactive, helpless, dependent nonalcoholic parent and following suit. Many people enter treatment having become just like the parent, despite having vowed not to; growing up has meant modeling themselves in the image of unhealthy parents. Remember what Kagan tells us: the child will accept whatever standards are modeled and will establish harmonious relationships on that basis. No wonder many ACAs have a

sense of terrible foreboding as they approach adulthood. Novelist
Sheila Bihary spells out this dilemma:

> A mentor is someone who shows you the ropes by which you hang
> yourself.

Others seek treatment because they are stuck. Development
stopped short of emotional separation, to ward off becoming like
the parent. These individuals often live very restricted lives, to ensure control, or they move into adulthood with an adolescent identity locked in place. They can't *really* move ahead, for lots of reasons,
all of them negative and terrifying. To be like the parent is a death
sentence, a self-destruct button that inflicts harm on others close
by. To not be like the parent is to be guilty of abandonment and
rejection, of leaving needy, helpless parents behind and becoming
orphaned in the process. What's the outcome?

The continuing attachment, which becomes the focus of exploration, is harmful, but separation looms as more devastating.
For ACAs in treatment, life is, in some important way, on hold.

> I didn't leave my home, I joined it. I went through the motions of
> rebellion, but had actually adopted the self-destructive behavior
> of my parents. I loved being with my family after I started drinking
> with them. It seemed so comfortable and familiar. I knew I'd never
> leave. Everyone was rotting, but it felt warm and good.

Another individual reflects on the painful tension she experiences between attachment and separation, in regard to marriage
and children:

> I want so much to have a good marriage, a good relationship, and to
> have children. But I know deeply that I am not equipped to do this. I
> feel chronically angry at the world and want nothing to do with most
> people. I can imagine what a good mother would be like but it's not
> me. I am sure I would harm my children, no matter how much I want
> it to be otherwise.

Another ACA echoes this woman's sense of herself, adding the
feelings of despair and depression she carries most of the time:

Coming to group is not a Mrs. Fields cookie. It's emotionally draining and hard work. I feel like I'm dragging my parents around with me here and everywhere. I live my life as if my parents were still in charge.

This is a pretty discouraging picture. But there's a bright side. These individuals are in treatment, which hurts. But they are getting help to challenge and change the very core of this unhealthy view. It's not easy and not quick, but ACAs do "come round again," to grow up healthy on their second try.

Let's go now to ongoing recovery, and follow ACAs' progress in growing out and coming home.

14

Ongoing Recovery

WHAT'S IT LIKE FOR THE CHILD?

We've seen that it is difficult, if not impossible, for a child to challenge the parents' view of reality without the support of a significant other, who shares the deviant but accurate view. The same support is needed for the process of ongoing recovery. Without it, the child cannot continue the challenge of beliefs and behaviors begun in early recovery, nor can it rebuild, or build anew, a different family "story" and a radically different personal identity.

Early recovery is often characterized by an atmosphere of urgency and a focus on new behaviors to replace old impulsive actions. In ongoing recovery, new behaviors are more stabilized, so the focus shifts to the challenge of deeper beliefs and patterns of relationship. There is continuing acknowledgment of parental alcoholism, and the realities of what happened, past and present, are incorporated into a new family identity and a new view of self.

As far as we know, children who are moving in a process of ongoing recovery also have parents in recovery, or they have one parent or significant adult who confirms the new view of reality and actively supports the child's changing view. Still, it's difficult for children to challenge the family's "story" and rewrite family history, if one parent continues to hold on to the old version of reality. Children may feel terribly caught—invited to see things in a new way by one parent, but threatened at the same time by the other. Such a split within the family causes a split for the child. There is simply no way to win. Children are faced with betraying a parent, no matter which point of view they settle on. When this kind of split occurs, it's understandable that children cannot welcome the move into recovery. It looms as a great loss, rather than a healthy new beginning.

The degree to which the normal, appropriate tasks of development—attachment, identity formation, autonomy, and separation—did occur, or can now occur, depends on many variables: the child's age at onset of alcoholism and onset of recovery; which parent(s) is alcoholic; which parent breaks denial; whether the family is intact; the new family "story" in early recovery and how it unfolds and changes in ongoing recovery. Although the uncertainty that characterized early recovery will be less dominant as the new "normality" is established and stabilized, other questions loom: Has anything changed, or has nothing changed? What is the family environment like now? What is the relationship with parents like? Is there a new, stable base of parental behavior, belief, and feelings to which the child can make an attachment and safely begin a process of repair? Or, is the trauma of the past enduring, so that issues of trust and safety remain at the forefront?

These variables and questions are critical to understanding what the process of recovery is all about for each individual child. What ongoing recovery will be depends entirely on what the child experienced during the active alcoholism and what the child experiences during the family's recovery.

WHAT'S IT LIKE FOR THE ADULT?

The task of ongoing recovery involves solidifying the identity as an ACA and the new behaviors that support it. The individual becomes more comfortable and adept at detachment and disengagement from the beliefs and behaviors that maintained a very unhealthy bond to the first family. The ACA has more distance, with fewer occasions of "fits and starts." Less and less does the individual consider chucking it all, giving up the new identity to run home and reestablish a "connection" based on sharing the old version of reality. For the ACA in ongoing recovery, the old version is like an old shoe: it doesn't fit anymore, looks shabby, causes blisters, and just plain hurts.

With new behaviors and the new identity as an ACA in place, the individual can begin the ongoing process of rewriting family history, incorporating the realities of the past, and constructing a new, healthy identity in the present. The issues that dominated early recovery remain critical themes, but now are within the context of a different kind of change. The ACA now focuses on challenging defenses, the maneuvers and traits that were adaptive during childhood but have proved to be enormously restrictive for the adult.

Ongoing recovery involves expansion. ACAs literally "grow out" as much as they "grow up" again. They open up; they broaden their awareness of their feelings, attitudes, beliefs, and behaviors in the present. They move from a limited, narrow view of the world, required and reinforced by the family's defenses and distorted version of reality, to a wide-open, expansive stance. ACAs will now take in what's out there, integrating a new version of the outside world with a new version of the inside world.

This slowly developing, ongoing process is fraught with anxiety, for most people. ACAs whose parents and first families are still drinking feel especially threatened, because the process feels like a betrayal and a loss of core attachment. The foundation of this expansion process is the challenge of the safety mechanisms adopted during childhood to cope with the disturbed family. If the ACAs are to successfully change, they must experience and question, in the present, the validity and usefulness of the defensive traits that were lifesaving to them in the family. The ACA in ongoing recovery will concretely challenge denial, the emphasis on control, all-or-none thinking, and the faulty assumption of responsibility.

This challenge occurs within the context of a new attachment or new "family environment" that provides the necessary structure and support for the new beliefs and the reconstruction process. The new attachment may be to an individual therapist, a therapy group, or a self-help group, and to the individuals within that setting. This new person or structure represents the new version of reality and thus serves the function of the supportive other. The therapist or the self-help group may not have a committed view about any person's particular reality, but they stand ready to represent the ACA's challenge of the old view. They are the welcomers, as the ACA enters into an environment that supports the challenge of denial about the past and the present. The new environment offers the ACA a "holding pattern" until the bonds that tie the individual to an unhealthy past can be broken. As we've seen throughout, questioning old beliefs and perceptions, without support, is very hard and very threatening; deciding, once again, that it wasn't so is too easy. The popular ACA movement, through books, articles, and films, has given countless individuals the written "supportive other" they needed to start this pulling-away process.

THE WORK OF ONGOING RECOVERY

During ongoing recovery, attention shifts from a singular focus on the alcoholic parent, and what happened, to a much more consistent focus on the self. ACAs are ready to challenge their own behaviors and the deep, faulty beliefs they learned from imitating and identifying with unhealthy parents. The alcohol focus, now more symbolic than concrete, anchors the individual's emerging and developing sense of self. Because the identity as an ACA is now much stronger, the alcohol focus forms the foundation for the main work of ongoing recovery. A pair of processes comes first: the challenge of deep beliefs and the challenge of defenses. Together, these ease the way for an expansion in perception, thinking, and feeling. The narrow range of awareness that was essential to maintain the family's defenses can now be slowly expanded.

The developmental themes that were part of the work of early recovery remain central issues throughout treatment. In ongoing recovery, they are related closely to the expansion of the sense of self and of relationships with others. Many of the most serious problems individuals face as adults are related to interpersonal attachment and close relationship.

THE DOMAINS OF CHANGE

In contrast to early recovery, which is largely supportive and strengthens the new attachment, identity, and beliefs, ongoing recovery involves deep challenge and deep change. ACAs find that they *must* revise and perhaps even completely relinquish their most cherished and most relied-upon thinking and behavior. This shift is far less pronounced than for the alcoholic or the chemically dependent person, who must actively focus on behavior change to deal with strong impulses to use a substance. For the ACA, the emphasis on behavior—responding to the pull of attachment and of old, unhealthy behavior patterns—continues throughout recovery as a struggle with underlying issues that are central to development. The old behaviors that symbolized attachment remain as a potential threat in relationships with parents and as a real problem in adult relationships with others. When the behaviors, attitudes, and beliefs adopted to cope and survive in the family become the behaviors, attitudes, and beliefs of adulthood, severe problems result.

In the process of deeper uncovering, the individual begins to question the past, the family, and the self in a stronger, more revealing light. By retelling family history, the ACA makes new connections and gives new meaning to the past and present. In Goleman's frame, the ACA creates radically new, personal versions of experience that affect literally everything: behavior, deep beliefs, feelings, perceptions, and relationships with others. A focus on alcohol and an acknowledgment of the reality of parental alcoholism govern this redevelopment process.

In developing a new personal and family "story," the ACA brings together the domains of the environment, the family system, and the primary developmental issues of attachment and identity formation.

The Environment   Like an alcoholic in A.A., an ACA in a 12-step program or in psychotherapy begins to tell a different story. None of the realities of parental alcoholism or their impact on the child and family is left out. The ACA goes backward to the past, remembering exactly "what it was like."

When ACAs remember what happened factually, they begin to feel the emotions that match the reality. This is a painful and, typically, a slow process. ACAs put together fact and feeling in small, incremental steps, because, for most of them, each new memory or insight represents some degree of loss.

The equation of recovery with loss is strikingly evident when an ACA who has parents in recovery joins a group. Regardless of the new person's own experiences, most other ACAs, with parents still drinking or dead, feel intense envy for what they conclude the ACA must now be getting from the sober parent. Imagine having the *permission*, and the example from parents, to write a new family history!

ACAs hold on to their fantasy that healthy recovery can be a family affair. They visualize the entire family moving together, over time, through ongoing recovery. A rising orchestral theme and "The End" would fit their fantasy nicely.

There are such recovering families, but they are very much in the minority. For the most part, ACAs journey alone and struggle continually with loss.

The System In remembering "what it was like," the ACA also unravels the beliefs, roles, and patterns of interaction that held the family together. The ACA begins to grasp how parental alcoholism organized family life and how everyone learned to explain what was happening in a way that denied it completely (or partially) and allowed it to be maintained. Eventually, the ACA arrives at the core of the family's pathological double-bind: There is nothing wrong here, and don't mess with it or fix it.

In reconstructing the dynamics of the active alcoholic system, the ACA must challenge deep beliefs that no longer fit. Recognizing that parents' insecurities, fears, and defenses, all related directly to alcoholism, literally shaped and maintained the family's stability is a painful experience.

ACAs find it terribly threatening to recognize that the reality of parental alcoholism was known unconsciously by all to be the single brick that, if pulled out, would topple the entire family structure. In recovery, the ACA bears the guilt and loss that go with pulling out that brick. The ACA must deal with a family structure that does indeed topple, or with the anger and disarray unleashed by the ACA's challenge. Many ACAs fear that their families will fall apart, which sometimes happens, or—a more frequent result—that the family will close them out. ACAs become outsiders in their families, left alone in the company of their revolutionary beliefs, actions, and feelings.

In ongoing recovery, ACAs maintain a stronger hold on what the family system was like and challenge their behavior and beliefs in the present. Ongoing recovery is revision—then and now. ACAs

learn, particularly in an intensive therapy setting, how they repeat
very unhealthy patterns, what these patterns are, and how patterns
of behavior and relationship are guided and reinforced by deep,
faulty beliefs.

Developmental Issues   In rewriting family history, the individual
also rewrites his or her personal identity—perhaps the most anxiety-
provoking task of recovery. To tell "what it was like" at home, and to
make sense of the disturbed family system, the ACA must look at
"Who am I?" and "How did I get to be who I am?" It's hard to recall
the truth about the environment and the system, without questioning
one's own deepest development.

   Simultaneously, the ACA begins to grapple with the puzzle of
the self and to pull away from his or her first family. If this process
of personal redevelopment and identity is to be completed, the
beliefs that maintained the parent–child attachment and provided
the model for very unhealthy identification must be challenged.
The ACA rebels, maybe for the first time, proclaiming, "This is
my reality, and I will hold it, regardless of the price." Then the ACA
begins to challenge old behaviors, beliefs, and meaning in every
sphere. For some, a new beginning, not a reconstruction, is under-
way. For all, it means breaking old ties with the past while actually
claiming a valid history and therefore giving oneself real roots. The
ACA begins to write an annotated truth.

   The issue of control is an important centerpiece of this uncovering work. Like the alcoholic moving into abstinence, the
ACA moving into recovery accepts, on principle at least, the loss of
control. ACAs come to terms with the reality that no matter what
they do, think, or say, they cannot will the parent to stop drinking.
This is extremely difficult for ACAs whose fragile sense of well-
being continues to rest on the belief that they can fix their parents, if they can just figure out the "right" approach. This belief
prompts many ACAs to seek treatment. Rather than recognize
their own "loss of control," they hope that treatment will give
them the answers they have been unable to supply on their own.
Many ACAs cannot grasp the deeper meaning of relinquishing
control, because it represents a horrifying capitulation, an
unimaginable rupture in defense. As we've seen, the ACA is so
dominated by the need for control that it's impossible to step

outside of it, to reflect on it, or to ponder the idea of giving it up. What does this central issue of loss of control mean for the ACA, and how does it happen?

In ongoing recovery, some individuals can accept their inability to control or change a parent, but they cannot transfer the concept to their relationships with others. Two group members, Harvey and Ted, illustrate this dilemma:

> I know you cannot tolerate my style and I know as soon as I speak you will attack, belittling me and calling me weak. But I keep trying. I just can't give up the idea that somehow I can get you to see me differently, like me, or at least have a dialogue. I can't believe I really can't change your view of me.

The individual speaking had great difficulty with the notion of powerlessness and his inability to control others. The person he couldn't control struggled with his need for control as well, but the focus was different. The latter could not relinquish or alter his all-or-none view of the world. There were good guys and bad, winners and losers, and strong people and weak. In the all-or-none view, the goal in life is to be able to separate the good from the bad, the strong from the weak; to identify with the winners and reject categorically the losers.

In the group, the two repeated their patterns of relationship without resolution. Although both were able to understand the dilemma intellectually, neither one of them really "got it." They couldn't reason or fight their way out of the bind.

Eventually, Harvey could see that his persistent belief in his ability to get Ted to like him was just like his efforts with his father. Ultimately, Ted could see that his categorical view of the world protected him against recognition of deep feelings of need and rage and a fear of becoming the bad, weak loser if he stopped warding it off.

Ongoing recovery involves the work of uncovering and the painful process of coming face-to-face with one's deepest beliefs and defenses. The ACA experiences how the beliefs that facilitated survival in the first family are now *the* central problem. No wonder ongoing recovery sometimes feels so sluggish, like pulling teeth, and so downright frightening. It really is like pulling the bricks out of my own house, starting from the foundation! Many ACAs get stuck periodically; intuitively, they feel that their next move will be the one that pulls the house down.

As I've stressed, this process is greatly enhanced by the support of others who are also challenging the very foundation of their lives. Individuals involved in self-help and 12-step recovery programs acquire a new language of recovery that structures behavioral change and the uncovering of deep beliefs and feelings. A language of recovery provides a sense of order and a vocabulary to describe and validate what was previously denied. As powerful and helpful as this new language is, it's also problematic because it is oversimplified. ACAs in recovery must go beyond the vocabulary, giving meaning to their own experiences in their own words. This adds to the difficulty, but it also reinforces the absolute uniqueness of the process for each person. The ACA is developing a new, healthy, independent sense of self that is personal and one-of-a-kind. It's not "yours," or "ours," as it was when growing up; it is "mine." This process of becoming a healthy person is very frightening, and "fits and starts" continue. Becoming a separate person had always meant becoming like the parent, destructive to self and others.

> So now, in ongoing recovery, I'm going to accept that I don't have any control? I'm supposed to loosen the "unhealthy" bond to my parents? You must be kidding!

ACAs in 12-step programs get to face this dilemma of stepping off a cliff into a void with a swing rope secured by a "higher power." Many find, within the programs of ACA, Al-Anon, and A.A., a structure that eases their growth and development on a new foundation: the relinquishment of control. Individuals learn repeatedly that the only persons they can control are themselves, and that control is a paradox. The belief in the ability to control oneself and others is "turned over" to a higher power, but the "higher power" is constructed by the individual! At the center of the work of ongoing recovery, for individuals involved in 12-step programs, is the development of a personal philosophy or belief that includes a relationship with a higher power.

Let's now follow the individual in treatment, to see how the brick-pulling and the reconstruction take place.

TREATMENT: THE PROCESS OF EXPANSION

Prominent early themes continue throughout recovery. Since this
is a process, with no discernible finale, the issues related to family
ties take their place as part of the individual's history and part of
the new identity. Their intensity and their interference in the ACA's
life are dramatically reduced. Like other significant symbols of
family life, issues related to parental alcoholism may come back to
visit at important times, but they no longer provide the dominant
influence in shaping the ACA's sense of self and relationships with
others. But all this is still down the line. For now, the individual
continues to struggle with issues of attachment, trust, role reversal, identity formation, and separation within the context of an
expanding framework of the self.

With the break in denial of parental alcoholism, the ACA
opens the gate to let in the truths of the past and the present. Because of the long emphasis on defense and the tightly closed family
system that resulted, most ACAs don't have a broad base of perception, thinking, and feeling available to them, when denial is lifted.
As kids, they stifled their naturally expanding awareness, in order
to accept the parents' rules about what could be seen and known—
which wasn't much, for many ACAs. Many ACAs incorporated their
parents' view that the world was dangerous, so their limited awareness and range of feeling were warranted. Most importantly, ACAs
learned by observation that freedom of expression was deadly:
they watched chronically out-of-control parents and vowed never
to be like them.

No wonder, then, that the process of challenging defenses
hardly looms as liberating. Instead, the idea of expanding one's
behaviors, perceptions, and feelings seems equal to becoming out-
of-control, just like the parents. Yet, ironically, this is what treatment is all about and this is what brings many people for help. The
defenses are now causing more harm than the potential changes
might bring. The ACA is in deep trouble and can't willfully stop,
change, or fix the problem.

The process of recovery involves challenging defenses through
expansion on three levels: behavioral, cognitive (including both
awareness and judgment), and emotional. Let's look at how this
works for ACAs in a long-term therapy group.

Behavioral Expansion   Expansion really means trying new ways of seeing and behaving. It may involve broadening one's horizons within the same general framework, or launching out in a new or opposite direction, or widening one's range from brand new premises. The identity as an ACA is an example of a brand new premise. Once this major shift in identity occurs, much of the behavioral change occurs step-by-step within the same framework, directed now by the new identity and the acceptance of the reality of parental alcoholism.

After attachment to the therapy group is firm and members can tolerate feeling vulnerable, the process of expansion begins. Carl shows us how the apparently simple steps are taken with great difficulty.

> Betsy realized she had taken Carl's regular seat and offered to change places. Carl accepted, stating how important it was to him to have the stability of the point of view represented by this same seat as he explored new ideas and feelings. Carl described his life-long attempts to be different from his father, in order to define a separate identity and "base" in his family. He was good in science and math—subjects in which his father did not excel—as another way of defining his differences. A constant place in the group gives him a similar kind of defined difference, safety, and predictability. The one chair gives Carl a certain point of view which he has grown to like. The risk of changing seats carries with it the imagined threat of losing his newfound ability to feel and express himself.

Several months later, Carl chose another seat. To everyone's surprise, he noted:

> I feel like it's time to take a look at things from a different perspective.

Another group member, Paul, experimented with a new behavior that was inconsistent with his beliefs about commitment.

> Paul suffered great distress as Tony got up and walked out of the meeting. Paul maintained that Tony had broken the ground rules. Members were to give the group high importance, show up and not leave. Tony's departure and the therapist's refusal to run after him jolted Paul.

Paul could imagine only two alternatives to disagreeing—violence or leaving the group forever. Tony was gone and he would not be back. Tony's leaving reminded Paul of his father, who abruptly blew up and stormed out of the house. Nothing could ever be talked about or resolved.

At the next meeting, the therapist reported to the group that Paul had called to say he would be absent because of a "conflicting appointment." With a good deal of affection, group members joked that Paul wasn't coming back, although they suspected he was trying something new. Paul returned and, over the next few weeks, explored the impact of his decision to miss a group:

> I was certain I would never be back, if I once decided not to come. Commitment is forever. It's all-or-none. But that's not what happened. I still felt like a member of the group and I had no trouble coming back.

Trying this new behavior had a monumental impact in allowing him to explore his deepest beliefs related to attachment and autonomy. Paul longed for a close, committed relationship, but felt that having one meant losing himself. Being able to choose to miss a group meeting opened up the possibility of a wider range of interactions within a relationship that would still signify commitment.

A final example of behavioral change related to expansion involves the issue of dress, a common arena for symbolic expression about one's beliefs and identity. Ken often came to group in a suit and tie, which others saw as a statement that he was closed, arrogant, and superior. Will, however, longed to be able to don a suit and tie—to him, the symbol of becoming a man—and not lose sight of his feelings. One day he arrived at group wearing a suit, tie, and tennis shoes. He decided to "try it on," to see what it felt like. For much of the meeting he was guarded, still, and wary. He explained that he was quite anxious and uncomfortable, because he was afraid he would lose his "feeling side," the hard-won openness to himself and others that proved to him he wasn't shut down like his father.

Losing his "feeling side" was not the only threat. Will needed to monitor himself constantly, to make sure he wasn't closing down *or* opening up too much! Wearing a suit and tie equaled becoming a man, which equaled becoming drunk, violent, and emotionally inaccessible. At the end of the meeting, he sighed, pleased that he had survived. He noted that the tennis shoes were a concrete reminder that he still had feelings, in case he forgot.

Cognitive Expansion Cognition refers to the way we see things—how much we see and what we see. It involves what we take in (perception) and how we explain what we take in (thinking and reasoning). We saw cognition at work in the behavioral expansion examples, as ACAs explored the deep beliefs that kept them from trying new behaviors. Paul had very restrictive ideas about commitment, and Will believed that becoming a man equaled being out-of-control. These ACAs restricted themselves behaviorally and symbolically (in the way they dressed), to match their deep beliefs.

To tell a different story means to challenge perception and thinking. ACAs must dig within themselves to understand what their deepest beliefs are, then challenge the validity of those beliefs, and, finally, give new meaning to the past and present. One of the ways this occurs is through dreams, which often play an important role in the loosening of controls.

After many weeks of difficult interactions in the group, with members feeling stuck and unequal in the "pace" of their uncovering work, several reported dreams.

> In Brent's dream, he was being pushed and challenged by the group about his "surface" responses and his denial of any feelings. He finally told others to shut up and leave him alone. To his amazement, they did and he began to cry. He was astounded that he could defend himself and that others would listen to him.

After Brent related the dream, he told members how relieved he was to know that, deep down, he does feel. The content of his dreams—the criticism of others and his ability to protect himself—illuminated the source of his fears in the group. He could see that he felt defenseless in the face of hostility and criticism from others. Following this dream, he began a more open exploration of memories, linking the chronic threat of danger in childhood to his sense of ever present danger in the group. When he saw the parallel, he could separate the two experiences, testing the present situation to see whether the threat of danger was warranted.

The themes of belonging and safety are also related to expansion and the loosening of controls. Following weeks of struggle in the group, several members reported dreams.

> Wendy: I was huddled up in a corner freezing in the snow. Then it slowly changed to mud.

> Paula: I've been afraid to read the summary because I was afraid it would be full of negative judgments. I did read it and saw it was neutral. Then I dreamed I wrote my own summary and reported it to the group. I was amazed that I could write my own view of what happened here.

> A newer member (chuckling): I'm not there yet. I dreamed I was swallowed up in a tornado the night before the group.

Dreams are also a gauge of how progress is defined by each person. In group interactions, Katie frequently focused on her feelings of powerlessness and helplessness, in the face of others' dominance and control. To be involved with others, especially to allow oneself to rely on others, was equal to ensuring destruction. After several years in group, Katie reported the following dreams:

> I was riding in a car, with my mother driving. She was drunk and missed a turn. I yelled at her to pull over so I could take over. This was a sign to me that I have more control than I think and I can take care of myself when I'm involved with others.

> In another dream, my husband was drinking and wanted my attention. I simply told him I was busy and would pay attention when I was ready. Can you imagine? I really am improving in my ability not to get caught up in taking care of others.

Emotional Expansion Emotion is feeling—technically, affect. This is the "rumble in the stomach," the body sensation that, when permissible, will be known and experienced as joy, sorrow, hatred, anger, love, laughter, or grief, to name only a few emotions. Most ACAs are afraid of feeling in the present, because it signals being out-of-control, and most couldn't feel in the past. Feeling wasn't permitted, or, if it was, it couldn't be named because reality couldn't be named. In ongoing recovery, ACAs experience, name, and connect deep feelings to the past and present.

Frank never dreamed and never felt, and was frequently amazed at the others' capacity for emotion. After many months in group, when Frank said he had a dream, everyone cheered. He gave details:

> I saw my father as helpless, embraced him and cried. It was at an earlier time in my life. I woke up and had all the feelings I must have felt back then. I felt like I belonged to the group, finally, and that there really is a depth of feeling I have absolutely no conscious access to.

Sometimes dreams herald a shift in feeling that's on the way; they're like a preview that prepares the individual for the change and the outcome. In one group, members talked about anger abstractly for several weeks, accenting their fear of it in themselves and others. Matthew then related a dream:

> I was participating in a boxing match that was restricted by a screen between the fighters, with only a small opening through which the hands could go.

Group members chuckled at the image and the external conditions of control necessary for experimenting with greater feeling. Later, Matthew gingerly challenged another member. He and others recognized he was trying out his "boxing" in the group.

Feeling is frightening and not necessarily welcomed. After Peg began to feel anger and sorrow, others spoke about the pain involved in changing. They envied her and, at the same time, felt embarrassed watching her. Peg wondered:

> How can this be progress? It seems like going backward. I can intellectually see that growth requires expanding the range of what I feel, but it also feels horribly out-of-control and awful.

Another member added:

> It reminds me of the way my parents looked when they were drunk. They would yell and scream and then cry, slobbering about how sorry they were. As far as I was concerned, there was too much feeling in my home and none of what counted.

TREATMENT: THE CHALLENGE OF DEFENSES

Expansion in behavior, cognition, and feeling can't take place beyond a certain level, unless denial, control, all-or-none thinking, and assumption of responsibility, the attentional and rational gatekeepers, are directly challenged. The first move is toward the idea of a middle ground, the grays. Finding a middle position is often the main subject of the working group in ongoing recovery. Eventually, ACAs get past the gatekeepers and are permitted to roam deeper behavioral, thinking, and feeling levels. The gatekeeper defenses are formidable. Let's explore how the process of expansion gets past them.

Denial   In recovery, ACAs no longer deny that a parent was or is alcoholic, but they may still deny much of the reality. They may not yet comprehend the meaning that they attributed to their childhood experience, and they may claim that they have no feelings about much of what happened.

Or, they may recognize meaning and feeling, but see them as "split off," almost belonging to someone else. This someone else is wearing their skin, but may have the role of an observer, or an "acter-outer"—someone who does it and says it, but is clearly "not me." One group talked about this notion of "splits." As they discussed it, they had the experience of bridging their own rigid controls and denial in the group, giving themselves a "middle ground."

> Members recognized that there was an unusual feel to the meeting today. They were exploring new territory, revealing new information, and testing the impact. In the gingerly, tentative process of revelation, members glimpsed a middle ground they could only imagine previously. A few weeks later, Will reported that he had done an amazing thing: "I empathized with a colleague. It felt good to me and phony. But it opened up our discussion. Then I talked about feeling like he did, something I'd always denied. More than that, I'd always felt condescending toward him. Then I got scared. I began to worry about whether I could control the degree of intimacy. Would I be able to stop him from talking or revealing too much?"

Listening to this, Ken, whose absence of feeling was a source of chronic irritation to others, noted:

I always thought my feelings were in my head and that's what I'd describe. Now I know my sweaty palms and the rumbling in my stomach are pertinent to what I'm feeling. But will they come out like a volcano?

Control   Here come the nasty intruder again! The issue of control is a constant through the entire process of recovery. It's more than a defensive maneuver; it's the hub of the wheel around which the process of expansion in recovery takes place.

The threat of loss of control and the threat of expansion are linked to the spontaneity of feelings and the range of behavior. Brad reported with amazement a deep, ongoing sense of fear on behalf of his cat:

I am constantly watching, to make sure my cat doesn't get out of the house. I'm certain something terrible will happen if she wanders out.

Prodded by others, Brad drew a parallel to his own sense of fear in the group:

Yea, I guess I'm my cat. I really am frightened in here. I'm afraid to let my feelings out "baldly," just as they are, without first having a conceptual framework to explain them. I can't risk experiencing an unknown feeling because something bad will happen.

The need for a "conceptual framework" is a common theme. It is often expressed as a wish for rules or for a map that will chart the course for uncovering. The "rules" or "map" provide a false reassurance that nothing surprising or out-of-control will emerge. This illusion of security quickly vanishes, as the group deepens its uncovering process and members experience anxiety. The lack of a rule or an explanation alerts members to the reality of unknown feelings and memories yet to be recalled:

There's a dark pit down there that seems bottomless. I know I have to look, but I resist. For the time being, I need to stay on top and scan it with a flashlight.

The prospect of opening the "pit," or the "black hole," is recognized by many as the core of their work in group. Yet, they must continue to reassure themselves of their ultimate control. Despite the strength of defenses developed to cope, the slightest hint of feeling or slip toward the "pit" feels like a total loss of control.

The possibility of loss of control over the uncovering process is also expressed in discussions of "pace" in the group. One member complains:

> The pace of things has been too intense in here over the last several weeks. It feels spontaneous, frightening, and out-of-control. Suddenly, the group reminds me of my family, and I am overwhelmed by a sense that something could go wrong at any moment.

Group members also focus on control interpersonally. They are terrified of being controlled by others, yet need to be able to realistically set limits with others. This limit setting is really the middle ground; it allows the ACA to maintain autonomy and legitimate boundaries, without having to manipulate others in order to control them.

Joe showed us his need to set limits, and asked others not to try to "fix" him, in case anyone had an urge to jump in:

> I realize that I need to feel rotten today and the group needs to let me, without getting into a dispute or attempting to convince me that I'm really a good person.

His request engendered in others fear of loss of control. Several members spoke about feeling very depressed and bad about themselves today. Others refrained from challenging Joe, and the group "hung" in an atmosphere of depression. Jack spoke about his difficulty in resisting the pull to cheer everyone up:

> It's hard to sit still. I run the risk of feeling just as bad and depressed as everyone else, because I identify and understand so readily. It reminds me of being around my depressed, drunken mother. If I couldn't fix it up, I was always in danger of getting dragged in.

All-or-None Thinking   The issue of a middle ground, a gray zone, reappears continually in the interactions of an ongoing group. It arises in relation to the expansion of thinking and in the emergence of feelings. Bonnie, long frightened about revealing herself, sighed:

The act of talking seems out-of-control. I found myself very open with dinner guests, and wondered why I was revealing so much. I watched in amazement because it felt so out-of-control. As soon as I open my mouth, I feel like my words and voice are running away with me and I can't stop them. I'm either silent, or I create devastation by the wrath of my words.

Bonnie had difficulty with talking, because she felt deeply and intensely angry. As she heard herself become engaged with others, she became frightened and suddenly on guard, lest her deep rage and "venom" escape. It was all-or-none, in Bonnie's view.

Ken, who continued to be challenged by the group about his underreaction and his minimal range of response, had a similar problem. He was afraid of being like his mother, who manipulated people by wearing different "faces" to achieve her ends, and who was frequently "out-of-control." Ken's narrow range of feeling and his lack of responsiveness to others reflected his protection against a double threat: manipulation by someone else, and being manipulative and out-of-control himself.

Ken lived a rigid, vigilant existence and had a narrow band of perception, feeling, and roles available to him. Life seemed like a tightrope: he had to negotiate the rope with excruciating care, a small step at a time; the threat of total destruction loomed large, waiting for one false move. There was no room for experimentation or for widening the range of his moves. His tightrope required precision and a watchful stance toward the world. As Ken became more and more aware of his restricted range of interaction, he began to take broader steps in the group, to feel a little more, and to entertain the notion that things were not "all right" or "all wrong." Later, he mused:

The group has given me a net so I can risk falling and it won't be the end of the world.

The challenge of the all-or-none defensive frame also occurs in relation to role or structure, inside the group and out.

Bonnie had always achieved a strong sense of identity, well-being, and purpose as a helping professional. But she also found herself more and more limited in making autonomous decisions and in career advancement. After much deliberation and anxiety, she decided to give up her profession: "My profession has given me a positive structure and a good sense of myself, but it's also grown very limiting. In letting go of this security, I am opening myself to unknown feelings and a new view of myself. I feel like it's time to be a 'clumsy adolescent,' exploring myself and the world within the safety of a supportive family—this group."

Over several months in the group, she struggled to hold on to her new, more vulnerable, sense of herself as an adolescent. But it was hard:

I feel hurt to see Paula be insightful, because that was my role in here for so long. But as the group observer I paid a price, because I never felt like I was taking care of my own needs. I got to be "right" and "strong" by helping others and not revealing myself. I hope I'll be able to go back and forth, helping and being helped, but so far it's one or the other. I'm more involved with my own feelings and the parts of myself I don't like. I also feel more confused and inarticulate. For now, I feel totally on the "none" side of the equation. I have to remind myself that these changes are important for me and that I'm making progress, because it feels like I've lost a great deal.

Bonnie joined the group because she was terribly concerned about her inability to tolerate an intimate, committed relationship with a man. She had achieved a sense of stability by constructing a narrow environment in which she could always determine what was "right." She longed for more, but always became anxious and depressed at the possibility of a closer relationship. Bonnie became aware of her need for control, and the limits of the narrow world she had constructed, when she joined a singles group:

It's wonderful and awful. I have lost my "mooring" and my identity by getting out of my usual structure. I am attracted to a man and have let myself feel dependent on him, even though I am constantly scared to death. This is an amazing experience. I realize I want to let myself be more dependent and give up control, but I fear I'll be hurt. I am opening up many feelings I haven't had in my adult life because I've so carefully constructed my environment. I have to get away from my careful control, to realize how frightened I am. I've been having a lot of nightmares as well, and recognize I was terrified as a child, something I am never aware of as an adult. Right now, I keep grappling with my belief that I can't do this in small bites. I keep expecting to blow up in front of myself.

Several years later, Bonnie showed how the shift in the all-or-none position occurs, when she reflected on the changes she had made:

It's incredible that I could tolerate living with someone, much less learn to deal with his unpredictability, mood changes, wishes, and needs. I feel naked, establishing a new identity for myself. It's like I've opened up the half of me I always had to deny. The world seems bigger and richer, though still scary.

Assumption of Responsibility   The final defensive trait that is challenged in ongoing recovery is the inappropriate, sometimes all-consuming, assumption of responsibility for everything and everybody. As ACAs question the validity of this premise, they come face-to-face with the purposes it served. Underneath a facade of responsibility, many individuals feel unworthy, deeply bad, and unlovable. Being responsible is an apologetic presentation of one-self to the world, a way of not being rejected out-of-hand. The ACA says in essence:

Whatever bad happens, I caused it and I will take the blame, so don't reject me.

If something good occurs, it's luck or somebody else's skill or genius. The ACA may feel diminished in the company of another's success.

The assumption of responsibility may also permit success. Some ACAs deal with their tremendous sense of survivor guilt, and with the reality of breaking unhealthy family ties, by maintaining a deep belief in responsibility. In this way, they can move ahead but not abandon the tie to first families who are still suffering and who would be left behind by the ACAs' relinquishment of blame and duty. In essence, these ACAs continue to believe:

If I feel responsible, I won't be guilty of the crime of abandonment, yet I can go after some of what I want, too.

Shirley put off joining a group for ACAs for a long time, because she believed that doing so would only make her responsible for everybody in the group and even more on-call to her first family. She had achieved a stable distance by forcing herself not to think about the family too much. When she did, she felt horrible and had to compulsively reach for the phone, to make sure they were OK. As Shirley progressed, she became more and more able and willing to question her feelings of responsibility. As she did so, she began to read more about ACAs and to attend Al-Anon—seemingly small, but actually major, steps out of her narrow range of belief. She reported to the group:

> I never could read anything or listen to others in meetings, because the more I learned the more I felt responsible for everyone. To inch out into the world always meant a greater loss of myself. I am finding very slowly that I can share my own experiences more fully, and those of friends, without having to feel responsible.

In a group that was deepening the level and intensity of its work and expanding its range, members finally agreed that they were all feeling responsible for Mike, who could not empathize. Members felt they had to get Mike moving with them, or they would feel too threatened and vulnerable to continue their own exploration. Finally, one exasperated member angrily spoke up:

> It's difficult for us to continue to dig when you refuse to feel, and deny that you could feel any pain at all. Why are you here? The experience of being in group has been painful. I've reopened memories and feelings from childhood—things I couldn't feel or know, growing up in a disturbed family. I was so controlled and responsible for everyone else, my emotions were unavailable. It's OK with me if you can't empathize with what I'm feeling, but it's not OK that you feel superior because of it. I grew up with that. I don't need it here, and I'm sick of trying to get you to change so it will be safe for me.

In the process of ongoing recovery, most ACAs will deal with deep feelings of all kinds—joy, sorrow, anger, grief. They are all difficult, but frequently anger looms as the most dangerous. Feeling responsible keeps this nasty emotion at bay, or at least directs it

back at the self. If everything is "my fault," then "I've only myself to
be angry at."

Shifting the target of anger from the inside to the outside is
frightening. Initially, the ACA may simply reverse unhealthy patterns. ACAs who are no longer going to blame themselves for everything will blame their parents instead. This reversal is directed by
a strong all-or-none frame. The ACA moves from being the bad kid
to being the good one. Eventually, this polarity will be mediated by
the development of a gray zone, after the ACA sorts out what was
good and what was not good about parents and about themselves.
This capacity to contain goods and bads at the same time doesn't
come until the defensive traits are challenged.

The ACA's repudiation of responsibility may first come as an
attack, a refusal to empathize, or a direct, forceful shove at others
who might need an ear or active help. On first glance, such a stance
is likely to be interpreted as selfish by everyone, including the ACA.
What kind of progress is this? By ongoing recovery, group members cheer the ACA's refusal to be pulled in, manipulated, or controlled by others' inappropriate expectations or needs. The ACA
can listen to others more easily *and* be supportive, because the line
has been drawn that protects the ACA against the total loss of self.
Sherri, quiet for months, finally "let the group have it":

> I am angry at all of you and don't want to help you in any way. When
> is it my turn? You talk about your feelings and your needs, and I sit
> here and boil. I have to sit on my hands not to jump in and take over
> to fix you. I don't feel sympathetic. I just want to shut you up and tell
> you to stop complaining. Isn't this amazing? What I really want is to
> have feelings and needs too, and I hate you all because you can.

As Sherri let herself dump on the group, she smiled, clearly
relishing her newfound ability to express herself. Yet, she cautiously wondered whether everyone would now hate her, because
she didn't care about them *and* because she was breaking her part
of the "relationship bargain." Sherri now could see that to be involved with others automatically meant that she had to be responsible for them and herself. There was no equality, and no sharing of
responsibility.

For a time, Sherri maintained her anger, straight-arming the
group to hold them off. Then she was able to relax her stance and

began to experience the gray of mature relationship: both give, and both get.

As the ACA pokes at the structure of defensive traits, things get better. But not without anxiety, as we've seen. Over time, individuals look back and, in amazement, find they've loosened up and expanded their horizons in every domain. They see, think, and feel in much less rigid ways, and are more tolerant and forgiving of others. Life and relationships are no longer adversarial.

Nobody wakes up one day to find this new, strong base magically in place. It gets there only through hard work, which is what recovery is all about. Let's conclude our journey through recovery by reviewing what it's all about.

VI

Summing Up and Moving On

15

What Is Progress? Growing Up, Growing Out, and Coming Home

PROGRESS

Prior to treatment, and many times during treatment, individuals wonder what it is all about, what kinds of changes are possible, and how they will know when they are finished. Initially, ACAs enter treatment with an idealized sense of what they want for themselves and from others. Often, they think of treatment as a reversal of everything bad, a magical transformation of painful memories and experiences into a live-happily-ever-after scenario. Cinderella meets her Prince; the Little Match Girl is rescued. This view of recovery is not only idealized, but unrealistic. It maintains the picture of the ACA as a victim who will triumph in the end, through rescue.

The ACA was indeed a victim to everything about parental alcoholism, but recovery is not a rescue, even though it may feel that way whenever support, understanding, and acceptance are offered.

What is so painfully difficult is to begin to appreciate, and then face head-on, the reality that behaviors, beliefs, values, and attitudes have been developed that have actively prevented any movement out of the victim position. To survive and cope with the alcoholic family, ACAs learned unhealthy views about themselves and the world that cannot simply be tossed aside, when they no longer serve the ACA well.

Because of the strength of defenses, the ACA entering recovery initially conceives of change in an all-or-none fashion, equating progress with simple reversal of past beliefs and behaviors. Individuals hope to feel safe instead of frightened, anxious, and unsafe; good instead of bad. They expect to be able to have needs instead of taking care of others' needs; to have a close, loving relationship with another who is responsive to those needs; to feel in control; to have feelings that are comprehensible and manageable; to make order out of chaos; quite simply, to not feel bad anymore. Hard work and time in treatment are needed, to recognize and comprehend the depth and complexity of the reconstruction and new construction processes. The foundation for significant change that they will form is quite different from feeling good instead of bad.

ACAs begin to *really* understand the concepts of personal responsibility and "incremental risk" when they realize, first, that expansion, challenge of beliefs and defenses, and changes in behavior come from within, and, second, that none of these changes is possible without a safe context that reinforces the new identity as an ACA, the reconstructed reality of the past, and a new understanding of the present.

Deep changes usually do not occur in isolation. They do not come as a "fix" from someone else, and they are not the result of finding the right formula, manual, or how-to guide. Deep change comes from within. For ACAs, the most significant change begins with the acquisition of the ACA identity. It proceeds with the reconstruction process of "making real the past" and the development, from this base, of a separate, healthy sense of self.

Individuals are bound by the attachments, beliefs, and defenses constructed to maintain and survive a pathological family system. Recovery is a developmental process of challenge and separation from these pathological bonds. Initially, the promise of reconstruction, of developmental repair, and, ultimately, of emotional separation is experienced much more as a threat, because it is all-or-none. Growth is equated with isolation and loneliness; the challenge of belief and defenses and the expansion in cognition and feeling carry a fear of abandonment. To step out of the family system, to challenge one's view of what happened then and is happening now, is equal to losing the attachment entirely.

Progress is a funny thing. ACAs often feel more anxious, vulnerable, and guilty as they move *away from* the past. It's hard to feel too great about an improvement that hurts as much as it heals. As individuals struggle to find that middle, gray ground of compromise, life sometimes feels more confused, fuzzy, and uncertain than ever before. The fact that life can be this way is tough to accept.

The uncovering of deep core beliefs is also an uncomfortable part of progress. Sometimes, ACAs straddle a threshold of change, moving back and forth between the "old me" and the "new me." Sara feels poised between two different views of herself.

> Sara said she had an important dream, which helped her make sense of her current feeling of being very split—it is as if she is holding on to two different self-images at the same time. In her dream, two perfect people fall in love. Sara is on the "outside," observing and feeling badly that she can't be perfect herself and therefore will never have a love relationship. Sara survived by seeing herself as someone alone and she cannot alter it now, to be able to perceive herself in a close relationship with someone else. Sara survived by dissociating herself from her family. She could decide that she did not belong and be an outsider by virtue of that decision. "Belonging" always meant the loss of herself. Would she ever be able to have a relationship where these truths would no longer hold?

In ongoing recovery, ACAs struggle with integrating complexities and with giving up their idealized hope of a magical "cure" or a new family that will be perfect. Instead, they experiment with a broader range of feelings, beliefs, and behaviors that includes the ability to tolerate uncertainty, grays, and even some contradiction in one's relationship with oneself and in relationships with others. "Interdependent" relationship becomes a viable concept.

As they stick with the process, but see no clear results, group members often ask themselves, "What is progress?" Most agree that change sneaks up on them. Suddenly, they realize that they are not feeling the same or seeing things in the old, familiar, distorted ways. They are baffled as to how they got there. Instead of telling newcomers what to do in A-B-C fashion, they say it's more uncertain. They describe how they made a commitment and then settled in to revise their whole view of their life and their world. "You've got to allow for unknowns and surprise," they say, "or you'll simply control the 'rewrite' of your own history." "Letting go" is impossible to contemplate, or to *will* to happen, but it happens. ACAs do settle in with friends, sometimes with lovers and family, with self-help support groups and therapy. They find a net for what is, in the beginning, a dangerous tightrope venture.

Progress shows up in subtle ways, at first; for a while, the ACA feels like two different people. Openness to others and a lack of defensiveness tell ACAs that they are at ease with themselves and the world. They don't have to have all the right answers, and they can be surprised. They can also be curious, perhaps for the first time; it's OK to look, to sniff, and to wonder about things. The ACA is often astounded at this taste of freedom. Group members, saying goodbye to a long-time member, thought about all of these things.

> When Charlie arrived, he said it was important to him to say goodbye to everybody in person. It was also extremely difficult. He noted that, in the past, he would have decided to go and then left immediately, closing the door on all feelings and everything left behind. This time, because of what he's learned in the group, he decided to allow himself to feel whatever it was that came up. He would stay, say goodbye, and listen to what others had to say to him.

In starting this Part, we briefly explored recovery as a developmental process of "growing up, growing out, and coming home." Let's build on that analogy now, to encompass the ACA's growth and change. Let's look at what these tasks mean, in the context of treatment.

GROWING UP

In undertaking the process of recovery in a therapy group, in individual therapy, or in a self-help, 12-step program (or in all three), ACAs begin a process of breaking denial, then reconstructing a new family story based on the reality of parental alcoholism, and finally separating from attachments that are often very primitive. These relationships are still bound by the shared beliefs, role reversal, and identity formation required to maintain the family system. Many adults specify a desire to separate from the family of origin as their key reason for seeking treatment.

"Growing up" involves going back to childhood, remembering what happened, and challenging the beliefs and behaviors adopted to cope. It means intensifying an emotional bond with the first family that may have been helpfully muted by adulthood and enforced distance. Many ACAs do not understand the importance of awakening the past and purposely intensifying the tie to parents, in order to achieve the specific goal of later emotional separation—this time from a much healthier base. In "growing up," the ACA will write a new story and create a new family album, now saying "what it was like." This rewrite of reality is the beginning of truth-telling. The ACA focuses on the environment and begins to explore and question the patterns of the family system as well.

"Growing up" also involves forming a new attachment to the therapy group, the therapist, the ACA or Al-Anon 12-step group, a sponsor, or the principles of ACA or Al-Anon. This bond might also include a church affiliation or some other kind of support that provides the security or net that enables ACAs to challenge their unhealthy bond to first families.

The defensive traits are still alive and well, providing the continuing false security necessary to undertake this process at all, but also framing the early work of recovery.

"Growing up" is issue-oriented: trust, safety, and dependency are often central. Many ACAs struggle with the issue of control—whom or what can they trust or depend on—and frequently translate the idea and the need to another person.

> Jack was quiet and withdrawn for several weeks. Finally he noted how upset and devastated he had been by an interaction with Jess a few weeks back. "Jess and I had a 'special' conversation in the parking lot after the meeting. I felt honored and privileged by his confiding in me. But, the next week, Jess couldn't remember the details of the conversation and clearly did not have the same depth of involvement that I had. I was so disappointed, because I thought it was really special. Jess's failure to remember reminded me so much of my alcoholic father. I was repeatedly disappointed in my hopes of what my father could give me or be for me."

Another group member noted his reaction:

> I feel humiliated on your behalf, Jack. You are trying so hard to get a
> reaction, but nothing comes. Your behavior reminds me of the way I
> throw myself at people who can give me nothing.

A new member had a unique sense of safety.

> Brent always remained quiet until Sherri arrived, had spoken, or in-
> vited Brent to speak. It became clear to him that, without Sherri, the
> group was dangerous and he could not participate. In examining this
> reality, he noted: "I've always been an introvert, going through life in
> a brown paper wrapper. Now I feel it's possible for me to emerge, to be
> seen by myself and by others. But not unless Sherri is here."

Relinquishment of control usually signifies total dependence
on another human being, which is terrifying. Thus, the sense of personal control, of being "in charge" of oneself and one's life, is often
relentlessly grasped and defended. The crux of many severe interpersonal problems rests on this very issue. Individuals view the
relinquishment or lessening of their need for control and for the
all-or-none view as a submission that will result in annihilation or
harm to themselves.

Control and a Higher Power   The concept of an inanimate higher
power to whom control is relinquished provides the means to move
beyond polarized interpersonal struggles. For most people, the
idea of a higher power is something religious; indeed, many members of 12-step programs refer to their higher power as God. Many
people balk, reaffirming their belief in their own control as op-
posed to the perceived need to adopt religious beliefs. Most people
need a long time in recovery, to become comfortable with the
concept and the language and to actively construct a higher power.

Belief in a higher power solves a number of interpersonal
dilemmas. It interrupts the all-or-none framework for viewing relationships, by elevating the issues of trust, safety, dependence, and
control to an abstract level. Instead of expecting other people to
meet these needs, the ACA shifts that expectation away from the
human realm. Individuals develop a submissive, deferent sense of
self in relation to a greater-than-the-self power that is defined by

the individual. Paradoxically, ACAs maintain control of constructing their higher power while relinquishing control to it at the same time.

By constructing a power greater than the self and then vesting one's dependency needs in that abstract entity, individuals are frequently able to see themselves as equal to others and to detach from familiar but unhealthy dependent or codependent relationships. As one ACA put it:

> By putting all my deepest needs somewhere else, off of my boyfriend, I could see him so much differently. He seemed benign all of a sudden, not out to get me or to withhold his care from me, which is how I felt for a long time. I'm beginning to grasp that love does not mean total care from your partner.

The tendency to form destructive dependency relationships is always a threat, when primitive longings reemerge through the course of treatment and ongoing recovery after treatment. These early wishes are especially strong in this "growing up" phase, when ACAs go back emotionally to childhood. Yet, these same longings are probably quite normal for all of us. Who hasn't wished for a magic "cure" or a feeling of total care and comfort offered by another? One of the most important and gratifying experiences for members of 12-step programs is the sense of being "embraced" by the group. It is an experience of being held safely and nourished by other recovering individuals or simply by the context of the meeting. Vesting these deep longings in an inanimate higher power provides a resolution to what may have seemed an unresolvable, win-lose situation:

> I am either alone, totally dependent on myself, or I am lost—swallowed up and ultimately destroyed by depending on another.

In treatment, issues of spirituality and ideas of God are often discussed in relation to themes of trust, attachment, or dependency. Shirley found it hard to trust a deity:

> I want to believe in a loving God, but if I do, I risk feeling bewildered and hurt, like a picture of a Hiroshima child. I would like to trust in God and think that God meant well for me, that I could expect not to be hurt. But I always anticipate a trick instead. I can't make sense of

what happened to me as a child and believe in a loving God at the same time.

A fundamentally inherent concept or experience of God is often uncovered in treatment. Integrating the contradictory elements of her experience with "God" was a central feature of recovery for Ellen:

> I remember way back—I must have been seven or eight—to the horror of my family. I can see an image of fear, doom, and despair, as I waited for the next round of violence. Then came the sexual abuse. I can remember "going away," simply leaving that place and reassuring myself that God would take care of me. I think that saved me. I really did believe there was something bigger, kinder, and more well-meaning than my family. I still believe that, or rather, want to believe that, but I can't let go and really experience the safety I know would come with trusting.

What happens to people who do not believe in God, or who reject membership in a self-help group because they equate affiliation with a requirement to adopt religious beliefs? The central core that sustains any individual in ongoing recovery is relinquishment of a belief in self-power, a false belief in one's ability to control oneself *and* another. A belief in loss of control is central to the individual's new identity as the child of an alcoholic. People who have difficulty constructing a belief in a higher power may be advised, like the alcoholic in A.A., to remove themselves from a self-centered orientation; to do so, they must acknowledge a power greater than the self. For many, it is less difficult to accept the notion of universality—a "higher order" to the universe that is outside of one's personal control or authority—than it is to adopt specific religious beliefs or language.

Initially, there are alternatives for those who continue to struggle with what appears to be the religious bias of 12-step groups. Many fear that membership, like organized religion, carries an already defined conception of God, which must be accepted. Newcomers often are reassured when they find that the only higher power they must believe in will come from inside them. What a baffling paradox at first!

Individuals in A.A. or Al-Anon are encouraged to put their trust in the power of the group and the established traditions of the group's conscience (*not* the individuals within the group). The function, not the form, of the relinquishment of self-power is important.

Ironically, the pull to believe in the power of self results in a return to an unhealthy position. The ACA is caught between a reliance on self, which gives a sense of superiority, and opposite feelings of need, inadequacy, and inferiority during a desperate search to find a "higher power," a caretaker, in another person. Constructing a belief in an abstract power greater than the self establishes equality among individuals. Dependency needs are legitimized and vested outside the self or others.

GROWING OUT

The break in denial, acquisition of the label ACA, and beginning treatment imply a move away from home, away from the unhealthy tie to parents and first families. Problems in the early bonds of attachment within the family, including role reversal, made "growing out" a difficult or impossible task, because the child perceived that its independence would ensure parental destruction. By assuming responsibility for whatever was occurring or not occurring in the home, children solidify unhealthy emotional ties to their families of origin. During the course of treatment and recovery, ACAs must face repeatedly intense feelings of guilt for leaving the still sick family behind. Primitive ties maintained long into adulthood interfere with the establishment of new, mature, primary families. A hope of fixing the needy parent may continue, or a wish that the "fixed" parent will take care of the now grown but still needy "adult child." Fears of being a parent, or becoming a parent oneself, may activate these conflicts, forcing the individual to seek help.

"Growing out" involves the development of a healthy sense of self. Issues of attachment, dependence/interdependence, boundaries, limits, modeling, and identity formation are at the hub of this entire process. Individuals begin to recognize, first intuitively and, later, quite concretely, that they indeed are arrested in their development. By holding off becoming an adult, they are warding off self-destruction or harm to others that they believe would accompany their own parenting, if they were to actively identify with destructive parental figures.

The process of recovery includes breaking down the barriers to identification that were established in the interests of survival. Individuals must begin to incorporate what was warded off, search for pockets of healthier parental behavior or belief, or reinterpret actual parental behavior and belief from a new perspective. Sue found that memories could still intrude.

> Sue's parents are moving to a smaller house and have given away many pieces of furniture to their children. Sue chose a special rocker she liked as a child but became anxious as she brought it home. "It's sitting in the middle of the floor in a 'decontaminant' phase. There are so many painful memories attached that I'm not yet ready to incorporate the rocker as part of me in my home."

Carla registered her amazement:

> I don't see why you'd even want it! Get rid of it!

Sue replied:

> I'm looking for ways to symbolically incorporate my family into my life in some kind of neutral way, rather than categorically rejecting everything about them.

Another member was looking for "healthy pockets."

> Alice notes that her new way of thinking magnifies her separateness from her family. Yet, she is beginning to be able to feel the depth of her need for her mother. "I am looking for back roads to connect with her—for ways not to be different or separate that will not kill me."

Several other members had made progress in "growing out." Tony's perspective had changed:

> My father believed that life is shit—it will all come out rotten. I didn't want that attitude, but I became the family problem anyway. I realize now—I can't change his attitude or view of life, but I can change my interpretation.

Drew made progress over the course of several years in group. In early recovery, he recoiled from group discussions about maturity, success, and adult partnerships. He maintained his belief that being alone was the only path possible for safety and integrity, even if the price was loneliness:

> You know what success is? You know what relationships are all about? I can remember driving to the club in my father's brand new shiny Lincoln, with my mother propped up beside him so she wouldn't pass out on the way. That's what being an adult is. They were like mannequins—propped up and smiling for the world.

Several years later, Drew reported a different sense of being an adult.

> On a recent visit home, Drew was quite pleased because he was able to tolerate being with his parents without becoming overly anxious or getting hooked into old patterns and responses. He was even able to be in a restaurant and not feel humiliated on behalf of his father. He recognized for the first time that he is a different person and he is not behaving badly himself.

Continuing to recognize and accept the reality of parental alcoholism is also a part of "growing out." ACAs often have to remind themselves that their vigilance is now more important than ever— a letdown, because they had hoped they could relinquish their guarded stance. The pressure from the family to deny and to "see" reality in a distorted fashion continues, and they must actively resist it. Group members revealed strategies they have developed to cope with a family environment and system that do not change.

> Members discussed the notion that contact with parents is all-or-none. Several said it is not possible to maintain one's independent identity and positive feelings about themselves and have any contact at all. Carla reminds herself that she has a "difficult parent" and that's the way it is. This helps her remember that she will come out the other side still intact. The loss of herself is always a great threat.
>
> Jack notes that he used to think of himself as a "visiting psychologist" when he came home, in order to get enough distance.
>
> Group members agree it is hard to feel good about themselves, because it requires a letdown in vigilance. They still need to be watchful and vigilant, lest a parent intrude.

The issue of modeling is critically important to ultimate separation. Individuals recognize and express their deepest and clearest awareness: healthy, autonomous development does not take place in a vacuum. Many report having looked for models in teachers, ministers, the parents of friends, or literary and film characters. ACAs need guidance in becoming an adult emotionally. They may have determined many times previously that they would not replicate the patterns of their parents, only to find they could not will themselves to be different and to create new patterns.

Therapist modeling is an extremely important issue throughout the course of group. Several members, always very anxious about feeling or expressing anger, were able to begin to explore these feelings in themselves, following the group's confrontation of the therapist:

> The whole time we were challenging you, I expected you would get angry and tell us our view was not correct. You would tell us that you know what is real and that it is not OK to disagree with you or even see things differently.

> I was so relieved when you were able to accept our criticism and not retaliate. You seemed to survive and not be diminished by accepting the reality of your error. I need to learn how to do that. And I need to learn how to be angry as well.

The therapist is an important model in all kinds of ways, but especially for legitimizing and demonstrating the acceptance and expression of difficult and painful feelings. In the course of a long-term therapy group, the therapist will experience a tremendous range and depth of feeling, in direct response to the reality of what is occurring in the group. It is not appropriate for the therapist to "work through" these feelings in the context of the group (that work belongs in the therapist's own therapy), but it is important that the therapist be emotionally present and responsive. A therapist who doesn't feel or who won't share his or her perceptions and reactions to what is happening feels too much like the defended, emotionally unavailable parents and may well unwittingly reinforce the ACAs' unhealthy beliefs and defenses.

The therapist is human and, like anyone else, is susceptible to bias, vulnerability, and imperfection, which the ACAs will be watching for. ACAs also will be sizing up the therapist's capacity for self-acceptance, humility, and equality with others. Is this someone who has something to model, to teach? Can I allow myself to learn from this person?

Ironically, the written summary provides a peek-hole into the therapist's strengths and weaknesses over the years. One long-time member, saying goodbye to the group, told everyone that she had long ago given up an idealized view of the therapist, which was painful but ultimately very important. After all, how could she continue to see her as perfect, when she routinely made mistakes in writing the summary? Group members laughed, but Peggy continued, with emotion:

> It may sound silly, but one of the most valuable lessons I've learned in all these years is how to tolerate my own imperfections, how to accept challenge gracefully and be at home with both my strengths and weaknesses. If it's OK for you, I've learned it's OK for me too.

The process of "growing out" includes learning from others alternative ways of behaving and of constructing reality, and then experimenting with those different ways.

> Karen spoke on the subject of "successes." She too is marveling at the different sense of herself she has been having recently. She now has new options, ideas, and even feelings open to her that before she just could not incorporate into her sense of herself. For example: her parents are having an anniversary party and expect her to be there. Up to now, she would have felt that her only option was to go, even though it is a very painful, unsatisfying experience for her. Or, she might have been able to stay away, but only with an excuse. Now she can decide not to go simply because she doesn't want to. Karen is getting a sense of separateness for herself that allows her to consider new options. This sense of being separate also applies to her feelings and her beliefs. She smiled as she said a new "truth" is "creeping up on her." This truth is the reality of her parents' alcoholism. The fact that her father still denies he is alcoholic no longer matters; it is her truth that he was and is. Now she can survive the disparity.

The group moved into a discussion of "What is progress?" and "What is different?" Doug summarized:

> I can now meet my own needs, rather than thinking that others always come first. I can speak up in group and outside, and take the time I

need. I am able to hear the different opinions of others without closing down. I am able to tolerate my wife's withdrawal without going after her or interpreting her need for distance as anger at me. I have made these changes first by recognizing what I am doing, then experimenting with a new behavior or different idea in here, and then transferring these new ways of thinking and being to the outside. It hasn't happened overnight and most changes are subtle. In a way, it's like reversing figure and ground. Shift an old belief a little bit this way or even turn it over, and there's a whole new perception on the other side.

COMING HOME

Individuals actively involved in reconstructing the family history reach a point of readiness to identify and separate. They often have a greater ability to incorporate complexities of the parents and to allow a parental portrait to include more gray. Parents are no longer all bad or all good, any more than the ACA is.

"Coming home" may include a capacity and readiness for acceptance, forgiveness, and perhaps feelings of love for parents that are rekindled and are now possible as part of an integrated, more complex view. "Coming home" may also include confrontation, an active breaking of the attachments and patterns of behavior that bound the individual to the past. ACAs may "announce" their separation by advising parents about their membership in a group for ACAs. Sometimes, such an announcement is the first time a parent's alcoholism has ever been acknowledged. Or, individuals may refuse to participate in denial, or in the distorted logic of the system, by going around it or stepping back from it.

> For many years, Ellen survived by refusing to see herself as like her father in any way. There was nothing positive about him and she had closed the book on him long ago. With progress in her recovery, she became ready to open the book. She made a visit home and interviewed relatives. Returning to the group, she felt a new sense of calm and a new, broader picture of her father.
>
> Ellen said she no longer feels chronically angry with men. She sees this change as part of a cycle of progress occurring over the course of many years of work. She has opened exploration of her father in an attempt to find a deeper portrait of him—beyond his alcoholism and illness—that she can incorporate into her own sense of self. In

talking with relatives, Ellen found that her father had many friends and was noted for his intelligence. Ellen smiled, now able to relate her own keen intellect directly back to him. "I finally have a healthy tie to him, one I can be proud of."

"Coming home" also involves grief. Throughout the process of recovery, the ACA struggles with deep feelings of loss. As we've seen, each step toward health also is felt as a step away from the family, which signifies abandonment and isolation.

Once "home," that is, once stabilized on the firm ground of a much healthier self, the ACA can tolerate seeing and feeling the whole of the past. The ACA can accept what it was like, what happened, and what it is like now, as A.A. and Al-Anon members put it. The individual can accept what was missed growing up and deeply grieve what is now lost: illusions, false beliefs, and self-destructive behaviors that maintained family ties. The ACA also grieves, ironically, for what is won: healthy survival, but at what a price! For most ACAs, developing a healthy self is a bittersweet victory.

For a few individuals, "coming home" may involve a real return to parents who are now sober and engaged in recovery programs themselves. Such an outcome is rare. It is more commonly experienced within a new "family," such as the group, or individual therapy, or the support network of ACA 12-step or Al-Anon programs. The recovery or treatment "family" represents the new haven for safe passage through recovery, and the new beliefs and behaviors that one can always come home to. Warren, in group for five years, "came home" to his real family. Both parents had been involved in A.A. and Al-Anon for years.

> Warren spoke with joy, wonderment, deep relief, and even sorrow. His weekend with his family had been wonderful, beyond his hopes and dreams. His parents were able for the first time to talk about what really happened and what it was really like for all of them during the course of his mother's active alcoholism. He and his family spent the whole visit remembering events, episodes, and the general atmosphere of what it had been like. In essence, the family rewrote their history together, with everyone now incorporating the reality of his mother's alcoholism and what had happened to each of them as a result. Warren said the acknowledgment of the reality of what is was like was profoundly important to him because now he felt like he really had roots.

Another member, who did not have a real recovering family to return to, recognized her formal treatment was over as she mused in group:

> Who will I tell my story to? Who will know what it was like and what happened to me?

She smiled and added:

> I know and that's enough. It's my story now. I have made it real and I have made it mine by coming here. Now I'll take it with me.

Epilogue

What more could be said? What experience, or memory, or dream, still uncharted, could provide a last word of hope? We have covered a virtual lifetime, following ACAs from childhood to all-grown-up, to starting over and growing up again. We've gone back to the past and peeled the onion, layer after layer. We've cried for the truth we always knew and for the loss that comes with making it real.

What hope is there for ACAs still unnamed and unknown? What encouragement might be given to ACAs who are just starting and to those struggling through the recovery process? John, long years into recovery, sums up their goal:

> There I was, sitting calmly, sorrowfully, amid the bones. Just skeleton remains. I was going nowhere. In this dream, I was stationed underground, in the grave, a sentry and a partner. This was my company, my life, my mission—to watch over the bones.
>
> And then slowly, but quite purposefully, I got up. I walked away and climbed out of the grave, into the sun and the wide expanse of the world that was there waiting for me. I turned one last time to say good-bye. The vigil of the bones was over.

References

Ackerman, Nathan W. (1956). "Interlocking Pathology in Family Relationships." *In Changing Concepts of Psychoanalytic Medicine.* New York: Grune and Stratton.

Alcoholics Anonymous. (1955) New York: AA World Services.

Bacon, Seldon. (1945). "Excessive Drinking and the Family." In *Alcohol, Science and Society.* New Haven: Quarterly Journal of Studies on Alcohol (special issue).

Beck, Aaron, and Gary Emery. (1985). *Anxiety Disorders and Phobias.* New York: Basic Books.

Beletsis, Susan, and Stephanie Brown. (1981). "A Developmental Framework for Understanding the Adult Children of Alcoholics." *Focus on Women: Journal of the Addictions and Health,* 2: 187–203. (Reprinted in Brown, Beletsis, and Cermak (1989), *Adult Children of Alcoholics in Treatment.* Orlando: Health Communications.)

Black, Claudia. (1981). *It Will Never Happen to Me.* Denver: MAC.

Blane, Howard T. (1968). *Personality of the Alcoholic: Guises of Dependency.* New York: Harper & Row.

Bosma, W. (1972). "Children of Alcoholics: A Hidden Tragedy." *Maryland State Medical Journal,* 21: 34–36.

Bowlby, John. (1980). *Attachment and Loss: Volume 3.* New York: Basic Books.

———. (1985). "The Role of Childhood Experience in Cognitive Disturbance." In M. Mahoney and A. Freeman (Eds.), *Cognition and Psychotherapy.* New York: Plenum Press.

Brown, Stephanie. (1985). *Treating the Alcoholic: A Developmental Model of Recovery*. New York: John Wiley.

———. (1986). "Children with an Alcoholic Parent." In N. Estes and M. E. Heinemann, *Alcoholism: Development, Consequences and Interventions*. St. Louis: C. V. Mosby.

———. (1988). *Treating Adult Children of Alcoholics: A Developmental Perspective*. New York: John Wiley.

Brown, Stephanie, and Susan Beletsis. (1986). "The Development of Family Transference in Groups for Adult Children of Alcoholics." *International Journal of Group Psychotherapy*, 36: 97–114. (Reprinted in Brown, Beletsis, and Cermak (1989), *Adult Children of Alcoholics in Treatment*. Orlando: Health Communications.)

Brown, Stephanie, Susan Beletsis, and Timmen Cermak. (1989). *Adult Children of Alcoholics in Treatment*. Orlando: Health Communications.

Cork, Margaret. (1969). *The Forgotten Children*. Toronto: The Addictions Research Foundation.

Cermak, Timmen. (1986). *Diagnosing and Treating Codependence*. Minneapolis: Johnson Institute Books.

Cermak, Timmen, and Stephanie Brown. (1982). "Interactional Group Psychotherapy with the Adult Children of Alcoholics." *International Journal of Group Psychotherapy*, 32: 375–389. (Reprinted in Brown, Beletsis, and Cermak (1989), *Adult Children of Alcoholics in Treatment*. Orlando: Health Communications.)

Chafetz, M. E., H. T. Blane, and M. J. Hill. (1971). "Children of Alcoholics." *Quarterly Journal of Studies on Alcohol*, 32: 687–698.

Engel, Lewis, and Tom Ferguson. (1990). *Imaginary Crimes*. Boston: Houghton Mifflin.

Erikson, Erik. (1963). *Childhood and Society*. New York: Norton.

Fine, E. W., L. W. Yudin, J. Holmes, and S. Heinemann. (1976). "Behavioral Disorders in Children with Parental Alcoholism." *Annals of the New York Academy of Sciences*, 273: 507–517.

Fox, Ruth. (1962). "Children in an Alcoholic Family." In W. C. Bier (Ed.), *Problems in Addiction: Alcoholism and Narcotics*. New York: Fordham University Press.

———. (1963). "The Effects of Alcoholism on Children." In *The Proceedings of the Fifth International Congress of Psychotherapy*, Vienna, 1961. Part 5: 57. Basel, Switzerland: S. Karger.

Goleman, Daniel. (1985). *Vital Lies and Simple Truths*. New York: Simon and Schuster.

Goodwin, Donald W. (1984). "Studies of Familial Alcoholism: A Review." *Journal of Clinical Psychiatry*, 45(2): 14–17.

Guidano, Vittorio, and Gianni Liotti. (1983). *Cognitive Processes and Emotional Disorders*. New York: Guilford Press.

Jackson, Joan. (1954). "The Adjustment of the Family to the Crisis of Alcoholism." *Quarterly Journal of Studies on Alcohol*, 15: 562–586.

———. (1962). "Alcoholism and the Family," In D. J. Pittman and C. R. Snyder (Eds.), *Society, Culture and Drinking Patterns*. New York: John Wiley.

Janis, Irving. (1983). *Victims of Group Think*. Boston: Houghton Mifflin.

Jellinek, E. M. (1960). *The Disease Concept of Alcoholism*. New Haven: College and Universities Press.

Kagan, Jerome. (1984). *The Nature of the Child*. New York: Basic Books.

Kaufman, E. (1986). The Family of the Alcoholic Patient." *Psychosomatics*, 27(5): 347–360.

Krystal, Henry. (1978). "Trauma and Affects." *Psychoanalytic Study of the Child*, 33: 81–116.

Lidz, Theodore. (1973). *The Origins and Treatment of Schizophrenic Disorders*. New York: Basic Books.

Mahler, Margaret, Fred Pine, and H. Bergman. (1975). *The Psychological Birth of the Human Infant*. New York: Basic Books.

Miller, Alice. (1981). *The Drama of the Gifted Child*. New York: Basic Books.

———. (1984). *Thou Shalt Not Be Aware*. New York: Farrar, Straus, Giroux.

McCord, William, and Joan McCord. (1960). *Origins of Alcoholism*. Stanford: Stanford University Press.

Niven, Robert. (1984). "Children of Alcoholics: An interview with NIAAA Director." *Alcohol, Health, and Research World*, 8: 3–5.

Nylander, I. (1963). "Children of Alcoholic Fathers." *Quarterly Journal of Studies on Alcohol*, 24: 170–172.

Piaget, Jean. (1970). "Piaget's Theory." In P. Mussen (Ed.), *Carmichael's Manual of Child Psychology*, 3rd edition. New York: John Wiley.

Reiss, David. (1981). *The Family's Construction of Reality*. Cambridge: Harvard University Press.

Rosen, Hugh. (1985). *Piagetian Dimensions of Clinical Relevance*. New York: Columbia University Press.

Steinglass, Peter. (1980). "A Life History Model of the Alcoholic Family." *Family Process*, 19(3): 211–226.

Steinglass, Peter, Linda Bennett, Steven Wolin, and David Reiss. (1987). *The Alcoholic Family*. New York: Basic Books.

Twelve Steps and Twelve Traditions. (1962). New York: AA World Services.

Wegsheider, Sharon. (1981). *Another Chance: Hope and Health for the Alcoholic Family*. Palo Alto: Science and Behavior Books.

Weiss, Joseph, and Harold Sampson. (1986). *The Psychoanalytic Process: Theory, Clinical Observation, and Empirical Research*. New York: Guilford Press.

Yalom, Irvin. (1985). *The Theory and Practice of Group Psychotherapy*. New York: Basic Books.

Resources

Alcoholics Anonymous
P.O. Box 459, Grand Central Station
New York, NY 10017
(Local offices and meetings of A.A. are listed in the telephone
  directory.)

Adult Children of Alcoholics
P.O. Box 3216
Torrance, CA 90505
(213) 534-1815

Al-Anon Family Group Headquarters, Inc. (also Alateen)
P.O. Box 182, Madison Square Station
New York, NY 10010
(For family members of alcoholics, including ACAs.)

Children of Alcoholics Foundation, Inc.
540 Madison Avenue
New York, NY 10022
(Dedicated to increasing public awareness and education.)

Families Anonymous
P.O. Box 528
Van Nuys, CA 91408
(For families and friends of people with drug problems.)

Nar-Anon Family Groups
P.O. Box 2562
Palos Verdes, CA 90274-0119

National Association for Children of Alcoholics
31582 Coast Highway #B
South Laguna, CA 92677
(Open to membership; provides a newsletter; dedicated to
   education; state associations also open to membership.)
(714) 499-3889

National Clearinghouse for Alcohol Information (NCALI)
P.O. Box 2345
Rockville, MD 20852

National Council on Alcoholism
12 West 21st Street
New York, NY 10010
(Many local affiliates of NCA serve as information and referral
   agencies; listings in local telephone directories.)

National Institute of Alcohol Abuse and Alcoholism
5600 Fishers Lane
Rockville, MD 20852

Index